SUMMER LIGHTNING

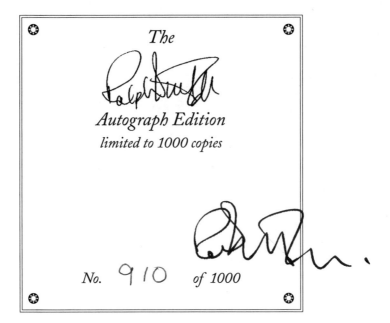

The

Autograph Edition

limited to 1000 copies

No. 910 *of 1000*

RALPH McTELL

✺

SUMMER LIGHTNING

AUTOBIOGRAPHY VOLUME TWO

amber waves

from heartland publishing limited maidstone england

First published in 2002 by Amber Waves

Amber Waves is an imprint of Heartland Publishing Ltd.,
P.O.Box 902, Sutton Valence, Maidstone, Kent ME17 3HY, England
www.heartland.co.uk

ISBN 1 902684 03 6

British Library Cataloguing-In-Publication data
A catalogue record for this book is available
from the British Library.

Book design by Jeff Horne
Typeset in Adobe Caslon 11pt

Extracts from the following songs are used with
kind permission of the publishers:
Summer Lightning ©1974 Misty River Music Ltd
All Things Change ©1969 Onward Music Ltd
When I Was A Cowboy ©1972 Westminster Music Ltd
Heron Song ©1974 Misty River Music Ltd
Nanna's Song ©1967 Westminster Music Ltd

Printed and bound in Great Britain by Biddles Ltd., Guildford
on acid-free paper manufactured from sustainable forests.

For Mick 'Henry' Bartlett

It's not a storm at all
It's only summer lightning

– Ralph McTell, *Summer Lightning*

CONTENTS

PART FOUR: MUSIC

PART FIVE: PARIS

introduction

Most of my songwriting is autobiographical. The incidents described in them have become songs because it has been possible to contain the poetry or symmetry within the confines of the song format. The episodes recounted in this book also have a kind of poetry, insomuch as there had to be a reason for writing them down other than pure chronology.

The first story I wrote for this memoir was called 'Picnic on the Playnies'. It is about a day out with the kids in the street when we attempted to cook over an open fire by the farm (the sewage farm!). The 'poetry' in this story was centred on the young boy (me) observing Maureen, who had decided to be mother to us all and do the cooking. When she cuts herself preparing the food and her blood drips into the chip pan, her small sacrifice becomes a mystical communion as one by one we receive the chips. It is the nearest we will get to sharing her body (except for Bobby Best, if he is to believed...). The blood and body of Maureen in a starling-whitewashed arbor of elderberry bushes. Adolescent stirrings around the fire. Laughter and smoky tears. Far too much to put into a song.

I loved recounting these moments and experienced a total suspension in time whilst writing. I could clearly hear the voices of the characters mentioned. In some cases, even smell them! So lost was I in the writing that I was transported back and confused by time and memory. Sometimes this was a wonderful intoxicating experience and sometimes there was a hangover and a melancholy for lost moments. Some names had to be changed to protect the guilty, and regrettably a few incidents omitted to protect the dignity of the innocent. No matter how difficult recounting some stories were, writing them down was pure pleasure. In some cases those who know my songs will recognise in these incidents the basis from which they were distilled.

More episodes began to arrive as I wandered back and forth from my first memories at eighteen months to the time when I met my wife Nanna in Paris in 1966. All these stories were sent to Nick and Jeff at Heartland Publishing, who were keen to publish them. The problem was in the editing: there was so much material that we all wanted to keep, and often chronology was needed to make sense of the incidents and to connect the narrative. I'm grateful to the editorial team at Heartland, particularly Jon Horne and Sarah Hall, for all their help.

In the end we decided to divide it into two books. The first volume, entitled *Angel Laughter*, came out in October 2000 and deals with my childhood, from my earliest recollections until, after serving six months in purgatory, I left the Infantry Junior Leaders Battalion of the army in 1960 at the age of 15.

This volume deals with the next five and a half years. It is an account of my adventure as a teenage boy approaching manhood. Music had always been an interest, but from where these memories begin, music, and more particularly the guitar, takes over my life and turns me towards a direction I am still following.

Within a year of meeting Nanna in Paris I was introduced to a music publisher (Essex Music) and a recording contract followed. These events have been chronicled in Chris Hockenhull's biography,[1] and I have no interest in elaborating on Chris's thoroughly researched work. From that point on my musical career ran in tandem with my life with Nanna and my family, and that is *our* story.

This, however, is mine.

I have to offer some thanks, firstly to my mum, who against family advice borrowed the money to get me out of the army and thereby allowed all these other events to take place. Next to Jack Elliott, whose marvellous

---

[1] *Streets of London*, Northdown Publishing, 1997

guitar playing and singing started my proper striving in music. To Woody Guthrie, for his inspirational songs and for planting dreams of the road and travel, combined with a political outlook that gave dignity to the working man and proved that you did not need to be a great musician to be a great songwriter. To all my blind black dead heroes, like Blind Boy Fuller, Blind Blake and the Rev. Gary Davis, for their joyous, complex, fascinating, *sexy* exploitation of the acoustic guitar. To Bob Dylan, for combining the Guthrie directness with the seductiveness of Jack Kerouac, and street attitude with a kind of majesty (and also for the introduction of the harmonica harness into this country and freeing me from the limitations of a bent wire coat hanger and a chest of drawers...). And to Wizz Jones, Davy Graham and Bert Jansch, who proved that British lads could make valid guitar music and songs.

Above all, though, is the Cast of Thousands—the friends who moved in and out of my life through music. They know who they are. But if I had to single out one from them all, it would have to be Mick ('Henry') Bartlett, who died in 2001 and whose name appears over and over again in this book. Henry's passion for music and his encouragement and enthusiasm for my early efforts were so important to me. To paraphrase Bill Shankly, music wasn't a matter of life and death to him—it was more important than that.

Henry was involved with music right up to the end, and indeed was awaiting the release of a follow-up album to the 1960s 'Famous Jug Band' records. He played a bit of double bass, but was most well known on the jug, from which he was able to produce wonderful percussive rhythmic bass effects. He accompanied me on my early recordings and lots of live work as well. We drove all over the place to listen to this piano player in that band, or that trombonist in another, or some interval band at Eel Pie Island. With just a few bob in the pocket we were accompanied by music, laughter and friendship. It is to these essentials, and to Henry in particular, that these episodes are dedicated.

As far as I can tell
Is all that I can say
A million miles on down the road
Twelve thousand days away

Mirror held to mirror
As far as I can tell
At this glimpse of eternity
I fumbled and they fell

Between these shards restored
Lies truth in splintered cracks
As far as I can tell
Remembered light refracts

And shadows cast by doubt
Move by the soundless bell
The sun tolled ringing earth reveals
As far as I can tell

PART ONE

CROYDON

tech

I walked from West Croydon station with my small bag of possessions, and with every step relished my familiar surroundings. It was the late autumn of 1960; my summer leave seemed an age ago and I took delight in the rattle and noise of the town. The contrast with the weekly visits to Oswestry was marked, the noise of the terminal gradually diminishing as I walked the route of the 64 trolley-bus. With each step homeward I left the life of the last few months further behind me.

Even as I write of these moments some forty years later, I can think of no subjectively longer six month period. My army days seemed more like two years; it had been a quantum leap towards manhood, as had been the jump from the relative gentility of the Waldrons, where my first memories began, to the Mitcham Road estate, where the warm feelings I held for it almost overwhelmed me. I could already see the giant gasholder under whose shadow we lived in Miller Road. It looked fat and friendly as I headed expectantly in its direction.

Familiar streets, familiar smells, everything was different and yet nothing had changed. As I walked over Pitlake Bridge I bumped into someone who did not even know I'd been away.

The traffic noise subsided as I approached the walk up Factory Lane past the working men's hostel. No cars passed me. The throb of the B power station grew louder then diminished, drowned in the hissing of the old wooden cooling towers and the clatter of the trucks into the council dump. Familiar sounds singing me home.

As the end of Miller Road came into sight my pulse rate quickened at the thought of number 17a and seeing Mum and Bruce again. The last few steps towards the gate produced a great grin of expectation at the welcome I would get as I crossed over the threshold of our upstairs two-bedroom flat and on to the green, green linoleum of home.

Against everyone's advice, my mother had borrowed the money from her boss Mr. Waters to buy me out of the army. She had made it clear to me that I would have to pay it back, and that I would also have to return to school in order to complete my O-level studies. I had readily agreed to this. I had served my time (six months), successfully pleaded my case to my dear mum, and not attempted suicide or self-mutilation (several lads had done this and about twenty were AWOL when I left Parkhall Camp).

The doorbell was answered by Bruce, grinning a toothy hello. I hopped up the stairs in three steps to give my mum a homecoming kiss.

"You'd better put your things in your room," she said rather coldly after a perfunctory peck. I realised that, far from being any kind of hero, my return was regarded as failure, and she had decided not to make my transition to civilian life a smooth affair. I have to say this pained me, and not for the first time I was shocked at my inability to convey the hell wrought by my own demons to others.

I contented myself for the first few days renewing old acquaintances. Just about everything was different to the way I had left it. For a start my little brother was now quite big and had already established himself at his grammar school. He had new friends and was playing rugby for his year (I had absolutely no interest in any team games at this time); he had recently discovered that he had hair and was combing it; he was wearing long trousers and his voice had broken. We never went about together after this, at least until my musical adventure became professional.

Re-establishing friendships was difficult. So little had happened to my mates and so much had happened to me. Just walking down the road together, I wanted to break into a run. I was teeming with energy, and the feeling of freedom was so prolonged and heady that I managed to put my cool welcome behind me. I took delight in everything around me and was sure I could make up lost ground at the college. Most of my mates were already at work and settling into the 'light and bitter, brown and mild' routine, We soon drifted apart, also forever.

The deal I had struck was that I would attend college—Croydon College of Technology, with a one day release for an A-level in art at the adjoining art school—and attempt to salvage something out of what was, after all, a grammar school education. The plan was doomed to failure.

Croydon Tech was a state of the art establishment. It catered to a tremendously varied bunch of students, and their range of studies went from engineering to the arts and secretarial courses to English and girls (studied by exotic Iranians). The art college was bridged by means of the canteen and there was an air of exuberance and ease about the whole place. It is hard to think of a more different environment to that of the camp. A few weeks previously I had been a number and a name, I'd responded to a self-administered nickname ('Ray'), and was screamed at from morning to night by mad men and boys who wore stripes on their arms. Here my hair began to grow back to the Tony Curtis-style late teddy boy look. I was addressed as Mr. May by my tutors, and everywhere and on every stair, corridor and room were girls. Girls, girls, girls.

Pretty as pictures, all sticky out petticoats, heavy eye liner, back-combed hair, girls, girls, girls.

Giggling, smiling, whispering behind their hands, collecting in groups, sashaying into the canteen, dancing in the common rooms at their lunch breaks to *Hit The Road Jack* and *Rubber Ball* and *Midnight in Moscow*, girls girls girls.

Just swishing past girls in the corridors, traces of perfume or the scent of shampoo, the rustle of clothing, all these things had a devastating effect on the newly released prisoner from Shropshire. By the end of the first week I was in love with four girls and had not spoken to any of them. After a few days some of them smiled in recognition. I blushed until I burned. Concentrating on anything in lesson time I found nearly impossible as my eyes and thoughts would settle on some sweet thing in a soft sweater or pencil skirt.

There was also the matter of my £50 debt and the need to repay my mother's boss, Mr. Waters. Luckily work came in the form of a gardening job for a certain Mr. Tickle who had a small electrical winding factory near to mum's chemist shop.

The Tickles lived in a beautiful house in Riddlesdown Road, in an outlying area beyond south Croydon. It had a huge, well ordered back garden with a large lawn, greenhouses and carnation beds. The soil was chalky and hard to dig, but I was still fit from the army; I liked being out in the open and I enjoyed the bike ride to and from the place.

There were two Mr. Tickles, father and son, and both were bird fanciers. Around the garden were aviaries containing all manner of parrots, cockatiels, amazons, and mynah birds. There was also a family pet named Joe, a very old African Grey parrot who was allowed to wander up and down the apple tree branches, and spent most of the time saying, "Come on down you naughty boy."

He found it difficult to climb down the tree and would, when distressed, order himself back into his cage with, "In your cage, Joe."

On my first morning, anxious to impress, I threw myself into my work and had not noticed the passing of time until Mrs. Tickle called me for a break with some tea.

"Ralph!" she called in a clear high voice, and from that moment on the mynah birds called my name at random so that I never knew whether it was her calling me or not. Even when they went out I would beaver away as hard as I could in case I got fooled into assuming it was the birds calling me. These same birds could perfectly imitate the sound of the car pulling up and the application of slightly squeaky brakes, so for me there was no chance of pausing to relax even to smoke the odd Park Drive.

Once unbeknown to me a young couple were staying at the house when the family had gone out. I kept up my normal work rate all afternoon, and just before the Tickles returned, the young bloke came out and asked me if I ever slowed down or took a break. He said they had been watching me from a bedroom window. I was pleased to be so commended for my efforts, and it was only on my way home at the end of my eight hours' work, when I could hardly push the pedals on my bike, that I found myself wondering what he'd been doing in a bedroom all afternoon while I sweated away behind the old lawn mower and rake.

Oh well, the first part of the journey home was all downhill and there was Saturday night to look forward to. There is always Saturday night to look forward to.

Saturday night seldom lives up to expectation; I suppose that's why we look forward to it, the next forever holding the potential to be better than the last. Ours would be spent at the Gun or other local pubs where I renewed old school friendships with Derek 'Les' Lester and Vernon

Burford. We would catch a jazz band somewhere, or shoot up west to Goodge Street and Fitzrovia.

Traditional jazz was enjoying its revival. I had liked this music since I was introduced to it by Vernon when I was eleven years old. His older brothers had quite a few records by Chris Barber and Lonnie Donegan; I knew these tunes and could identify the difference between a trombone and a trumpet, and to my new friends must have seemed quite knowledgeable.

There were all sorts of different dance steps available to the uninhibited, from the intricacies of the Cy Laurie steps, done against the beat at a furious speed, to the more ungainly 'skip jive' favoured by ravers. There do not seem to be any filmed records of these dance fads, but I thought them very stylish and sharp, especially performed by some of the couples. The added attraction was that girls were swirled around very fast and revealed all sorts of hidden paraphernalia of stockings and suspenders to the delight of leering students.

There were a couple of real creepy blokes who could not dance but asked girls to join them in the breaks in the common room, and these girls accepted. I couldn't believe how uncool these geezers were. I was too laid back to show any enthusiasm for this venture and although I had made the beginnings of fumbled exploration whilst 'away', I was still hopelessly shy. I decided to make notes and practise some steps in the privacy of my own bedroom.

The problem here was that I did not have my own bedroom. There was only a foot or so gap between my bed and Bruce's, and this hardly allowed room enough for the rather galumphing prancing about required for Trad. Nevertheless, I practised my reverse turns, often cracking my shins on the old iron bed runners. Once I rehearsed a few steps out in the yard one evening until spotted by Mrs. Bradley, who surprised me whilst silently taking in her washing and observing me from behind the privet hedge. It is very difficult to convert a full flying Trad jive with an invisible partner to the earnest search for something you have mislaid around the dustbin area of the yard, and my sheepish grin did not do much to convince her that I was all right. She bolted the back door once inside.

There was a parallel interest in Thirties jazz around this time, and a band called the Temperance Seven played a dance at the Denning Hall. The evening was called, somewhat inexplicably, 'Votes for Women 1913'.

The admission charge was two bob and the evening was subscribed mainly by the art school students. I thought the event was fantastic; I enjoyed the high camp of the band, but mostly I loved the music. The musicians were fabulous. They even had fabulous names like Alan Swainston-Cooper and Cephas Howard, and Whispering Paul McDowell, the vocalist, was so cool. The band performed in what looked like Edwardian costume and their playing was peerless. Soon the Temps had a number one hit with *You're Driving Me Crazy.*

Amongst the audience were some beatnik types from outside the college, including one quite famous raver called 'Little Ray'. The kids at the art college were different; they wore strange clothes—and what were those fabulous jeans they were wearing and where could you get them? Levis were forty two and sixpence a pair, which was double the cost of their rivals. Some boys had been to Paris to buy them. I had wanted a pair since I saw my first James Dean film.

Somehow I secured a small grant to assist Mum with my education and this was in part used to pay back some of the money I owed her. This meant that with incredible frugality I could spend some of my money on the odd item of clothing, usually from Millets, and buy my smokes and an occasional 45 record out of my gardening wages. I was one of the poorer kids at the college—but not as poor as Squeeb.

Squeeb came from New Addington and was a very bright lad full of confidence and fun, with jet black hair and slightly puffy eyes which gave him a frog-like appearance. He had small teeth and his hands trembled, but if he was nervous he certainly did not show it. I fell in with him, and being from the same social class we hit it off quite well. Squeeb chatted in a matey way to everyone and they responded to him in a usually friendly way. There did seem to be an enormous gap in social standing with the majority of kids coming from posh outlying areas of Croydon, but this did not daunt Squeeb, who bantered his way with them all. With boys and girls it is not all one way traffic and I guess some of the girls were interested in finding out about the new kid (me). They did this through Squeeb.

I was still at the stage of colouring up whenever I was spoken to, and although these girls were so pretty, they were out of my class and I looked elsewhere. As far as appearances went, I resembled more the boys on day release from the engineering school, who were proper lads, but I was with the kids who were studying the arts. Somehow the class structure seemed to prevail and like sought out like, except for Squeeb who pitched at everything and went out with no-one. Somewhere in those first few months I went out with Judy, Jenny, Angela—and eventually Roberta. But the first one I remember was Cleo.

girls

Cleo threw herself at me at the end of a dance. Actually, she nearly threw up on me, and because she seemed a little worse for wear I walked her home. My affectionate little goodnight kiss did not end there as she suddenly sobered up and pressed me in a scary clinch that I managed to self deny, playing the double bluff that if she was that pissed she would not remember it and I could deny that it ever happened.

Judy was addicted to dance. At lunchtime in the common room, to the sound of a cheap record player, she would perfect her laconic, languid routine. Boys did not dance in the bright midday sunlit room that was reserved for us to spend our lunch hour in, so Judy danced with Susan, who was quite possibly the sexiest fifteen year old I have ever seen, before or since. They had the knowledge, of men, that is, in the biblical sense. Or so I thought. I was wrong about both of them, but more wrong about one than the other.

Susan was stunning in every regard; her naturally very blonde hair was parted down one side so that the majority of her fringe fell across her pretty face. She was forever pushing it back and unselfconsciously putting it behind her ear, which had the effect of making her look gauche and vulnerable. Her small blue eyes were nearly always smiling and she had teeth that were white and prominent; not quite Brigitte Bardot but also not quite Joyce Grenfell.

She had a husky laugh and a wonderful figure with huge breasts. Every boy in the place fancied her gutless. Both girls were working class but Susan fancied the most drippy boys in the college, hooray Henrys and chinless wonders from the suburbs. I stood no chance. I went for Judy.

Judy was something else; slim to a ridiculous degree, and her bust was almost non-existent. Her grey eyes were sleepy and heavy-lidded, and her hair was thick and styled in what was beginning to be known as the Mod girl look. She had a slight stoop to her shoulders and showed just the right amount of disinterest to make her interesting.

We went out quite a few times but it was all a bit fraught; at sixteen I was still encumbered with virginity, and although I once wormed my way into Judy's sleeping bag, I only ever got inside her bra—and there wasn't much there except two rolled-up handkerchiefs.

She did accompany me once down to Brighton on a rave and we shivered underneath the pier on the cold pebbles in March. A sleeping bag is like a giant condom, for unless you plan well ahead there is nothing much you can do once you are both in it except try to keep warm. So much for another Millets bargain! We slept, I suppose, but the next day, tired and unfulfilled, was the beginning of the end. Judy ended up going out with (and eventually marrying) one of the boys in engineering.

Jenny was sweet: she reminded me of a Sunday school teacher I once had. She loved me because I comforted her when Ricky Tyrell packed her in.

Ricky was a boy from the other side of the tracks, confident beyond his years and extremely funny. He had straight, wispy hair, tiny slits for eyes and a square English face. He wore a sports jacket and straight trousers and looked quite conventional, but his sense of humour was wicked. Once whilst watching a particularly ungainly girl jiving around the common room, he turned to me and said above the noise of the Dansette, "My God, Ralph, she looks like a ruptured camel with his hump on fire!"

One day a rumour started circulating around the college about some film extra work. We found there were auditions taking place somewhere near Dulwich. I was only too ready to try our luck, as the amounts being talked about were up to five pounds a day.

We embarked on a bus and train journey that took about two hours, and finally arrived at a tiny one-roomed office above a tobacconist shop, where a middle-aged lady with dyed black hair and a deep masculine raspy voice sat behind an overflowing ash tray and told us she hadn't the slightest idea what we were talking about.

"You are an agent aren't you?" asked Ricky. She replied that she was, but had no extra work, although she thought that we were two nice boys and she would put us on her books.

"What are your names?" she asked.

"Ricky Tyrell," answered my friend.

"Don't I know that name?"

"Yes," said Ricky. "My great- great- great- great grandfather Louis Armstrong shot the two little princes in the eye in Epping Forest and is known in history as one of the most heinous and vile aristocrats of all time. He was imprisoned in Thornton Heath clock tower before being transported to Virginia where he made some amends and a small fortune by discovering the pork pie."

We never heard from her.

I don't know if it was the disappointment at not launching his movie career, but things quickly fell apart with him and Jenny after this. Jenny had saucer eyes as big as my mother's, and to see her cry brought back painful memories. Gradually she replaced Rick with me in her affections and the responsibility was too much for me. One day she pointedly told me that she had fallen for someone else, and although I guessed it was me, I pretended to be happy for her and wriggled away from the situation.

When I told Ricky of these events he said, "Christ, how must she feel being rejected by two of the best looking blokes in the college?" I could not believe this remark for he was no oil painting either. The two of us began to drift apart after that, and apparently Jenny cried for a fortnight.

Angela had enormous breasts, but I was put off by her very thin legs. She was pretty and outgoing, with masses of curly dark hair, and had a lovely laugh that cracked when she chuckled. She was adored from afar by Spike, who had a Plan. He had found out that Angela was interested in me, and as he was besotted with her, persuaded the three of us to go to the cinema together. When I turned up he had quite a pretty girl in tow, and somehow engineered it so that I sat next to her whilst he sat with Angela.

Immediately the movie started, he fell on Angela, who resisted for a while but, assuming we boys had cooked this up between us, eventually responded to Spike's advances. Meanwhile I sat glumly with Gina. The poor girl was upset at my lack of interest as she had rather liked me, and Spike persuaded me to write to her explaining things. I helpfully sent a brief note along the lines of 'one man's meat is another man's poison', which I am sure helped to restore her self confidence in no time.

Roberta was quite simply the most stunning looking girl in the Tech. She was taller than any of the other girls at about five foot nine, with huge eyes and flaming red hair. She was on a secretarial course. She had a beautiful figure and always dressed as if she was going dancing instead of going to school. Her friend Tina was smaller with massive back-combed hair and wore more eyeliner than Dusty Springfield. The two girls were inseparable, and in a way Tina successfully minded her statuesque friend as she moved about the college attracting wolf whistles and remarks from just about all the boys. Like everyone else I fantasised about Roberta; you simply could not help it. Those huge blue eyes and that figure, and in spite of everything a gentle shyness about her. Tina strutted along basking in Roberta's reflected presence, and some of the more astute lads reckoned that Tina was a teaser and probably would never come across. The two of them danced together and sat together in the canteen and walked together, Roberta in pastel blues and Tina in dark greens. They were impressive.

One day I was sitting with some friends in the canteen when Tina strode over to us and rolled up her sleeve to reveal several finger-sized bruises.

"Can you see these?" she asked.

"Yes," we chorused.

"Do you know how I got them?" she demanded.

"No," we all chimed.

"From her," she gesticulated with a nod of her head in Roberta's direction. We all looked at Roberta who blushed prettily and turned away towards the door.

"Every time she sees you," she said, looking at me, "she grabs my arm and says, 'I want him!'"

There was a loud "Phwoarr" from all my mates.

"Please ask her out, Ralph—she's hurting me and she really likes you," implored Tina.

The lads on my table were guffawing and slapping me on the back. I was grinning stupidly and you could have lit a match from my burning cheeks.

"Go on!" roared my mates. "Go and ask her, go on, get stuck in!"

I was embarrassed, frightened, flattered and excited. I smiled foolishly at the wonderful Roberta and lip-read the word from her across the crowded canteen.

"WOOF."

I thought perhaps she couldn't pronounce her Rs properly and was trying to say Ralph. A small speech impediment was not going to stand in the way of a possible revealing of unthinkable delights to come. She smiled at me and for the rest of the afternoon I thought about her and her impediment, wondering if I should address her as 'Woberta' to put her at her ease. I met her later that day after lessons and asked her if she would like to come out with me for a walk before she took the bus home.

"Woof."

"My name is Ralph," I said.

"I know," she said. "Woof woof."

As we walked away from the college, some of the boys were calling after us. Roberta took no notice; she was used to producing this kind of attention. I looked at her again.

"Woof woof," she said.

By the time we had crossed the road she had hold of my hand. Cars were switching on their lights and the winter evening was drawing in. I had no money and nowhere to go, so we headed for the Town Hall gardens and sat on a park bench.

"Whereabouts do you live, Roberta?" I asked.

"Woof woof," she replied.

Then she said, "Norbury."

"Oh, what bus do you have to catch?" No answer. I tried another tack.

"Why do you keep saying woof?"

"Woof woof," said Roberta.

"Roberta—" I began.

"Woof woof woof," she said and then as I made a slight move she kissed me. This was a big kiss. It went on for a long time. Christ she was powerful. And probably the same weight as me, although I did have a slight height and reach advantage. But the first round was definitely hers.

Eventually I staggered from the Town Hall gardens and saw Roberta on to the bus and said goodnight.

"Woooof," breathed Roberta.

I commenced my walk home. I was aware of an aching below the belt which had started somewhere during the tenth round, and by the time I crawled through the front door I was in agony.

In the morning at college I resisted the opportunity to satisfy my leering mates with details of my encounter and simply told them that I had walked her home. We went to the pictures later in the week, but the story was much the same and with nowhere to go I felt I had lost that bout and Roberta's stamina and strength had finally won the day. I decided to throw in the towel, much to the incredulity of all the blokes I sat with. I told Roberta I had met someone else.

Years later I met her in the post office in Croydon when my first son Sam was in his pram. We chatted and she was just as sweet and lovely as I remembered her. I said how nice it was to see her, and we just said goodbye.

Woof woof Roberta.

guitars

I was gradually learning not to burn up every time a girl smiled at me (I haven't quite got it cracked yet, but I'm getting better). I had plenty of new friends and was moving easily about the college and in the main attending my lessons, which had nothing like the strict discipline of school. The freedom was intoxicating. Instead of the smell of Lysol and carbolic and the rub of serge trousers and clatter of army boots, this place flounced with pretty girls and perfumes and the ease of jeans and desert boots.

I became involved with the culture of common room and refectory. What interested me was the jazz club, which took place on a Wednesday evening after last period. There were a few who were only following the current musical trend through the trad jazz revival, but there was a small minority intent on taking the club towards the very modern—and even that floundered when Dave Brubeck got into the charts with *Take Five*. We just stood around chatting whilst listening to the likes of Thelonius Monk and Eric Dolphy and secretly hoping for some King Oliver or Freddy Keppard to relieve the intensity. Anyway we felt fairly hip.

Mostly the blokes wore the usual jeans and stuff, and even collars and ties like the Modern Jazz Quartet, but some also wore corduroy jackets and woollen sweaters or ex-military gear and combat jackets. Some of the lads cut their own hair with razors and a comb, or got their mates to do it for them. Footwear was mainly brogues, plimsolls, or winklepickers. Levis with a combat jacket and Clark's desert boots became my gear; I blended in almost anywhere.

One evening at the end of a jazz club session the DJ, Robin Langer, played an EP called 'Muleskinners' by Ramblin' Jack Elliott. It practically cleared the room, but I was captivated. I wanted to hear it again and again, and finally I prevailed upon Robin to let me take it home with me. A journey that would last the next forty years had now begun.

A few months before joining up in the army, I had acquired a guitar from Kennards, the big department store in Croydon. It was the cheapest of the cheap and was made of plywood by 'Egmond Frères' of Belgium, and it cost £5. It really was a piece of crap and could barely be held in tune, but there was that twang to it and I loved the ritual of stringing it, and the packets the strings came in, which held the promise of Superior Tonal Quality from the manufacturer. I had bought strings from the old boy at the store before, one at a time for my one string fiddle that Grandad had given me, but at fifteen now felt ready to start playing on six strings. Unfortunately the guitar was almost impossible to play and eventually it was put to one side.

That night, when I returned home from the jazz club, I played *San Francisco Bay Blues* from the EP on my pathetic little turntable about twenty times. Finally I picked up the plywood guitar that had been lying dormant for so long while I'd been away and painstakingly tuned the strings to something like concert pitch. I realised that Jack Elliott was playing in the key of C—but what were these other chords?

Slowly—oh so slowly—I worked out all the changes, and found chords that I had never found before. Looking back, I was lucky to have been able to do this, because I discovered how to make the notes without chord diagrams. For years I did not know the names of the chords I was playing. After a couple of days, I could play the tune recognisably enough to know I would have to get a better guitar. The strings had started to cut my already sore fingers, and if you cut your finger tip you can bet that the wound will perfectly accommodate a guitar string—very nasty.

My mission in life now was to find a guitar that sounded like Jack Elliott's. This proved impossible, but I settled on a £15 Voss guitar from Potters Music in South Croydon. It stayed in tune and I could not put it down. My college work suffered terribly, but I was lost in this wonderful music. I took the instrument to college and played it every break and lunchtime in the stairwells between floors, my coterie of pals sitting around smoking cigarettes and encouraging my efforts. I worked my way through all the songs on Elliott's 'Jack Takes The Floor' LP; my favourite was *Cocaine Blues*, which I found I could copy from the record quite easily, even though it was the first fingerstyle guitar piece I had ever heard. My pals were even more impressed.

Suddenly we were into mock O-levels. I took French, English, Maths, History, English Literature and Art.

I only passed English Lit and that because I loved poetry (not something you bragged about in Croydon). My worst failure was with maths: eight per cent for the entire exam. I was not altogether surprised that I was summoned to see Dr. Waring, our head of department.

"Well Mr. May," he began, "I expect you know why I have asked to see you."

"Yes sir."

"I am afraid that I won't be entering you for the actual exam."

The thought of failure and disappointment for my mother's sacrifices welled up in me.

"Why can't I take the exam sir?"

"Because you only got eight per cent."

"But surely that shows I got something right sir?"

"Mr. May, I am aware of your circumstances and I took the trouble to try and work out your thought processes in all stages of the paper. I am afraid, however, that they eluded me and although you showed your thought processes they defy logic in the mathematical sense. You simply cannot be creative with maths; there is only one answer and that is the right one."

"Yes, I accept that sir, but surely there is a glimmer of hope," I said as a weak smile spread hopefully across my anxious face. "After all, I did get something correct. I mean eight per cent is better than nothing."

"True," said Dr. Waring. "But the only thing you got right was the date and your own name, and as I've never awarded zero before I gave you eight per cent out of pity."

My crest had fallen to the floor. "I see," I murmured.

"Good luck with the rest of the exams," smiled the benevolent doctor as I scooped up my crest and pushed it into the back pocket of my newly acquired Levis. At least Mum would understand, as she was no good at algebra. I then resolved not to say anything about the mock exams but to wait for the real thing.

Two of my more important haunts over the next few years were the Whitgift Arms, a pub at the foot of Scarborough Road in Croydon old town area (of which more later), and a small but influential coffee bar called 'Under the Olive Tree'. The Olive was somewhere we used to go to after a few drinks at the Whitgift, and was run by an upper class couple called Parker.

In the ground floor sitting area was a splendid juke box which contained records by Muddy Waters, Woody Guthrie, Big Bill Broonzy and Howlin' Wolf. There was a coffee machine and one-armed bandit, rumoured to contain a £40 jackpot of sixpences visible behind a two-inch thick glass plate. Bruce, my younger brother, was working behind the bar with another school friend called Rick, and apart from having fun and meeting girls, they were also making a little pocket money.

Downstairs was a tiny parquet dance floor with a small raised platform round the outside, and on several nights a week a remarkable DJ called Dave King played even more remarkable records that must have been flown in from the States exclusively for him. I heard many future hits at the Olive Tree long before they ever got heard on the radio.

I have to say that I was less than interested in the music of the day, having by this time heard Ramblin' Jack, Jesse Fuller, the Carter Family and even old-timey banjo playing. Almost every waking hour my guitar was glued to my hand as I struggled to unravel the mysteries of the acoustic instrument that had taken over my life. I had developed a type of fast bluegrass flat picking, which may not have been of much musical value but impressed the shit out of my friends. I was never as moved by this stuff as much as the real mountain music, but everything I heard led me on to more wonderful discoveries, and as I was drawn deeper into the music I met more and more people who miraculously liked the same things.

My rambles with Les 'up west' to Soho and the area round it had brought us into company with lots of new acquaintances. For the most part we wandered around the pubs and bars of Fitzrovia. Sometimes we would hear a bit of music emanating from a bar or pub and go in to check it out.

That's how I first saw Buck Polly and Pete Brown. Both these two had busked around Europe, and Buck had achieved mythical status through an outgoing cockney personality allied to a western-styled wardrobe and the ability to play some tunes on the twelve-string guitar. It is impossible to explain the effect all this music had on me—sometimes it was just the sound of the instrument that knocked me sideways. Buck was the first person I ever saw play a twelve-string.

On the air in and around Finches on Goodge Street was the sweet essence of marijuana, and without ever having tried it, I knew that was what it was. Through discreet enquiries we found the name of a bloke who sold ten-bob deals. When we tracked him down, far from looking the depraved monster of movie depictions, he turned out to be a bit moddy, with slightly back-combed hair and aged at least seventeen or eighteen. He wore a light blue raincoat and was somewhat smarter than the beatnik crowd that frequented Finches at that time. I realised, not for the first time, how out of place Les and I looked in our Croydon modes. He asked us for our money, which we handed over in a sweat, and from inside the mac he produced two deals beautifully folded in newspaper to an intricate envelope; he had a special poacher's pocket sewn into the lining for this purpose. Les and I nervously went outside to smoke our first spliff. We wandered around Great Newport Street, and there in an alley near the Lamb & Flag I joined the three papers together as I had seen others do. Les carefully emptied the whole of his deal into the Rizlas and I began to roll. Just as I was about to glue the parcel together, a couple of cops walked past and glanced up the alley.

"Oh shit," said Les as he noticed them. "Quick, we better go!" Suddenly the rollup split and the weed went everywhere and we started to run as the two cops returned to look up the alley. We had a good start on them and, charged with the extra adrenaline from our attempted criminal act, we made our escape into the Saturday night throngs of people in Soho. Relieved at our escape we both started laughing, especially as I had my deal safe in my pocket.

We retraced our footsteps to Goodge Street and there in some quieter back road we rolled up again. The joint was pure grass—we had not put any tobacco in it—and greedily we both started pulling away. The effect was pretty immediate and I felt a change in my perceptions quickly—although Les did not. This is often the case with first-time smokers, and his puzzled expression made me laugh—which made *him* laugh. Soon the pair of us were wracked with hysterical giggles, exactly as we had been in chemistry class when we made laughing gas and gulped in huge lungfuls of air. *Every*thing was hilarious. In the end we had to sit down on shop window ledges to get our breath, only to go off again at the slightest thing.

"Look at him!" Les would say, and suddenly an ordinary bloke would become an object of total hilarity and we would be fighting to gain control of our breath once again. The problem was exacerbated by Les's laugh, a deep rumbling chuckle. If someone has a laugh that makes you laugh what chance have you got?

I began to get scared. Would I ever return to normal? We began walking, trying not to look at each other for fear of starting to break up again. For a while we sat on the kerb on Tottenham Court Road just watching the traffic, the rainy streets reflecting neon and car lights.

I got back to Croydon still quite early and had a slight problem trying to give the ticket collector my bus ticket instead of a train ticket. There was a copper standing next to him which increased my temporary confusion, but soon I found the right item and began walking back to Factory Lane and home. Saturday nights would never be the way they were again.

By now I was taking the guitar down to the local pubs and playing quietly in the corner, the same tunes over and over. Gradually one or two other guitar players drifted in to the scene. I was getting a bit of a reputation as a flat picker; love for this music and that of the Carter Family and Woody Guthrie became almost an obsession. I tried playing with different materials like collar stiffeners from shirts so that I could pick up speed. I cut up my set square from geometry and made plectrums out of it. I used thin card and almost any flexible material would be worth investigating as to whether it had the potential to make me sound better. Then I got a thumb pick and some metal finger picks.

About the same time and unbeknown to me, other boys of my age had also signed up to this style of music. We would meet eventually at the Olive Tree, where I would make friends that would take me further into music and travel, and around this time I wrote my first fan letter to Woody Guthrie. I was already getting fed up with the sound of the Voss guitar and I knew I must get a better one. I now knew that the sound I was after came from what were called 'jumbo' or 'dreadnought' guitars, and the first one I heard was played by Max Faulkner, a brilliant flat-picking guitarist whose hero and sometime teacher was Steve Benbow. His guitar was a Levin. It was made in Sweden, not America, but it sounded like Jack's, Woody's and all my new heroes'. It cost £45 new, which may as well have been £45,000 for all that I could afford it, but I knew I'd have to have one.

Somewhere into the picture came Mick 'Henry' Bartlett. Almost everyone called him Henry because one night in the Duke of York, Horse-Head Clive happened to remark that he looked like Henry VIII, and the nickname stuck.

Henry's enthusiasm took us both all over south London in various battered old cars to listen to blues, R&B, folk or jazz in clubs and festivals, and just about anywhere music was played that fitted his exacting standards. He never learned to play a conventional instrument, but he formed numerous bands in his career and recorded on at least four albums, including two of mine. I don't remember him ever complimenting me directly, but by his willingness to share his musical passions with me I presumed he must approve of my efforts. Henry played the jug; a stoneware one was his favourite, although I do remember one time at a session down at the Folk Cottage in Cornwall he was forced to play the plastic container that contained the chemical fluid for the Elsan Rural karzi.

One day Henry took me up to the King and Queen, a pub in the Edgware Road near Marble Arch, to see two young guys play: Tony Wilson (last heard of as a music writer living in Dublin) on guitar and Phil Allacker on banjo. Tony was playing a Harmony Sovereign guitar, and to me it sounded even better than the Levin; it was also cheaper at £35 and it was made in America. I resolved to save for one of these.

Henry introduced me to Phil, a gentle, serious soul who, like me, believed that music could somehow save us all from whatever it was we all needed saving from. Phil's taste was purer than mine; the very mention of bluegrass music would cause his face to change shape and reveal his disdain for the corruption of frailing and drop-thumb banjo. We hit it off well, and soon worked out some numbers together. I don't know whether or not it was this that prompted Henry to take the plunge into promotion, but he later negotiated the use of the Olive for a Sunday afternoon folk and blues session. This was the first of many ventures into running music clubs in pubs, barns and village halls with no real intent to make money; the music always came first.

After nine months' work and frugal balancing I had saved up £29. The guitar seemed as far away as ever when a friend told me of a second hand bargain in Ivor Mairants Musicentre in Rathbone Place. He had a Sovereign in the window for exactly £29! I went up the next Saturday morning with more money in my pocket than I had ever had before. I walked in at opening time and Ivor himself served me, letting me into the little store room at the side of the counter. I sat down and started to play. It was like heaven, the bass strings booming, the top strings ringing.

After what seemed like a quarter of an hour Ivor tapped on the door and said, "Well son, what do you think?" and before I could reply he added, "Only we are about to shut the shop—it's a half day on Saturday."

It was not the first time that time itself had been suspended by music. I bought the guitar, and Ivor threw in a Hamilton capo and a soft case. As I journeyed home it would have taken a plastic surgeon to remove the smile from my face.

A week or two after my happy Saturday a friend came up to me in college and asked.

"Didn't you used to be in the IJLB, Ralph?

"Yes," I replied (already it seemed like another life ago).

The friend said nothing and handed me the Evening News. On the back page in the stop press was written:

"There is to be an inquiry into the Infantry Junior Leaders Battalion at Parkhall Camp in Oswestry following the suicide of a second boy soldier in the last two months. The Junior leader who has not been named belonged to 'A' Company and was enlisted in a Scottish regiment."

❧

brighton

Some people are born hitchhikers. I was definitely not one of them. The first lift I ever got was on a truck outside Plummer Barracks when I left the army. It was exhilarating for so many reasons, not the least being that Sam Weller and I were on the back of the lorry leaning over the cab as the wind in our faces blew away the dreadful memories of the past few months; it seemed to whistle freedom's song as we rattled and laughed to the train station and our homes.[2]

At college back in Croydon I had fallen in with a nice bunch of kids who were a little bit more daring than most of the middle class teenagers and late developers that attended the place. We all liked jazz and frequented pubs and clubs that played Trad, and two friends called John and Wendy (already a couple at sixteen) often danced the manic skip jive. It never looked cool, and it was certainly too elaborate for me. In spite of home practice sessions with half glances in the 'utility' wardrobe mirror, I used to mix up the bits that the boy was supposed to do, and anyway it was years before I would have had the nerve to ask someone up to dance.

I did think of taking lessons, but schoolboy memories of enrolling

---

[2] see *Angel Laughter,* page 286

with my mate Tom Shaw at Fred & Cynthia's School of Ballroom Dancing (over the top of Burton's the tailors in Crown Hill, Croydon) came flooding back. A desperate attempt to meet girls, it had proved to be an absolute joke, although it gave us the chance to dress up smart and to smoke in a debonair way and look sophisticated.

The natural selection process decrees that any girl who is halfway attractive will not have to seek out a mate, because sooner or later she will be approached by someone, and even if the attentions are unwelcome, she will begin to acquire communication skills in dealing with it. This is not so with boys. Of course it is easier to make an approach to a girl if you are presentable and are able to do so without frightening them, but what if your affliction is shyness? This of course meant that the girls at the dancing school were either there because they really wanted to learn how to dance or, as seemed more credible looking at them, had never received the attentions by normal means from the opposite sex for reasons of size, halitosis or contemporary standards of beauty.

However, most of the handful of lads that were at the dance lessons were, like Tom and me, reasonably nice looking but incredibly shy. Except for Gerald. Gerald wore thick glasses which still hadn't enabled him to see that his teeth needed cleaning, his sweater that had been sweated in was often tucked in his trousers and sometimes, even more off-putting, only tucked in at the back.

We all wore hair cream in those days, but Gerald used Vaseline—and even that couldn't damp down the dandruff that powdered his shoulders. Gerald had been to classes for years and was completely lacking in tact or inhibition when it came to girls. After the instruction period, there would be three dances to close the session: a foxtrot (which was always going to be beyond me), a quickstep and a waltz. My only hope was the waltz, which I could make a reasonable stab at so long as it was in a straight line. Tom and I would stand in the shadows at the back of the room watching the hideous Gerald dancing with the girl of his choice, invariably the one we had hoped to have the last waltz with.

After four weeks we both quit. Apart from the small selection of 'talent', Fred our perfumed instructor was having far too much fun dancing the girl's part and teaching the boys, whilst his colleague, a large lady who was always in her ballroom gown, danced solely with the girls. A peculiar case of role reversal.

Barney Matthews not only liked jazz but had interests along the lines of the Beat scene that was beginning to attract me. Of course my main interest was getting laid, but although partially liberated by my army experiences, I now had to learn new approaches to girls with names like Thalia and Glennis who lived in the posh suburbs of Woodmansterne and Tadworth. This was much harder than I thought it would be, as I know they viewed me as a bit of an oik. These were mostly the girls doing O-levels but the college was full of girls. As soon as I saw someone I wanted to get to know, I looked around and found someone I wanted more.

The influence of Barney, John and Wendy had a calming effect on me (unlike that of Les). Our trips around local clubs drew me into a wider circle of acquaintances, and soon we were travelling further and further afield for our entertainment. One weekend Barney and John suggested that we hitch to Brighton for a change of scene, as they had heard through the grapevine that something was happening down there. We agreed to meet every hour on the hour at the Palace pier.

I was partnered by Barney on that trip and I remember the buzz when we got our first car. It was only going twenty miles down the road, so we had to try again somewhere near Gatwick airport. What do you know—we stopped a Bentley. Beginner's luck maybe, but it's not the sort of thing you ever forget. However, it was not long before I found that I'd used all my luck on that first trip.

Our driver was a pleasant chap and very proud of his car. He took the machine up to ninety miles an hour, which was the fastest I had ever been moved in my life. As I leaned back in the big leather seats I began to feel that the world was opening its arms to me and that my new adventure was just beginning. Once at Brighton, we met all our friends and just hung about on the seafront shivering or crowded into steamy cafés to drink a cup of tea. The weather was cold and damp, but we felt free and full of life.

This jaunt became a regular event as winter gave way to spring in 1961, and for some reason more and more kids seemed to be making their way down to Brighton. Most excitingly for me, a good number of them were 'beatniks'. I had decided that these were the people I wanted to be with, and as my confidence grew, so did my hair. One day I was cutting the hedge around our flat and Mrs. Potter walked past up the lane and muttered as she passed, "You're looking more like yer mother every day Ralph!" I was *so* pleased.

Some of the kids had blanket rolls and were sleeping out overnight, so the next requirement was a sleeping bag which I bought from Millets for 37/6.

The first night I slept under the Palace Pier was in the March. I almost froze to death and my back has never been right since. It took me years to realise that there are two things you should never economise on: your shoes and your sleeping bag.

Almost every weekend we would travel down to the seaside and stay overnight. Soon I was travelling on my own, and gradually I got used to always being the last to arrive at the pier. By now I knew where to find everyone, and sometimes after hanging around all day in a windswept and interesting mode, we would find our way to the Three Pigeons coffee bar. There was an open fire somewhere in the place, and soon our young faces were glowing and our hands throbbing as life returned to frozen extremities. At length the dreaded journey back would have to be undertaken and we would slip away singly or in pairs to face the headlights of cars on the London road. Frequently I would walk well beyond the Brighton gates and wait for hours for a lift, but the weekend I decided to partner Les must have been the record.

Les was only marginally worse than me when it came to lifts but he was blessed with more patience. This particular day, there was not much happening and we had decided to meet some other friends at the Whitgift back in Croydon, so we left early.

Of all my friends at school I loved Les the most. He was a true individual and always went his own way. At the age of twelve Les was utterly fearless. He had a racing bike, stripped of all but the essentials, that consisted of two wheels and a front brake with a fixed gear rear wheel. The saddle was set right up in the air and the handlebars were set as low as they could be. I used to watch in awe as he mounted the machine and his legs slowly propelled him up to a fantastic speed. The road outside our school was on a very steep hill and as the one cog on Les's bike only had about ten teeth, by the time his legs were flying up and down at a sprinter's pace, he must have been travelling in excess of forty miles an hour. Sometimes I would see him from the top of my bus home as he gained on it down the hill and whizzed past on the outside. When I later asked him if he was scared, he replied that it was all part of it and even if he'd wanted to stop he would have been unable to. So, like a skier, if an obstacle got in his way, he simply went round it.

I was drawn to him through our shared sense of humour and his infectious, deep laugh, which when it started would set me off till tears ran down both our cheeks. Ironically it was tears of a different nature that brought us together.

It was during one of my few assertive moments at school that an argument developed between us. I am not a scrapper, but whatever it was about I wanted some satisfaction, and a scrap was proposed in the changing rooms, out of sight of the masters who patrolled the playground.

We entered the changing rooms and squared up to each other. I knew I would have to get in first, as once my anger had diffused I would want to call it off. I took a swing at Les, he ducked, and my fist crashed into the wall. I recoiled in pain and Les burst out laughing. My follow-through punch hit him straight in the eye, which shut him up completely. It was plain from the silence that followed that I had hurt him and that he couldn't see to defend himself, so I didn't hit him again. Instead I insisted that I walked him home with his bike as I nursed my bruised hand and pride.

By the time we got to his house we were getting on like the proverbial house on fire, and the next day when I asked how he was, I was delighted to find we were still friends. And friends we remained long after marriage, moves and music combined to split us up in our mid twenties. It wasn't long before I was going home to Les's house at lunchtime from school, where we listened to records and smoked roll-ups in bits of newspaper.

Eventually I gave my dinner money to his mum and she gave me the same as she gave Les. She was only a slightly better cook than the ones at school, but that didn't matter as at least we could have a laugh and a smoke in peace. She was a hard, thin woman but no disciplinarian; she knew we were smoking but said nothing. Mr. Lester was a round-featured man with thin grey hair and remarkably short arms which only just poked out of his jacket. His fingers were always extended as if to compensate, and like Les he couldn't say his 'R's properly.

In conversations about dads, our friends in turn spoke of their fathers' exploits during the war. I proudly revealed that mine had been a Desert Rat, and Les, who had said nothing at the time, afterwards revealed to me that his dad had been what he called a 'cellar rat' during the war. That is, he had gone down the cellar and not come up for the next six years except to impregnate Mrs. Lester.

The Lesters' eldest son Colin was a very bright lad, but had dropped out of grammar school and was working as a milkman. He said little, but usually could be relied upon to sell us the odd cigarette. Les's sister was a striking redhead of fifteen. To have a sister who was apparently sexually active whilst still underage filled me with optimism, as I fell in love daily with girls on the bus going to the school up the road.

All in all they fascinated me; they were quite unlike any family I had ever met. They seemed to cope with what life threw at them, and our lunch breaks were full of laughter and merriment before facing the uphill walk back to school.

As we ambled out of Brighton that Sunday afternoon, such thoughts were far from my mind. Here we were again on the way to 'find out', in trouble of sorts but neither of us could have cared less. I don't suppose more than half a dozen words were said without one or both of us chuckling. I can see him now, his slightly bow legs striding purposefully forward, a cigarette between his fingers, whilst his small bright blue eyes screwed up to pinpricks of merriment as we spoke in Stanley Unwin language to amuse ourselves.

As our inability to stop a car became more apparent, our laughter turned slowly to mild hysteria. Hours slipped by and we debated as to whether the best place to stop was where we were or back down the road—or maybe just around the corner. As it was, the two unluckiest hitchhikers in the world spent the next eight hours on the A23 trying to get a ride.

In desperation near the King's Head pub at Pease Pottage we jumped out in front of a Mark Two Ford Consul, whose driver gave us a lift to Redhill and lied that he had planned to stop for us anyway. We eventually arrived home after catching a Green Line bus, on which we both fell asleep, our 45 mile journey having taken thirteen hours.

From then on I hitched alone until I left for abroad with Max Faulkner in 1962.

One Saturday morning our friends had decided to travel to Brighton, and as usual I started out on the Purley Way just behind my house. After what for me represented a very short wait (about an hour), a van stopped and I clambered aboard. Lying in the back were two blokes who had hitched the van from further up the road. I had seen one of them before and knew him as Rod; the other one was unknown to me. After acknowledging my existence with a nod, they started to talk in a kind of beat shorthand which was a mixture of Kerouac, the Goon Show and the boogly boogly shoe.

Rod was disdainful in manner and was decorated in hip London garb, his hair was long and back-combed and he wore gloves with rings on the outside and a black jacket. Even before he cut his first record Mr. Stewart cut quite a dash. I got to see him in places up the West End on several occasions, but I particularly remember him at Brighton one day on the seafront. The beatnik element used to gather at a place called the old fish market and by now a few players would arrive on the weekends and play a little Trad. This always pulled a crowd, and many of the onlookers stopped just to gaze at the unwashed hordes who sat around trying to look interesting.

One of our number (Trev) suddenly got up. Without a hint of embarrassment, and using the deserted market as an echo chamber, he burst into a stagey version of *Nobody's Child*. The effect was incredible. Money was thrown from the people above, and some said that women had actually shed tears at his plaintive rendition. We all certainly looked like nobody's children.

After a half-hearted attempt to auction an alarm clock, a scuffle broke out and there on the beach in front of us a fight was in progress between Rod Stewart and a girl. We were all dumbfounded, but none of us could take our eyes off what we were watching. Like most scraps it was over in minutes, but my abiding memory is one of pity for Rod as he was in tears of frustration and rage and obviously very deeply hurt. He had no sense of shame at his crying and seemed oblivious to the reactions of the other blokes around him.

That of course is not how we described the incident to friends later. Rod was one of many names that were characters on this scene; in particular I think of Italian Tony and Horse-Head Clive, John the Road and Gnome Pat, as well as Steve and Terry from Croydon and Trev from the Cocalina coffee bar in George Street.

The Cocalina was the first real coffee bar I went to. It was owned by a Mr. Block and it had a small dance floor where I would watch entranced as boys and girls performed their strange, mannered dance routines. Fashions were changing once more, and a weird hybrid style was emerging.

The girls were wearing tight skirts and tops with their hair back-combed at the crown and fringes in the front. The boys were wearing suits of tailored quality, striped shirts with detachable collars, slim ties without Windsor knots and often handmade boots in dark green or blue leather.

Terry Atkinson was an adherent to this style, and so was his friend Brian Ash, who went out with a very striking girl. This couple were wonderful to watch, and together the whole group of kids at the Coke were known as 'Modernists'. They showed a degree of sophistication that would not be around again in youth culture for a very long time. Gradually they evolved into proper Mods, but their first incarnation was what impressed me most.

Having neither money nor scooter, Les and I adopted a style some-where between mod and Teddy boy as we couldn't bear to do our hair styles à la mode, and so clung to our traditional Tony Curtis cuts.

We started making regular visits to the Streatham Locarno ballroom on Wednesday evenings, but remained poor pathetic dancers in spite of that. It was actually torture to look at the incredibly pretty girls and still be too shy to ask them to dance. We would get dressed up in our Blake Brothers jackets and black cavalry twill trousers, black suede shoes and elaborate post-Teddy Boy hairstyles. These creations were held together with Brilliantine, sold in Woolworth's for a shilling a tin. You could sculpt your hair into amazing shapes, and it would normally hold up until you got really hot. Then a trickle of lavender-scented sweat and grease would run down from your sideboards.

Usually we went on the bus, and Les would stay over at my place. The order of the evening would be to wander around the gallery and gaze at the girls down on the floor, and for me to watch enviously as boys who were much more stylish and bold with their fashions would expertly swing, glide and turn, in what seemed the height of sophisticated, distracted elegance, with equally posed and pretty girls with bouffant hairdos and slim fitting skirts. After another circuit at floor level, Les used to aim for the bar, and in truth he did not seem to mind that he was as partnerless as I was as the end of the evening, because he was often quite merry by then.

My yearnings were soon forgotten as we reminded each other of particularly stunning girls we had seen on the dance floor. Each time I promised myself that next week I would get up and ask a girl to dance.

Once on the floor, all the kids had a way of seeming disinterested in their partner. It was as if being with someone enabled you to express your style in a way that would have been impossible on your own. It was the combined effect that was the art. Hands connecting, heads turned at the right time, and turns executed with unspoken understanding.

For my part I had to count. This was partly to remember my moves but also to distract myself from the intoxicating nearness of some lovely creature who had the power to turn me to jelly. The feel of a waist or the suspicion of a breast as your arm passed under hers to direct a turn. Of course inevitably even the most studied disinterested partner could hardly fail to notice my lips counting one- two- three- four or whatever, and this probably seemed as if I was talking to myself. I just could not manage the studied cool of most of the boy dancers. Still it was great to wander about amongst the kids of our own age and pose and smoke and fantasise.

There were two live bands at the Loc. They had a revolving stage, and at some point in the evening it would begin to rotate, with the other band, already playing the next tune, swinging into view. Some of these bands were really good, but even then the brief period when they played actual records was the one the kids loved best. As the bass notes of The Marcels singing *Blue Moon* started there was a rush to the dance floor that neither band could engender.

The kids who flooded the floor were terribly stylish in their south London chic. Some of the fashions and hairstyles had not yet reached Croydon a mere mile or two down the A23. The boys were beginning to back-comb their hair and were wearing cashmere polo neck sweaters, and some even had what looked suspiciously like bell-bottom trousers. Les thought they looked like poofs. In fact they were mostly tough South London lads with an eye for style, and some of them were starting to arrive at the Loc on super little Vespas and Lambrettas. All the boys wore suits and/or the fashionable sweaters or celluloid collars. None of them wore lavender scented Vaseline hair grease or bought their jackets from Blake Bros. of West Croydon. Les and I must have stood out like a couple of hicks.

This particular evening I had been watching the same blonde girl in a black shift dress all night. Most of the time she had been dancing with her mate, and once I was sure that she was without a bloke (I did not fancy one of the legendary punchups that sometimes occurred) I waited for a slow tune, then walked quickly over to her and asked formally if she would like to dance. That was the only time she looked at me, and after grinning to her even prettier mate we took to the floor.

All my 'between the beds' and 'back door' rehearsals for this moment had not prepared me for actually feeling the softness of a real partner in a shiny dress, and I managed to tread on her foot at least once as I affected the mandatory disinterested pose of the young dancers. I was erotically charged and hot, with a trickle of lavender scented perspiration running down my cheek and ready to propose marriage. However, before I could say anything to her she said 'thanks' and quickly returned to her mate, where they both sat giggling. I walked away with a strange walk in an attempt to hide my manhood and a broken heart. Someone later told me that the girls 'up the Loc' always turned you down after one dance to keep you keen, but how was I to know that?

Les was impressed, though more with my nerve than my expertise. Anyway, by now he had discovered scotch and orange and usually went home pissed and content.

∾

singer

More and more lads were turning up to the Loc on scooters, and some of them were spectacular. One bloke who always wore a brown suit and winklepickers had a Vespa GS whose panels had been electroplated in copper. He'd also had it tuned so that when the boys pulled away from the front of the venue after the dance, his machine would burn off the rest in a satisfying throaty purr. These little machines were very quick and considered not in the least unmanly.

Some of the boys had started wearing parkas, as the Modernists gradually metamorphosed into Mods. Les and I saw ourselves more as rockers at this time, but couldn't have afforded a motorbike (although I had driven a BSA Bantam down Factory Lane and loved the thrill). However, one day whilst looking in a sweetshop window we saw a car for sale, so we bought it.

It was a 1939 Singer Super Twelve with overhead camshaft, and we got it for ten pounds. The bloke that sold it to us never questioned our age, so I suppose we looked old enough. I can still see Les's look of con-centration as we pulled away round the block to test-drive it.

"You'll soon get used to that clutch," said the vendor.

"I had a little trouble at first," said Les, lurching round the bend.

"Yes, you have to mean it when you want to stop it, she's a heavy old girl. It's a lot of car for ten quid." We stopped millimetres from a parked car in front of us.

"I think I'll try reverse gear," said Les knowledgeably.

"You try anything you like mate," said the man, and as Les noisily found reverse he added, "One of the first overhead camshaft motors, you know."

"Yeah, it makes such a difference," said Les. Sitting in the back seat I had to look out of the window to hide my laughter as Les once again struggled to shift into the next gear.

"You'll find it best to double de-clutch going down through the gears," said the man helpfully.

"What about going up through the gears?" asked Les.

"Well yes, it helps if you do it going up as well." As I wondered what the hell a double de-clutch was, Les had lit a Woodbine to help steady his nerves, and the smoke was getting in his eyes as his lips gripped the end in concentration. With smoke now drifting up his nose and half blind, he suddenly sneezed, which caused his foot to slip off the accelerator and made the car lurch almost to a standstill.

"Ah, testing the compression," said the man, and turning to me gave a knowing wink. "There's nothing wrong with the compression, and it hardly burns any oil either," he lied.

Having sprayed the windscreen with his sneeze, Les endeavoured to clean it with a bus ticket, and then seemingly using all his strength to turn the wheel, he manoeuvred it into a suitable parking place and told the bloke we'd have it.

Les pulled out ten one pound notes (Les worked two paper rounds) and slowly—and I thought very maturely—counted them out. How he did it without laughing after the ballsup he'd made of the test drive I don't know, but by now the madness of what we were doing had taken us over, and we were in a play that would only end when the curtain came down.

And this was only scene one. As the chap handed over the log book and keys he said, "I'm probably selling it too cheap and in a few years it'll be a classic. There you go, easy come easy go." Then the classic remark from the man that's just sold you a pup: "Good luck with the car, boys."

"Thanks a lot mate," we chirped, and in a cloud of blue smoke and grinding gears we lurched off down the road.

I was very impressed with Les's ability, as he had only once before driven his brother's car, and then only down the street. And here we were, motorised! There was of course the small matter of insurance, and come to that a licence for which neither of us would have been eligible for another year anyway.

But this was the least of our worries as Les battled valiantly to keep our vehicle on a straight course down the road. There was about eight inches play on the steering wheel before the wheels were moved, so the faster we went the more stable the car became. Les had to move the wheel sixteen inches in each direction more or less all the time just to have some tactile contact with the direction in which he wanted to travel. We pulled up a couple of streets away from where he lived and parked the car. It was only then I noticed how much my friend was shaking.

We stayed put while we smoked a cigarette, and then Les said, "Right, let's go, I'll drop you home and have a chat with Colin about learning what a double de doobie is and we'll go for a drive tomorrow." With that we ground a bit more metal off the first gear cog and lurched off down the road to Croydon.

For a few days we were content to drive about locally and as a precaution against getting a tug from the police had borrowed the full driver's licence of an acquaintance. As we drove about Croydon with Les double de-clutching beautifully, we would repeat the mantra:

Here we are in the Singer Super Twelve
Nineteen thirty nine
With plush interior and overhead camshaft
With Derek J. Lester driving
On Patrick B. Bowman's licence.

After about a week we were ready to venture further afield. Not really having a better idea I suggested Banbury, where my pretty cousin Christine lived. With only a glance at the map we were off. At one point the car achieved the heart-stopping speed of between 65 and 80 mph (the speedo needle oscillated violently between the two marks). It sure was thrilling and we cheered the old girl on as we trundled towards Banbury.

Once there I telephoned Christine, who must have been surprised to hear from me, especially when I told her we were in town and would she meet us in a little pub near the Town Hall. She agreed, saying she would bring her friend Eileen. Les and I rolled up to the pub, majestically parked the old car and went inside.

We ordered two light and bitters and sat down in the corner in the shadows. We attracted only the attention any stranger attracts in a small market town, and although by London standards we were pretty plainly dressed it was clear from our garb that we were from out of town.

We were only halfway down our drinks when a bloke in a mackintosh walked in and said in a loud voice, "Does anyone here own a Singer Super Twelve?"

My heart sank and Les looked anxiously at me.

"Say nothing," I mouthed.

"What if it's the cops?" Les mouthed back.

I shook my head and prayed that it wasn't, then in my anxiety spilled the best part of a quarter of a pint down my swish London gear.

"Does anyone here own a Singer Super Twelve?" repeated the man, louder this time. Most of the bar looked around at us as we buried ourselves in our pints.

"All right, suit yourselves," said the man with just a hint of exasperation in his voice, "only it's on fire outside."

Les and I looked at each other, then jumped up at the same time and rushed to the door to find smoke pouring out from under the bonnet. On lifting it up it was clear that there had been a short circuit of some kind, as all the wiring to the headlights was burning like a slow fuse on a cartoon stick of dynamite. As we stood there helplessly, a helpful local asked for the keys and after jiggling them about in the ignition managed to stop the burning.

"Don't worry boys, she'll still drive but you'll have to wait until tomorrow as you won't have any lights."

"Oh good," said Les.

"Thanks mate," I said, and we trooped back dejectedly to the pub as Christine and Eileen arrived. Somehow we had a bit of a laugh and Les and Chris seemed to hit it off. When everyone had gone home and the little town was dark and silent, Les kissed Chris goodnight, I shook hands with Eileen and we crept back to our car. Starting it up, we limped with one lamp to a quiet street where we tried to grab a few hours' kip.

At first light we headed off back to London. Most of the way back Les was silent and even the mantra failed to produce the normal effect. The truth was that Les was smitten by my cousin Chris, and I felt a kind of glow for him.

Les and I eventually stopped going to the Loc. My wardrobe was changing from the pre-mod styles of the early sixties, along with my taste in music. I stopped using hair Vaseline and began washing it every day with egg shampoo from Mum's chemist. For spots I spent a fortune on Valderma balm that did not work, and I switched from Blake Bros. in the High Street to Millets at the top of Surrey Street market. There was a dress code even for the beat crowd.

Dances, however, were still the best places to mix with girls, and it was at one such evening at the college that I found myself talking to Susan. Of all the girls at college she was the most out of reach for me, as she was always deeply involved with one or two of the more sophisticated blokes. Currently it was Adam, a striking lad who unfortunately tucked his jeans into his black suede boots. He looked like Jack in search of a beanstalk, and he had landed the sexiest girl in the college.

Still, he had forsaken the beautiful Susan for a girl with shiny hair—which Susan pointed out was because she only washed it once a week, whilst her own was washed every day. I instinctively breathed in her hair aroma and was even more intoxicated.

She wore a perfume called Apple Blossom, and sometimes when walking past the fruit counter in a supermarket I am still reminded of her. She prattled on about this and that, and I was hardly able to believe that she was talking to me. She kept pushing her hair behind her ear like girls do when they are deep in concentration. The unposed naturalness somehow conveyed an unguarded, little girl look. Christ she was sexy in the dim light of the hall. She giggled, fidgeted and smiled, and all the time she was looking and talking with me. I leaned against the wall as much to hold on to something as to appear casually interested. She babbled on about Adam and her and I nodded where it seemed appropriate.

Suddenly she stopped talking and looked at me with a softness in her smiley eyes. It was not exactly a come-on but I found myself unable to stop, and I leaned forward and kissed her and she kissed me back and I felt like I was starting to float from the floor. I tried to appear nonchalant as I lit a Park Drive, which stuck to my lip on the first drag and pulled off a small but painful piece of skin. She didn't seem to notice, and I offered to see her home. I hardly recognised my own voice which seemed to have temporarily returned to choir boy pitch. Again Susan failed to notice. She took my hand and we headed for the door.

I was almost overcome with excitement as I sat next to the fragrant-haired girl whose head was lightly resting on my shoulder, and the six-mile, two-bus journey took no time at all. I dabbed at my torn lip with my bus ticket until it was quite specked with blood and wondered if she was thinking of me or Adam. Would she regret this move? Had she planned to make Adam jealous? I checked my packet of cigarettes to make sure that I had enough to last the night, and enjoyed her snuggled up form sitting next to me on the almost deserted upper deck rear seat on the 112 bus.

Soon we were at her front door and suddenly she was kissing me goodnight and it was the most wonderful moment and suddenly I was in her house and we were going to have coffee and suddenly we were almost out of control.

Then, in no time, I was having to leave and catch my bus, my un-touched coffee cold in her kitchen, the beautiful Susan waving and smiling on the doorstep, her hair ruffled and her small green eyes sparkling. The last bus had long gone and I had to frequently rest as I staggered home, my head full of plans, my heart full of hope and my loins feeling like they'd been kicked by the milkman's horse.

We were fairly cool at college because she was still sort of going with Adam, or at least not arousing his suspicions that there might be someone else. I was confused as to what my role in all this was, but our evenings compensated for our lack of contact during the day; in fact they made it more delightful.

Susan's mum seemed to like me, and we were always left alone in the front room. There was a pencil drawing of Susan's father on the sideboard. He had died a few years before and I imagined him watching us both as we got as near to consummation as she dared.

I think Susan liked me for what she perceived as my feral qualities. Certainly I was more rough-hewn than her other boyfriends. I had not quite developed into a Beat and I was not a Mod; I was rather drab in appearance, but I tried to be considerate and I did seem able to make her laugh. At this time, all I wanted was sex, whereas most of the girls seemed to want a long-lasting deep relationship. Susan, however, did not. It was as if she was prepared to learn about certain intimacies so as to be prepared for her Jack and the Beanstalk man. I began to feel a little used. She seemed more consumed by curiosity than either love or passion, and once or twice I caught her looking over at Adam in the common room where I was supposed to be cool and not show real signs of our 'togetherness'.

The so called swinging sixties were not all free love and sexual abandon. Most of the kids I knew at college were still virgins at sixteen; I felt light years away from most of them and indeed as far as life experience went, I could not relate to many of them at all. Even so, as far as virginity was concerned, I was in the same boat. There were a few steady couples that may have been having a more intimate relationship, but most of us were still at the fumbling stage, and certainly most of the girls I met had a sort of code as to how far they would let a boy go with them. In many ways this only added to the excitement. Most still lived at home, and the lack of facility to explore, and the certainty that even if you were left alone together there would be an authority figure nearby only added to the intensity and urgency of pre-Pill gropings.

At Easter, Les drove the three of us in the Singer to the Mitcham Fair. I wandered around the stalls and was amazed to find so many familiar faces still working there. The boy who wanted comics from me was now in charge of the rifle range, and I was relieved that he did not recognise me, but the old lady on the 'Pick A Straw' stall[3] was long gone. The hierarchy of the fairground remained, with the lads now my age taking change from the punters whilst balancing on the swirling whirling machines with Bruce Channel's *Hey Baby* blaring from distorted loudspeakers. The shrieks of excited girls and the posturing of young lads amongst the coloured lights was stimulating, as I searched amongst the weather-beaten faces and tattoos for people I had known from my short stay with the fair.

Les was patient and happy, occasionally slipping off to ride on some machine by himself whilst Susan and I wandered over the cinders, breathing in the smell of fried onions and candy floss on the air. Susan did not share in my nostalgia, and after one or two rides she said she was cold, and could we go back to the car. I thought this was a little bit odd but there was something in her eyes that suggested she really meant it.

I borrowed the keys of the car, and while Les had a few extra turns on the 'Whip' and the 'Waltzer', Susan and I climbed into the back seat. Soon the windows steamed up and there behind the trailers and caravans, amid the thump and smell of the diesel generators mixed with

---

[3] see *Angel Laughter*, page 183

the scent of apple blossom, leather, woodwork and chrome, Susan finally dared; and through the hubbub of swirling, heightened senses over the rattling loudspeakers, Little Richard expertly articulated the moment: "Awopbopaloobopalopbamboom."

∾

whitgift

Les was often quite moody at this time, partly I suppose because he couldn't see Chris as much as he would like, and partly because the car was getting less reliable. His mum had found out about it and naturally wanted him to get rid of it. One sunny evening we were driving through the old part of Croydon at the bottom of Scarbrook Road when the old girl came to a halt and refused to start again. This was really it, and after a great deal of swearing we pushed her round the corner, took our bits and pieces out of it and left her to the vultures on the estate at Salem Place. As we walked around the corner, the Whitgift Arms appeared in front of us and suggested that we went in for a cheer up drink.

The public bar was a long narrow room with a dartboard at one end and the gents toilet to the left. Just inside the door and to the right was an elderly piano and running away from it along the window was a settee. Further into the room was the bar itself and opposite it and extending all the way up to the toilets were benches. It was early evening and there were only a couple of people in the place.

As we walked up to the bar, a kindly looking bloke with a neat tie and Fair Isle pullover asked, "What'll it be, gents?"

I looked at the prices that were scrawled in chalk on the barrels that rested on the counter as I felt around in my pocket for change. As well as a few coppers, I felt the reassuring weight of a half crown. I can still remember the prices:

Bitter @ 1/10d per pint
Gaymers cider @ 1/2d per pint
Coates cider @ 1/3d per pint

"Two pints of cider please," I said, pointing to the barrel of Coates. The barman turned the squeaky spigot on the cask and dispensed the liquid into two rather greasy glasses.

Hot from our efforts to start the car, we drank the stuff far too quickly and Les ordered another. Cider is so easy to drink when you are young; it's only a short stop from apple flavoured cordials. We were only halfway down the second pint when the alcohol kicked in and for some unaccountable reason the bloke next to us started to twitch and nod his head quite violently in agreement with nobody.

Les found it very funny and as usual I found Les's laugh dangerously infectious. At first it was under control, but the more we tried to stop ourselves laughing the more hilarious it got, until Les finally broke out with a huge "HA HA HA HA HA!" and the flood gates opened. I joined in and soon we were near helpless with merriment. The bloke next to us nodded and twitched knowingly and gave the barman a wink which said the cider's got to the young fellows. The barman nodded and the bloke next to us said, "W-W-Well aren't you going to let us in on th-th-th-the j-j-joke?"

As he spoke his head twitched violently to the right and left then once up and down.

His friend leaned round to look at us and blinking in an exaggerated way added, "Come on lads what's so funny?"

This was all too much for us. When Les did manage to get a word out, all he could say was, "Blimey there's two of them," and then more laughter.

I managed to come up with, "It's our motor, it's just blown up and we're just seeing the funny side of it."

The two regulars half smiled, twitched, blinked and resumed drinking and I helped my friend outside into the bright evening sunshine. We wandered off towards south Croydon with a really great cider buzz on and resolved to meet back at the pub for more of the same the next evening.

The two men we met that afternoon were Big Eddie, who was a kitchen porter, and Reg, who worked for a firm called Skinner's Removals. The landlord was called Maurice and his wife was called Rene (pronounced Reen). They were a kindly, tolerant couple, and thanks to Les and I, their little cider pub became a hang out for half the dropouts and art students in Croydon. Most of their regular clientele were in advanced states of cider addiction but there was hardly ever any trouble there.

Cider was so cheap that for 3/9d (three pints) we'd all be "silly as a box of night lights" as Georgie would say. Georgie was a dustman and a perfect Teddy boy, who'd never given up on the old style and music. His authentic appearance was only diminished when he opened his mouth to speak: poor Georgie's voice had never broken and he sounded like a five year old who had learned to swear. He was in most nights and always spotless with a clean neckscarf tied sailor-like round his throat. Then there was Danny, an Irishman from Cork city who no-one but me could understand because of his accent (my childhood neighbour Mr. Connaughton came from Cork, so for me it was fairly easy). To finance his drinking Danny did a bit of caddying up at Croham Manor golf course.

Gypsy Tony was a tiny man almost bent double with a curvature of the spine. He was about seventy when I knew him and had been a soldier in the 1914-18 war.

"I was in Kitchener's army in the Pioneer Corps 'cos I weren't too fit an' they 'ad me pickin' up bits o' bodies an' puttin' 'em in bags out in France. I said fuck this an' I took a penn'orth. They tol' me I was lucky not to get shot them bastards. For desertin' you see."

Tony was a sweet guy and I always sat with him for a while down the pub. He had lost part of a finger in the war but had never had the amputation done, so from where his first joint should have been a piece of stained bone protruded, which was a bit grisly, but which he seemed to use to his advantage in rolling cigarettes.

One night after a few drinks in a serious moment he reached over and clutched my arm and said, "You're an educated chap Ralph an' I want to ask you somefin'. Do you fink it's wrong for a man to interfere wiv hisself?"

At first I wanted to burst out laughing, but then I saw the concern in his eyes; this dear little old man was really troubled.

"You see I'm a caflick and the church says that a man should not interfere wiv hisself."

I knew from previous conversations with Tony that he was once married and that his wife had died. I looked into his sad deep brown eyes and with all the authority I could muster at sixteen or seventeen said, "If you believe in God and he gave you eyes to see and you didn't use them or legs and you refused to walk or a tongue and you refused to speak, what would God say? When you do whatever you do perhaps you think of your wife and in a way you celebrate her memory and the things you once had, how could any god be angry with that?"

I looked him in the eye and he looked straight at me, still clutching my arm as his large brown eyes filled up with tears that splattered unchecked down his cheeks on to the table.

"Thanks Ralph," he said, wiping his face on his cuff. He turned away and we never spoke about it again.

Bill Coomber made up the trio with Big Eddie and Reg and every night they joined in close harmony and sang. Bill struck me as officer class; he was always immaculately dressed and wore a bow tie every evening. He always sat in the same place at the end of the bar and kept an eye on the rest of us. Bill had a natural ear for close harmony and sang instinctively a third above the melody line against Eddie's clear baritone and Reg's crooning tenor. I loved these goodnight songs that eased us all into the night as we went our several ways home.

> *"It's long and thin*
> *It dangles down your chin*
> *Have a guess, Yes yes*
> *It's spaghetti"*

they sang, and then the *Whiffenpoof Song*:

"We're poor little lambs that have lost our way," they warbled, oblivious of the plaintiveness and accuracy of the description.

Big Eddie had a solo:

> *"When I was a wee wee tot*
> *They took me from my wee wee cot*
> *And put me on my wee wee pot*

To see if I could wee or not
And when they saw that I could not
They took me from my wee wee pot
And put me in my wee wee cot
Where of course I weed a lot."

He sang this nearly every night and always with the same response: everyone laughed politely at the end and Eddie accepted the applause with many a nod and twitch. One night, his Northern Irish wife who had been waiting outside for him for ages came back in and demanded that he leave with her now.

"Away w-w-with you w-w-woman," he said playfully and gestured with the back of his hand his feeling that she was trifling with more important work. As she stormed out of the bar Eddie burst into the *Wee Wee Tot* song. As he reached the last line, she strode into the bar, grabbed a full pint of cider from the counter and poured the whole lot over his head. Eddie just kept singing, his last note held as never before. That was the best it ever went down.

"He shouldn't have done that," said Bill Coomber in my ear.

"Why?" I asked. "You mean he should have shown her more respect?"

"No," said Bill, "that was my pint she poured over him."

News of the Whitgift spread quickly. There was a happy mix of younger and older generations united by the need for cheap drink and good company. Guitars appeared some nights, piano players on others. We always deferred to the older crowd and they in the main tolerated us. Drunkenness was common but was seldom followed by aggression.

Paddy from Dublin had also fought in the First World War. He was a passable pub piano player, but that job was usually done by an old boy with thick lensed glasses and a flat cap. He always blamed the cold temperature in the bar for his frequent mistakes, which was a cue for someone to buy him a drink. However Paddy the dep had another weapon at his disposal: he used to carry a chanter in his top inside pocket and would wail away on some forgotten named slow air or a jig if he had the puff. A chanter is the practice pipe of the uileann or Irish pipes and the sound is made by blowing through a small reed rather like an oboe; it has a mournful note when played without the drones and regulators.

"It was the gas in the war you know. The gas got me chest," he would gasp before breaking out into such terminal-sounding coughing that someone always bought him a drink.

"Ah no," he would decline, "A beer's no good to me, I better have a little Irish. It's the same price you know."

This little parlour trick usually resulted in the old devil getting two drinks for his performance, for if the benefactor went to pick up the pint to exchange it, the old boy's claw would strike out like a snake, and with surprising strength for one so close to death he would grasp the wrist that threatened to carry the drink away and rasp, "I might manage that if you give me a minute to get the whiskey down."

Over the next two years, hundreds of kids must have visited the place, and not just from our neck of the woods. Beatniks from London's Duke of York in Charlotte Street appeared, together with couples from Brighton, and kids from Mitcham and Purley, Carshalton and Streatham, Thornton Heath and Norbury. Art students and bikers, poets and rogues all crammed into the tiny bar.

Amongst the girl regulars were Pat and Cathy, in duffel coats and dyed black hair, Margot, who was Indian and very tiny, and the Croydon Beat chapter of Steve, Val Liloff, John Kercher, Brian, and, recently returned from Spain where he'd grown his hair long, Terry Atkinson, former Modernist and now complete beatnik with a travelling past.

Terry had actually done it: he had hitched to Spain, picked grapes for his living, and travelled along the Côte d'Azure. He'd written poems and philosophised about the travelling life and I was captivated. Terry was always complimentary about my guitar playing and come to that, my attempt at painting. He gave me the kind of support you can only get from someone who is older than you are, and it was through Terry that I met Max.

∾

SUMMER LIGHTNING

max

Max Faulkner was older than me by a couple of years, and when you are seventeen, two years is a big gap. He was a great character. At nineteen he had a face that was lived in and a voice that sounded like it broke in the womb. In reality he lived with his mum. He was certainly the biggest bloke in our group of friends, weighing I should guess fourteen stone (I weighed eleven). His hair was starting to go back at the temples and was combed forward, Nero-like, in a short curly fringe. He walked incredibly erect and sort of bounced on the balls of his feet, his step sure and his whole demeanour exuding confidence. His ever present acne would have turned a more sensitive soul into a monk in a silent cloistered order, and his crowning glory was his huge scarred nose.

If you didn't know him you would have thought "Who is this arrogant ugly bastard?", but because you did know him and because his couldn't-give-a-fuck attitude was genuine, and because there was no harm in him and he had such a great smile, all the girls loved him. If we were all left wing beatniks, then Max was a redneck. He loved cowboy songs and the Carter Family music and, without noticing any irony, the songs of Woody Guthrie too. We soon hit it off really well, learning all sorts of songs together. Max was the guy I taught *San Francisco Bay Blues* to, and he showed me an E minor chord in exchange. We'd often play down at the Whitgift and at other outings that somehow got organised.

Through him I met at least another dozen kindred souls and soon we were getting invited to parties if we'd bring our 'boxes'. This of course was great because we never had to bring any drink, and until I got too drunk to play I had a wonderful time. The down side to all of this was Max's party piece.

After picking the night away and having plenty to drink, he would disappear into some room in the house only to reappear naked except for his bush hat. I have tried to indicate that Max was a big chap, and he was big in all departments. He would march into the main room with lights full on smoking a Pall Mall cigarette without a hint of shyness, and enjoy the gasps of amazement from the girls and the looks of envy from the boys as he performed forward rolls on front room carpets all over south London. I can still see the slap of his tackle as he rolled head over heels amongst the Axminster and Wilton. At one do, a very bonny and well-endowed girl called Sally joined him in his display. They became more of a double act than Max and me, and if we were planning to go to a party or crash one the question always came up: "Will Max and Sally be there?" Not surprisingly, they became lovers.

As the summer of '62 washed over me, I moved through friends and acquaintances like a bird in some migrating flock. We were all travelling in the same direction but no-one knew where we were going. Sometimes I was at the front, usually around the middle section, seldom at the rear. The two years penance spent at college had been a bit of a waste; my second year attempt at improving my exam results had only produced an A-level in Art. Earlier friendships had been temporarily outgrown, and though I didn't realised it at the time, music was the force that would drive me from now on. This was the summer when people I had met in the Soho pubs turned up again closer to home. In particular Henry Bartlett, who has been a lifelong friend since those days. Henry lived in Mitcham, and his mum and dad were constantly warm and encouraging to this young guitarist.

One weekend we all went down to the river at Richmond. We hired a couple of skiffs and rowed them and hauled them up weirs and waterfalls to Hampton Court. On the way back, our boat suffered a glancing blow from a pleasure steamer and sustained damage that nearly cost us our lives, let alone our deposit. Somehow Les replaced the shattered wood by the rowlocks and balanced the splinters like a vertical jigsaw, and the owner failed to notice as we tied up just a little way from the boathouse. That night we slept out in the shelter at the back of the towpath. We had our sleeping bags, or in my case an old World War Two army blanket and a couple of safety pins, as I had decided that sleeping bags weren't cool.

I was cool all right and as usual shivered the night away. Eventually, as the morning arrived, I gave up on any sleep and looked over to where Les was lying in exactly the same position he had adopted the previous evening. He had borrowed a couple of deck chairs and after predictable slapstick setting them up, had managed to make some sort of bed. I shall never forget the look of total repose on his face as he lay there. Partly through envy, but mainly because I was still a bit unsure about the other 'friends' that were sleeping out with us, I woke Les up.

Once we'd had a cigarette, we determined our strategy for the day. We were both hungry and had no money as usual, so Les did the milk round (meaning picking up a pint from a doorstep before the householder brought in the bottles). By the time he got back, Max and Henry had woken and were smoking and coughing and getting adjusted. Les triumphantly presented three pints of milk to the gathering and without saying much we all took huge grateful swigs from the bottles as they were passed round. This milk business did not sit well with me. I often put myself in my mum's position, where the loss of a bottle of milk would have caused some hardship. The unspoken rule was that you never took a single bottle but if there were three or more on the doorstep you could take one.

From the corner of my eye I noticed Henry getting himself together. Henry had always intrigued me. At the tender age of seventeen he'd grown his first beard (or more likely had simply never shaved), he was a huge fan of the Mickey Ashman jazz band and lived for music. This morning he was clearing his throat and smoking his first Senior Service of the day. The large intake of milk first thing had caused a cloying sensation in our mouths and several of the lads were spitting manfully.

This was an art that I had mastered when young, and I could spit with alarming speed and accuracy. So when Henry decided to bring round a waste basket that was in the shelter and pose as a waiter with a spittoon, I saw a chance to impress him. I got myself ready and when it was my turn, I let go a gobbet that should have blown a hole in the bucket. Unfortunately I missed the receptacle completely and shot the contents of my mouth straight up his arm holding the bucket. I was mortified. Les started his distinctive chuckle, whilst my mumbling apologies were sounding wet, and in spite of my cool adoption of a blanket for my image I was looking pathetic.

Henry was determined to drag out the incident for all the comedy it was worth. Without once meeting my eyes—and sensing that everyone was staring at us both—he first looked at his soiled sleeve still holding the bin, then slowly looked at those on his right, then more slowly looked at those on his left, then even *more* slowly his eyes, beginning at my belt buckle, moved slowly up my body until they met mine—and then and only then I could see that his face was slightly contorted in an attempt not to laugh himself. Henry had an operation for a lazy eye when he was a child and when he looked at you a certain way, one of his eyes involuntarily looked upward and it was doing it now. It was all too much for me and we both just cracked up.

Max was his usual ebullient self. We picked away on our guitars, and in a fit of bravado started to play to the crowds walking over Richmond Bridge. At the end of a song, a bloke shouted to us and threw down a half crown. Then a few more coins clattered on to the pavement. We played another couple of songs and got some more coins and made fourteen shillings in three numbers. It was an absolute fortune, and as we went off and bought bacon sandwiches, Max said to me, "Well Woody," (he often called me Woody after the great man and it made me feel good), "I think we may be ready to hit the road!"

Plans were drawn up to go to Greece. Henry was to make his way with June and Stan would find his own way Max and I were to travel together and meet Beau and Sally at Munich main railway station. We left England in the September; I had never been more excited about anything in my life.

The fare across the channel to Ostend was £2-2s. We had decided to go that way for ease of access to Germany. As the boat pulled into the harbour after the four hour crossing, my eyes feasted on all the sounds and sights that greeted them. Everything was different, the cars, the clothes, the voices.

"Listen Max, they're talking in French!"

"That's because it's their language," he explained. The sarcasm was wasted because I was thrilled with everything I saw and heard. I had my blanket roll and a small duffel bag with nothing much in it and my Harmony Sovereign guitar in a soft plastic shaped case over my shoulder. Max had his guitar in a hard case, and a huge rucksack that was packed by his mum. On his head was a ridiculous bush hat and down in his boot was a bowie knife. He had actually written a list of things you might need on the road and one of them was this bloody knife. It worried me.

We found our way out of the port and on to the Ostend-Brussels road. In my pocket I rubbed my lucky farthing and we raised our thumbs in high spirits in anticipation of our first lift. After six hours and a whole packet of duty free Pall Mall cigarettes we had travelled about four hundred metres. I wondered if it was Max's big hat or his enormous rucksack. Perhaps they had X-ray vision and could see through his Levis to where the bowie knife was strapped to his leg. Now I ask myself, 'Would I have stopped for two largish men, one with huge hat, both carrying full size guitars, a duffel bag and a rucksack that could have passed for a double garage?'

Our attempts at nonchalance would probably have been seen as arrogance as we stood puffing away on giant American cigarettes. After the next ferry's shipload of travellers had been accommodated and we were still standing there, I decided to hide some of our gear in the bushes at the side of the road. Sure enough we got a lift in a lorry. Lesson one had been learned and we rattled our way almost to Brussels before the driver put us down and turned off the main road. An early evening mist had begun to fall and we were dead tired. The mist became a fog, and we were stumbling on blindly through it when Max said, "Fuck this for a game of soldiers, I think we ought to try and get some kip."

My heart sank as I fondled my blanket roll; I suppose I had expected that we might sleep under cover but it was no use, we couldn't see anything and the fog had muffled the sound of traffic. I was sure we were no longer on the main road, as what little traffic there had been had dried up to a trickle and no-one could see us until they were on top of us. Max's huge nose and hat would appear out of the fog at the oncoming drivers, which could only have made them want to hurry home to their wives and families and make themselves a comforting hot drink. That was certainly what I could have done with.

With the mist now turning into drizzle and not much of anything moving on the road, we stopped. Max opened his rucksack and pulled out a tiny two-man tent that he had brought with him without telling me. We put it up somehow, and after Max had installed his rucksack, the two guitars and himself, I was invited in with my damp piece of rag posing as a cool bedroll.

The night passed in moist misery. I became aware of the noise of vehicles passing perilously close to our little home, and I poked my head out of the tent flap to be greeted by a terrifying sight. We had only got halfway across a dual carriageway and pitched the tent on the tiny grass central reservation. Traffic was thundering past in both directions at less than a metre from each side. I woke the incredulous Max, and as carefully as we could we packed our gear and found our way to the right side of the road for Brussels. This time I hid in the bushes along with both guitars and Max's rucksack, and this became the pattern for the rest of the journey to Munich.

We arrived in Brussels, had a cursory look round, ate some chips with mayonnaise, and headed out on the Aachen road. That night the weather improved and we slept in the open by a bridge somewhere. For some reason it had seemed wise not to take a map, so I cannot say what our route was but the next city was Cologne. We did eventually find a free map in a petrol station and it helped a bit. Try as I might, I do not remember eating anything else on this trip. We were stuck by the side of the road waiting for lifts, and only if the driver felt like stopping for a coffee in a roadhouse would we get a chance to eat.

As usual I had hardly any money and what I did have (maybe a fiver) was meant for Greece in case we were not able to go busking. Until Frankfurt I survived on coffee and cigarettes, and mostly felt tired rather than hungry.

All my life I had regarded Germany as the enemy, responsible for the loss of a Dad and the misery of our poverty. I expected the Germans to be hostile, and frequently cursed them when they failed to stop for us. However they seemed to bear no malice towards us, and instead wanted to talk in English and to know all about us and what we were doing and where we were going and why.

I found it hard to explain my reasons, and must have looked and sounded very young and vulnerable. It took us about a week to make it to Frankfurt. There we picked up a ride with two American servicemen, who made cracks about the quaintness of the German language; in particular the word Ausfahrt amused them, and us too at first. Then they spoke of the obliging nature of the German girls and generally treated us like manly equals with much chortling and thigh-slapping.

A stye appeared on my right upper eyelid, and my gums started to bleed. My two packs of cigarettes had been consumed and I was now reliant on Max for smokes. He was generous at first, but soon I felt obliged to wait and ask for his 'twos-ups'.4 In Frankfurt we met a gypsy musician who noticed our big guitars. He struck up a halting conversation with us and suggested we go for a beer with him and play some music.

My instinct was to decline, but that was not what we came here for. Off we trooped to some place he knew. Once inside he was greeted like a long lost brother. His guitar was brought to him, drinks were provided and he started to play. It was a German Framus cello guitar, and he was one of those incredible players with a different chord for each beat of the tune. He sang in an unintelligible dialect with a voice that cracked and split in a way that indicated a life of cigarettes and shouting. He was impressive.

He signalled that it was our turn. Max and I removed our guitars from their cases and tuned up. I still hardly ever have a drink in the daytime, and at that age and starving, this beer had gone straight to my head. I played enthusiastically but not well, and after two numbers the people were talking to each other louder than we could play. I reached in my bag, pulled out my harmonica and harness and to much derision, strapped it on and we did a version of *Hard Travelling* that I thought was pretty good. At the end of it the Gypsy guy strapped on an incredible looking machine with six mouth organs fixed like spokes on a wheel. He could play in virtually any key and proceeded to play some unbelievable Austro-Hungarian type melody that made our efforts sound lightweight. With as much dignity as we could muster, we staggered out into the bright Frankfurt sunshine, half pissed and ready for some chips at least. We both fell asleep in a park and woke feeling rotten, but we did manage to get on the road south and spent a night in some trees at the side of an autobahn.

We spent the next two days at the side of the road with nothing to eat and in my case nothing to smoke. I had stopped asking Max for twos-ups and he was flicking his dog ends into the road so that I now had to climb over the barrier to retrieve them. I was beginning to get fed up with him; I had now got another stye on my other eye, my gums were bleeding every time I tried to clean my teeth, and I was running out of toothpaste as I was snacking on it from time to time in my hunger.

To pass the time, I wrote a diary for about five days and letters of description home which my mum failed to keep, saying only that it was good to know that I was all right. From that time on, I have only sent her postcards and she is happier with that than anything else I have ever done.

We eventually arrived in Munich and walked right through the imposing city. Finding our way to the railway station was easy, but we were very tired by the time we settled down with a beer. I managed to find some rolling tobacco, and in the hustle of the main concourse we were hardly noticed, looking for all the world like travellers ourselves, which of course we were. I say 'hardly' because the man who sold the 'warm Wurst und Brot' that was to be our diet for the next week had certainly noticed me, and whenever I looked in the direction of his kiosk his eyes were following me.

That first night we slept down some stairs but were awakened by the general noise of Munich waking up. We got washed in the public toilets that were conveniently near to our resting place. I remember finding it a little disconcerting having a lady sitting there whilst we took a pee, but like everything we got used to it and so long as we left some small change, she didn't mind us making the place our own. My eyes were slowly closing up with the appearance of more styes, my gums still bled, and I couldn't have weighed more than ten stone. My money was totally gone by now and I was beginning to realise that I would soon have to go busking or starve.

I was nearly sick with fright at the thought of playing in public. Max was still OK and had enough bravado for both of us, but he was not pushing too much the idea of playing live. Time, though, was running out. After five days of waiting for the London train it began to dawn on me that Beau was not going to show up. It was typical of the unreliable bastard. Finally one evening we struck up outside the toilets and nervously played our first session, making about eight marks.

This was a great morale boost, and I was able to buy some warm wurst from the sausage seller who was always looking at me. I should have been thrilled with the new opportunities, but I wasn't and I dreaded the next occasion when we would have to play.

I was sleeping in shop doorways wrapped in my pathetic blanket, and shivering the whole night long as merry Germans poured through the station concourse, while not so merry Polizei variously prodded and poked and on several occasions woke me with a boot in the side. My right eye looked as bad as my left, and I could now insert a match into the huge pocket that had appeared behind my front teeth. In spite of being able to eat the warm wurst I felt increasingly miserable. Each night the crowds of people coming through the station ought to have provided us with ample funds to travel anywhere we wanted, but my nerves just let me down and I cried off.

Neither of us could understand where all the people where coming from or going and then the posters advertising the 'Oktoberfest' began to make sense: we were in the middle of the biggest beer festival in the world. We decided to pay a visit. It was huge, on a scale like nothing I had seen before. Max saw it as a great opportunity to busk, but when at last I had the courage (after investing in a couple of beers) the little crowd that gathered thought we were playing out of general bonhomie rather than our lives depending on it. They clapped politely at the end of our couple of numbers and dispersed.

Still, I had to laugh; a couple of the styes had burst and things were looking up! After looking at the rides and the thousands of Germans happily swigging away on huge steins of beer, I began to feel resentment creeping up on me. Part of me, I am sure, knew that if I were able to ask for help or food, these people would have been just as kind as any other, but another part of me was angry. Couldn't they see my ribs poking through my shirt or see my infected eyes? Jesus, some of them were eating legs of pork that would have fed a couple of British families for a week. I mean who won the fucking war anyway? And, more insidiously, what were those songs that they were all singing as they staggered home through the station at night? It sounded to me like I'd heard those songs before.

Beau and Sally's arrival date came and went and Max and I soldiered on as best we could. Max had plenty of dough left but could not show it as it would only underline the difference in our two states. I think he had found some compassion for my situation, and although I know now that all these little distractions would have passed, when I suggested that we return to England he did not resist. I was heartened by this, and took it to imply that despite his bravado he wasn't confident to go it alone, or else he genuinely felt sorry for my predicament. We decided to go home via Paris and immediately perked up at the prospect.

Meanwhile in Greece, Henry had arrived and for the next several weeks dutifully went to the meeting place every day at twelve o'clock to be disappointed at our non-appearance. Stan, who had been out on the camp site with him, finally upped sticks and headed east, and none of us saw him again for nearly two years.

In Paris the two of us hauled our weary way to the Gare du Nord (why does every lost soul head for the station?). I remember nothing of our journey to France, because I slept as soon as I got comfortable or warm in a car. Not much company for the kind person who had stopped for me. Certainly by the time we had arrived we'd had enough and decided that once back in England we would take a train home from Dover. Max generously offered to buy me a meal and we settled on a small workman's café near the station.

"Well Woody, have anything you want," offered my friend.

"You know what I really fancy, Max?" I said. "Egg and chips."

"So do I," he replied and we ordered the meal. I didn't want to take advantage of Max's sudden generosity. Back home the cost of such a workman's lunch would have been about 1/3d. The food arrived and I noticed we had been given two eggs, but nothing prepared us for the shock of the bill when it was presented. The bill came to twelve shillings and sixpence for the two of us! In that time 12/6d was a day's money for a labourer! I felt awful and not having enough French to argue the toss we dejectedly left the place and tried to cheer ourselves up by visiting the Eiffel Tower. This in itself was no mean feat as we had to drag all our bedraggled belongings everywhere we went.

Visiting the tower was not cool (only tourists did things like that and we were road soldiers) but who would know if we didn't tell? We surveyed the city from the top and felt very distanced from the life that bustled below us. I threw a piece of newspaper off the top and watched it vanish as small as a postage stamp below and far away. It was time to go home.

∾

Outside by the wall
Where snails have crawled
Leaving tinselled trails
Shining in the moonlight
Pale
Lovers
Promising nothing will change
The things they share
Breathing promises
Of cloudy vapour disappearing
In the frosty midnight air

PART TWO

SOUTH

pad

The idea of leaving home again and setting up in Poole, in Dorset, came from Tony Dickinson, who I knew from college. Tony was the younger brother of Beau Dickinson, who was very nearly a true Beatnik in the sense that he had not an iota of responsibility, was not the slightest bit creative (except when it came to making up excuses as to why he had broken yet another promise), did not approve of work, and loved modern jazz.

Beau was a very handsome man and the girls adored him. He had black curly hair which he kept unfashionably short on top and a little longer at the back, and a luxuriant black beard to match, which made his beautiful white teeth seem even whiter. His eyes always sparkled with mischief, his nose was large, and he smiled all the time. Tony was a few years younger, and although softly spoken like his elder brother, was much less striking: his eyelashes curled upwards, and though his eyes sparkled just the same, they were smaller than his brother's; and if anything he had an even bigger nose.

Tony was very secretive, which I found annoying because I felt that he thought I didn't understand his allusions and inferences. But to be honest I thought him immature; his professed love of modern jazz seemed unreasonable in one so young, and I assumed he must be doing it for

SUMMER LIGHTNING

effect. Tony knew of my love of guitar music and I can only think that it was for this reason that we got introduced to this circle of people, as at this time there was a very healthy bunch of aspiring country blues players to which we were introduced almost immediately upon our arrival at the 'pad'.

Poole High Street was a very different place in 1962. It had a Georgian feel, and it was all a little run down. There was the usual selection of seaside cafés, cheap restaurants and small shops but no supermarkets.

The pad itself was situated over a betting shop down at the end of the High Street. Access was through a passageway, past the door that led into the shop and up a wide stairway to a landing. There was a bathroom with a bath which was not connected to the water supply. Up a little further to another small landing, where you could either turn left to the main living area or right to several other rooms on various levels and half levels. There was also a lavatory which was mercifully connected to the mains. The living room was L-shaped, with a primitive kitchen arrangement on the left of the door as you entered; the living area was round to the right where there were a couple of old chairs, a distressed sofa, and an open fire on which were burning some old fish boxes. In fact the whole place smelt slightly of fish and I soon discovered why.

The whole of the upstairs was deemed unfit for human habitation and was owned by a local fish shop who leased out the downstairs to the betting shop and for a very modest rent allowed the rooms upstairs to be used as an artist studio for one of the residents called Dick. Naturally enough when Dick saw how much room was available, he quickly filled it up with fellow students so that the rent was hardly felt by anyone and always promptly paid, which in turn meant that no-one ever checked up on us. At one time there were at least eight people living, cooking, playing, loving, and occasionally even painting in the place.

When I arrived at the pad I had about £2 to my name, a sleeping bag, a spare shirt and underpants, a toothbrush and razor, a towel and a Harmony Sovereign guitar with a spare set of strings and a capo, which were unsafely housed in a white hardboard case with a red lining. The clothes I stood up in were a blue cotton shirt, an old military combat jacket, a pair of genuine 28-inch waist Levis (priced 42/6), two pairs of home-knitted socks in green wool and a pair of suede moccasins.

As Tony and I shuffled awkwardly into the main room we were greeted by Phil. He was tall and slim with a huge brown beard and moustache that completely hid his mouth. He welcomed us into the place and introduced the others who were there. Sitting on the sofa was Dai and his girlfriend Sue, him with real red hair and her with masses of eye makeup. Next we met Dick, who was standing by the record player feeling the power cable (he hardly took any notice of us at all).

"For this thing to be bloody red hot," he said strangely.

The music playing was *Porgy and Bess,* and I asked Phil, who seemed to be the friendliest, who it was playing trumpet.

"It's Miles Davis with the Gil Evans Orchestra," said Tony before Phil could answer. One or two of the bunch seemed impressed and I was embarrassed not to have known.

"That's right," said Phil, smiling, and Tony blushed bright red.

On one of the chairs by the fire sat a very pretty girl with a very wide mouth and strong jaw line. Her hair was an unnatural red/brown colour and she too wore lots of makeup around the eyes. Perched on the arm of the chair sat a curly blond haired bloke of about 25, strumming loosely on an acoustic guitar.

"This is Anna and Pep," said Phil.

Anna said hello. Pep managed a nod, then asked, "What kind of axe have you got man?" I told him and he seemed quite impressed. Then, "What kind of music do you play man?"

I said a bit of Jesse Fuller and Jack Elliott, and within a few minutes I had the guitar out and was playing my small repertoire to an admiring audience. This was totally against my natural reserve, but whenever I moved locations during these early travelling days I was aware that it was a chance to assume a different identity, and although still terribly shy I could on occasions push that to one side, especially if I was among strangers. What made this show different was that Tony was with me and he knew me a little bit. Perhaps it was in defiance after not recognising Miles Davis.

"You blokes will have to share a room at the back," said Phil after a while and he showed us back out of the room and over the second landing to a cubbyhole with no windows except a small skylight about a foot square up in the roof. Fish boxes were piled up on one side of the room and there was an elderly army-type iron bedstead on the side under the skylight. Tony insisted that I had the bed, and he made himself a bed out of the upturned fish crates. We stacked most of the other boxes outside except for two which we used for bedside tables. There was no light in the room except what came through the skylight, but fortunately we found a light bulb the next morning for the single socket. That first night the boys fed us with rice and a sort of tomato sauce. We drifted off to bed very late.

Tony spent much of the time writing little stories in a childish hand, and although he wouldn't show them to me, I knew they must be very profound. Tony also would not reveal his age, and in company with the other blokes kept very quiet. To be honest I found him a bit of a bore and anyway, a bond was developing between myself and Pep. All the guys in the pad were middle class. Of the four, I suppose Dai and Pep were the closest to my own roots, although they too had accents that would have stuck out in Croydon.

Phil was very kind to Tony and me—almost paternal, or at least big brotherly. Dick was genuinely upper class; typically he was the most outrageous in his eccentricity and his descent into the squalor of the pad was total. He wandered about the place in a state of dishevelled undress, bearded and unkempt, and he had affected a mode of speech which several of the fringe of students were using. If he wanted to know the time he would ask, "For me to be wondering what time it's to be?"

After he had been told the answer he might add the construction, "For me to be thurbing into Bournemouth for something," by way of explanation.

'Thurbing' was a general verb that was used in place of any other. "What a bunch of dicks," I thought, but within a short space of time I was using the word myself.

Pep never used this mode of speech. He lived with Anna away from the pad and he had very strong opinions about everything—always sounding off about something or other—but what flattered me most was that he actively sought my company and took me around with him. One morning he took me over to the art college annexe to show me a marijuana plant that he was growing in a pot. He said the principal had adopted it and always paused to water it whenever he visited Pep at work. Pep loved the idea of someone in authority being duped into caring for a banned plant: "Stupid cunt," he said. His liberal use of strong language added to his personality; I'd never heard anyone who spoke so well swear so much.

Pep was a potter, but that title does not come near to describing his involvement with the craft. He didn't just throw pots, he lived and loved them. He was one of the first of the few men I have met that could inspire you with their passion for the work they loved; he taught me how to distinguish between Chinese and English porcelain and explained in breathy detail the secrets of different glazes. As he would speak of the ancient potters' search for the elusive red glaze, his voice would become dreamy and he'd show me pieces where there might be a hint of red on a pot after firing. He talked with real reverence about old pots that he had acquired, and years later prided himself that he'd been able to fool one of Sotheby's experts with one of his own imitation Siamese dishes (after he was happy with the glaze and so on, he tied the little dish to a piece of string and dragged it up the garden path to make tiny chips on the rim to 'age' it even more). I'd never even thought about such things before, and now I was becoming an expert.

Pep's second great love was country blues by the likes of Sleepy John Estes and other more obscure artists. He was always picking away on his guitar, but he was not very good; his timing was erratic and he sped up alarmingly. But he knew a few riffs and he also knew that he wasn't very good. He seemed to get a lot of pleasure out of watching me play and always wanted me to play my bit of Blind Boy Fuller or anything in my primitive ragtime. Sometimes we would play together, though I am sure he got more out of it than I did.

Pep's third love was Anna. He was passionate about her and very jealous; she was a little younger than me, and I was convinced that she was mad. Everything about their love was so intense, and Anna was constantly seeking reassurance or railing against some insensitivity that he had shown her; often she would be in inconsolable floods of tears. An empathy grew between us that became quite strong, and although I didn't fancy her, I enjoyed her turning to me until it finally occurred to me that Pep might get the wrong idea.

One day he took me over to Bournemouth to a pub at a place called the Landsdowne. There was a bloke playing a beautiful 12-string guitar and singing in an unbelievably loud voice, in a style not unadjacent to Leadbelly. His name was Jonathan, and he wore a little pillbox hat with a tassel on it. He spoke thurbish all the time, which was annoying, but he was a very good guitar player. His mate, who was just as posh as Jonathan, spoke the same way and played a stovepipe.

In those days blues records were as rare as rocking horse shit and all us would-be country blues players played the same songs, which were copied from the same few albums that were circulating. One such album was called 'Blues Fell This Morning' and on it was a track by someone called Stovepipe Number One. I'm sure when the recording was made it was supposed to be a novelty, but I can remember the earnestness with which they were discussing the correct materials to make the best bass resonance. Just watching other blokes playing was wonderful, and hours were spent soaking up music and chatter in the living room of our pad. I never got to know Jonathan better, but he came several times to the Poole house and played to an audience that were arguing with much passion about art, music and the meaning of life.

Somewhere beyond the High Street was a small pub called The Angel which sold cider. There was the usual assortment of characters that this kind of place attracts. It was here that the blokes went to relax further as everyone was pretty laid back anyway. Drinking was never really heavy as no-one had enough money to get really pissed, but somehow we did manage to get a drink and so long as it was not interfering with the other customers we were allowed to play guitar and someone always bought me a drink. At some time amidst the general friendliness of the place and the warmth of the drink we got introduced to Mr. and Mrs. Dawes, who had a lot of children aged from about seven to sixteen.

Mr. Dawes was an old-looking fortysomething with his hair swept back and a jovial demeanour; his wife was about the same age, with a wonderful Dorset accent and the looks of a Romany: jet black hair and dark brown, darting eyes. She was slightly stooped and had a protruding belly. These two saw nothing unusual in the set-up in the pad, and one or both of them often turned up for a coffee or a chat. Their kids were allowed to wander where they pleased, and several of them used to pay regular visits to see the 'beatniks'. Somehow we all rubbed along together, cadging roll-ups and wondering how long it would be before we had to get a job and start paying our way. We survived on coffee, rice and occasional spaghetti, but I don't really remember eating anything substantial until the arrival of George.

∾

george

One morning I rolled out of bed and was drinking some coffee in the kitchen when in walked a rumpled-looking chap somewhat the worse for wear.

Phil looked up and asked, "Can I help you?"

"Well that depends, brother. Where the fuck am I?" he demanded whilst scratching his belly through a large tear in his string vest.

"You're in a private flat in Poole High Street." answered Phil.

"Well thank gawd I'm still in the same town I started out in last night. Foulser's the name, George Foulser. I got pissed up last night and someone must have brought me here. Could I possibly have a cup of coffee, mate?"

"I'm afraid we've run out of milk," said Phil.

"Don't worry about that," said George. "Black'll be fine. With four sugars."

Then Dai walked in. "Good to see you up and about," said Dai. "How are you feeling today?"

George said he was pretty good and wondered how he got to be with us. Dai explained that he had been found outside asleep in the gutter at about 1 am. Dai and a bloke called Francois had dragged him upstairs and put him in an empty room, where at least he would be dry if not warm. Armed with a cup of hot sweet coffee, George roundly thanked us all for our great kindness. Then he tapped someone for a roll up, sat down on one of the fish boxes in our 'kitchen' and informed us that what we had done was in the true spirit of socialist and student/worker relations. Between noisy sips of his drink he began to take in his new surroundings.

"Who the fuck put that gas oven in?" he asked accusingly. When it was explained that Dick had done it, he pointed out that we could all be blown sky high, and offered to make it safe for us. The offer was gratefully accepted, but to tell the truth it didn't look much different when he'd finished. It was a fairly primitive bodge-up of hose pipe and jubilee clips, but it was true that it smelt less of gas in the pad than before.

George knew loads of things and had opinions about everything. That evening we went to the pub where he bought us a drink and we talked and talked. Several of the blokes got bored, but I just loved to listen and though I'm not a cockney, I found the sound of his working class accent reassuring and his colourful language inspiring.

"Blimey, this wire is red hot," he exclaimed as his fingers brushed the electric cable that powered the record player, and as his eyes followed the wire I noticed for the first time that the cable powered everything.

"Christ that's dodgy," said George. "That wire isn't strong enough to feed all the lights and the record player as well. I'll be happy to sort that for you if you like."

"Oh er thanks," mumbled Phil, preferring not to get drawn into the conversation about the electrics, for he had a problem about the morality of hot-wiring our place illegally from the betting shop downstairs. He needn't have worried; the wires continued to almost glow and nothing was ever done about it.

George didn't move in, as he had nothing to move; he just didn't go away. He was a political agitator and a published author. His book was called *The Seaman's Voice*, and I was delighted to find a copy some years later in the library. Until then I only had his word for it (but I believed him anyway).

George was a blacklisted merchant seaman and had just been rumbled and given his papers in Poole Harbour, off a small steamer that moved down the south coast delivering coal. So in time-honoured fashion he decided to drink his money and worry about what to do next when his hangover cleared. He appeared to own nothing and desired even less; all he seemed to want was someone to listen to him, a couple of drinks and the occasional bunk-up. He had to wait a long time for the latter.

As a young man full of the songs of Woody Guthrie and already a confirmed socialist, this was like having my own guru. No matter what subject came up, George was ready with an opinion and an intuitive socialist response. Much of what was said went over my head, and you can't really discuss much when most of us were left wing and agreed with everything he said anyway. Thus George was forced to take an even more radical line so that someone would disagree with him, and then he could get back on his horse again. It wasn't long before the words 'middle class' were being used as an insult, for George had no sense of tact as far as his student landlords were concerned. "Fuck 'em," he said defiantly.

Of course this led to a cooling off between him and some of the lads. But Anna, Pep and myself still enjoyed his company, though Pep often wound George up just to watch the sparks. And as Pep and Anna's relationship rocked on, soon Anna was confiding her troubles to George as well as me.

George was really a caricature of what you would expect a seaman agitator to be. When we found him, he was clad only in a shirt and working trousers and lace-up boots. But on the dust sheet of his book he was wearing a donkey jacket and roll neck sweater; his hair was a short back and sides 30's style, brushed straight back with the very shortest hair above his ears sticking straight out. His skin was quite pale for a drinking man and he had a nose like a potato stuck on his face; he also had several teeth.

He was soon convinced that Anna fancied him.

It is well known that there is a correlation between food and love-making. There was never any attempt to organise meals together; it would have been against the whole spirit of the place. However I was not involved in any relationship, and hunger was quite often on my mind. The cooker was mainly used for boiling kettles for coffee, but one day George blurted out, "Don't any of you lot ever eat anything? How does a bit of roast lamb and potatoes sound to you?"

It sounded great to me and I said so. It was soon pointed out that we had no money but George would have none of it.

"Let's have a whip round," he suggested and between us we raised about three or four shillings.

"That'll do," said George, and off he went, returning in about half an hour laden with groceries. He slapped his shopping on the table and pulled out a huge tin of peas, some Oxo cubes, a load of potatoes and some meat. We all stared in amazement, our eyes widening further as he plonked down enough change to buy a pint of scrumpy with as well.

"How did you manage that?" I asked,

"Well I'm glad you asked, Ralph, and I'll tell you. I paid for the veg what they was asking, but the meat I blagged. You've got to get the meat first, otherwise there's no point. What you do is walk up to the butcher's shop and stare at all the stuff in the window. Once you've been noticed by the butcher himself you scurry off for a few minutes and then come back and do it a couple times more until you are quite sure he's seen you. Then you go in and without looking him directly in the eye, you ask him if he's got sixpence worth of scraps for your dog. 'Course sometimes that's exactly what you get, and you can still make some sort of stew out of a tanner's worth, but if you go in at the end of the day and they've had a good 'un, they'll usually work out that you look so down on your luck that even if you'd had a dog you'd probably already eaten it so they figure you might be just out the nick or be really down on your luck and they'll throw in three breasts of lamb or a bit of stewing steak and there you go. Then you hand over the tanner and as you pick up your bundle you make sure you squeeze his hand and you say, Thanks pal I won't forget this, knowing full well that he won't forget you and so long as you don't take the piss you can go back some other time and do it again."

That evening we dined like kings; what a man was our George.

Things of course got tighter and various members drifted off to eat with friends in the evenings or else they stocked up in the college canteens. Tony got a job as a washer-up in one of the seaside cafés called the Galleon and usually managed to smuggle a few leftovers back to the pad, and I kept my eye on George to see when his next miracle might take place.

One evening when there was only him, me and Pep in the place, George suddenly burst out with, "Ain't there no bleedin' allotments round here?"

I looked nonplussed and so did Pep, then we both realised what he was thinking and I was appalled. I found myself thinking of my uncle Reg and his carefully nurtured rows of lettuce and carrots.

I blushed deepest red, but felt I had to declare, "That's stealing! I'm sorry George, but I think that's wrong—after all these are the gardens of the working man, the ordinary blokes who have no land of their own. You can't nick from them."

George said nothing but reached over and opened his tobacco tin and slowly manufactured one of his 'Black Beauty' rollups. Once satisfied that it was perfect he licked the glued edge, stuck it in his mouth, lit it, inhaled a medium sized drag, blew it out, luxuriously tapped the cigarette prematurely on the ashtray and looking sort of over, past and through me said:

"To each according to his need. From each according to his ability. I know I don't have to remind you who said that, and furthermore we won't be nicking from one geezer. For a start you notice I asked for an allotment not a garden, that's so we can take a little from all of them. All blokes with allotments grow more than they can eat, it's only natural, if you've got a certain amount of plot you're going to fill it up. Otherwise you're wasting it. You content yourself with the knowledge that you can be charitable and offer your neighbour some of your surplus, only the chances are he'll have too much left over as well and it'll get thrown on the compost heap anyway.

"The other reason for taking a little from all of them is that they can commiserate with each other about being pilfered from and in a couple of days they'll have forgotten about it all. It is quite legit socialistically speaking, after all our need is greater than theirs, so we take according to our needs. 'From each according to his ability' will be about our ability to climb over that bleedin' fence around the allotment."

George felt very pleased with himself after this and took another pull on his fag, which this time caused him to start another bout of lung-wracking coughing.

"I still don't think it's right, George," I said.

"Then you don't have to come," he said, leaning over the table at me and stubbing out his cigarette at the same time. "Now, who's going to tell me where the nearest one is?"

It is one of my small regrets that I wasn't one of The Few who went over the wall that night, for to see them when they came back covered with dirt and scratches, flushed and animated by their adventure, made me feel pathetically moralistic. Especially when I saw what a small amount they had taken: there were some carrots and a swede or two, some tomatoes and a few onions; but the biggest haul was of rhubarb.

The spoils were spread out on the table like harvest festival for us all to admire, and George promised us all a stew the next day. When I came in that evening the pot was bubbling merrily on the stove. This time George had got the stewing steak, and after crudely chopping everything up had thrown it all into the pot. Including the rhubarb. We still had a few spuds left: they were boiling away on the other burner, and the smell was fantastic. Eventually the meal was served up and I was duly offered a bowl. Nothing was said but I could feel George looking at me through his spoon.

"No thanks," I said, "I've already had something," and I went up to the room I shared, took out the guitar and seriously thought about leaving the pad and going back home. After a few seconds' strumming, I went back to the kitchen to claim my bowl, only to find that it had been democratically shared out amongst the rest.

Life drifted on. More and more people called by as the reputation of the flat grew, and although I sometimes felt as if we were viewed as freaks by our guests, I still loved it. No-one ever thought about turning in until 2 or 3 o'clock any night of the week and every night was like a weekend. One weekend Henry turned up with Linda and June and we all hung out together.

Until now I had survived on fresh air, cigarettes and the charity and kindness of the chaps at the pad—and George's odd miracle—but now that Tony had got a job, the pressure was definitely on me.

Living was cheap. Clothes were washed by hand and jeans were scrubbed in the yard with a broom and rinsed in the bath on the landing. One day it was brought to our attention that some of the clientele from the betting shop had been seen pissing in it.

This presented us with a dilemma; we did not want to rock the boat by complaining to the landlords, because we were not supposed to be living in the place anyway, to say nothing of the bath's water supply being disconnected. Nevertheless George had a bit of fun one day when we'd seen two fellows go up to our landing to relieve themselves in the bath. George slipped off his shirt and walked purposely into the bathroom with his moth-eaten old towel over his arm and my toothbrush in his hand as if about to perform his daily ablutions. His feigned shock and horror at what he found on entering not only produced a grovelling apology from the two embarrassed offenders but a couple of quid to get the place cleaned.

There was never enough hot water to perform anything more than a sponge down, but we managed to wash bits of ourselves at a time on an irregular basis. When I see how my own kids feel filthy if they don't shower every day, I often wonder what they would have made of the generation that bathed once a week whether they were dirty or not.

One day Les turned up at the pad. He had become very strange, and was living in a park somewhere in the town. He'd had a very hard time in Belgium where he'd been travelling and had been drinking rain water from puddles. He had formed peculiar opinions about the Belgian people and picked up some fleas. Large spots were clearly visible through his patchy beard and I was really worried about him. He was on a mission to find out about himself and there was nothing I could do to change his direction.

He stayed with us for no more than a couple of days, then he was back to the park and off on his travels again. If anything, Les's appearance probably added credibility to the presence of Tony and myself amongst our middle class hosts. They must have been alarmed by his appearance; he certainly scared me and I worried about him for a long time afterwards.

The Dawes kids, who were allowed free rein all over town, were less regular visitors to the pad, except for the youngest, Jeannie, and her older sister Shirley. We were something of an odd collection and the two kids were intrigued by our lifestyle. They were both very familiar and would wander into any and every room to see if we were in, and because we were all very young—more like older brothers than uncles—this did not seem odd to me. Little Jeannie would climb over any of us, laugh her little gap-toothed husky chuckle as she pulled the boys' beards or got us to play our guitars. She was very fond of Pep and Anna, and would crawl up on to the sofa between them for company.

Pep looked like a leftover-teddy boy; he had his blond curls pushed back and wore very tight jeans and desert boots, usually a workman's blue shirt and often a rollneck sweater. There was no attempt to impress his persona on people as he honestly couldn't have given a fuck what anyone thought of him.

Then Anna found she was pregnant, and, true to his unpredictable form, Pep married her.

 ∾

gill

As the pad became part of the established student tourist route, more and more kids from the colleges spent the odd night there; most however left before morning, and for most of the residents the novelty of staying up late began to wear thin. I was one of the last to give in as I was one of the last to get a job.

The wages at the Metal Box company paid about £5 a week after tax, but it made an enormous difference to me. I could buy George the odd drink and at least afford fresh tobacco. One day over the Angel, I sat down near the door with my drink and slowly took in the faces around me. Although I was firmly part of this little scene, I by no means knew everyone that gathered there. As I worked my eyes through the crowd, I suddenly noticed a girl that made my heart jump. She was without doubt the most beautiful girl I had ever seen.

Years later in *The Godfather* I was to read of the 'thunderbolt' that hit the young Michael Corleone during his enforced exile in Sicily when he first saw his bride to be, but at that time I had no words to describe the effect her appearance had on me. She simply looked stunning, her long blonde hair all the more blonde against a navy blue duffel coat, her smile somehow still unsure though huge, the slightly awkward way she held her cigarette; she was a little too clumsy in her movements to be obviously sexy, but she had a smouldering effect on me. I couldn't take my eyes off her and I couldn't understand why the boys weren't all over her. I knew she was middle class by the way she moved, and I knew that I was losing myself and I knew I must meet her and I knew it would not be tonight and what was her name and where did she come from and she didn't even notice me and she went out with some geezer and as she walked out she didn't even notice me again.

When I had judged a cool time had passed I ventured as casually as I could to ask (without my voice breaking up), "Who was that girl in the duffel coat?"

"Oh, that's Gill," someone said.

"What does she do?" I asked.

"She sort of hangs around the college."

"Is she a student?"

Phil looked up at me and said, "No, but she sometimes models for the photography class."

Something about the way he spoke indicated that he might have sort of fancied her himself. I decided that enough had been said and changed the subject. She was certainly lovely enough to have been a model and I knew her name. I would have to be content with that, but of course I wasn't. I had to get to know her—but how?

The pain of longing for someone is never so intense as when you are young; the effect that this state has on you makes your whole body and mind behave oddly. The intensity of feeling, the appropriateness of every silly love song to your situation and the deep dark knowledge that the object of your affection and the causer of your pain isn't even aware of your existence let alone your name, yet everywhere you look hers is written in huge capital letters, and even when you gaze out at the stars through the tiny skylight in your fish box smelly bedroom you see 'Gill' written in the sky.

The next morning I awoke in what I thought was a muck sweat. My sleeping bag and cover were soaked and I thought I was paralysed, as I could not move my head. With great relief I found I could move my feet and then, thankfully, all my other parts. I called to Tony to help me. He hopped out of bed and came anxiously to my side.

"I can't move my bloody head," I bleated.

"Why are your covers all wet?" he asked.

"God knows. I'm more worried about my neck."

Tony looked at my bed, and then his gaze went up to the ceiling. Suddenly he said, "No wonder you can't move, there's no bloomin' glass in the skylight."

It was the first night's rain since we had arrived at the pad. Not having any glass in the roof meant that it had just rained on me, and now my neck had locked. How could I approach the most beautiful girl in the world with my head locked securely on one side? Perhaps she would think I looked knowing or quizzical. I tried squinting, cowboy-style, whilst leaving my head at its jaunty angle. No, she would probably think I was deformed. She might go out with me because she felt sorry for me. Oh the pain of love. Oh the pain in the neck.

I kept myself indoors that day, but the next morning was horrified to find that I was no better. There was nothing for it but to go to the hospital. The doctor who examined me suggested a neck collar. I decided against that, and stumbled back to the pad. After a couple more days of misery, with just about everyone asking me what was the matter, George offered to help me out with some Chinese massage he had learned in Hong Kong. I declined, but he passed on the secrets of the Orient to Tony, who crept up behind me and, grabbing me by my forehead and the back of my neck, gave it an almighty jerk. It caused me to utter a rather unmanly shriek, but freed up the spasm.

Weeks passed and I never saw Gill. The atmosphere in the pad was changing. Phil was clearly under pressure either from work or the bombastic nature of George, who had by now become the patriarch amongst those who still hung on to every word.

We hardly ever saw Dai or Sue till early evening, and Dick was about his work and only showed up on odd days, recounting strange snippets of dreams. Once he said, "For me to have had the strangest dream the other night. I'd been plating this girl and I was sort of hiding from my mother with a huge dollop of cold cream on my nose."

Another gentle soul arrived at the pad; his name was Ian, and everyone reckoned that he was the best painter of all of them. Ian dyed his hair blond and was the first bloke I'd ever met to do so.

George had acquired an old typewriter from Anna and was busy tapping away in his room. His papers had finally arrived, and with much pride he undid a parcel tied up with string. After shuffling through piles of stuff, he produced an article he'd written for the *Observer* about the similarities between the Norwegian language and the Geordie dialect. He had noticed whilst on board ship that these two groups of sailors could converse with each other. It was just another bit of glamour that added to George's reputation.

I questioned George about what he was writing and he told me it was an article called 'The Pad At Poole'. I was terribly impressed, and when it was finished and sent off to town I waited anxiously for news of its impending publication. Once George had the bit between his teeth we hardly saw him. He locked himself in his room and tapped away at his article. When asked where all the concentration came from, he pulled a small bottle from his jacket containing some tiny pills.

"Ephedrine," he smiled smugly. "A great little helper, keeps the ideas flowing."

When we asked what ephedrine was, he told us it was supplied to asthmatics to help them breathe but it also was a form of speed and it was cheap. Though officially it was a prescription drug, with a rattling chest like George had, it was easy to find an old chemist who would sell you a few pills 'as you'd left ship without them'. Pep knew all about 'ephies' because of a real need, and though speed was always a popular recreational drug, I just did not fancy trying them in spite of George's offer. It was a long time before I even tried the 'purple hearts' that were only threepence each at the time.

George eventually received a rejection slip which stated that the article was not of the quality of his previous one, but that they would be pleased to hear from him if he had anything else to offer. George said he couldn't really give a fuck, though he seemed disappointed. He never let any of us read it, but he did tell me that we were all mentioned in it.

The novelty of George was beginning to wear a bit thin. Some of the blokes were deliberately avoiding him, and there were those who suspected that George, like the puppy, might just be for life. The whole point of being in a gang of your contemporaries is to debate and let off steam and not be constantly reminded of where you were going wrong, or that your arguments were based on false premises and so on. I can still hear Phil's voice cracking with near hysteria as he tried not to lose his temper with George. There was also the class thing—perhaps that was another reason that I continued to get on with George, as I think I still had enough Croydon accent to sound more like a fellow Londoner.

"You know what, Ralph," he said one day, "I'm beginning to think that you're bad luck. I ain't had so much as a sniff of a bit of skirt ever since I been in this place."

Is that right, I thought to myself—well some of us had been waiting considerably longer than that (unless I counted Susan, but she would have probably denied it).

I was still in touch with Henry and the gang from Mitcham and sometimes I would give him a call at his home just for a little chat when I felt low.

One day he said, "We're all going to the Richmond Jazz festival. Why don't you hitch up and meet us there?" Things were slow at the pad so I said yes, and immediately felt better. Once I got there and it was good to see all the friendly faces and to partly impress them by my authentic appearance. Linda was there, with June and a few other faces from home, plus some from our flirtations with the West End scene who were more stylishly attired.

The day was overcast but intense. There were skip jivers and Cy Laurie dancers; a sea of combat jackets, beards, berets and cider. I wandered in and out of the company through the grounds when suddenly, walking by herself smoking a cigarette, clad in Levis and a loose sweater, I spotted Gill.

Sometimes in life one is hardly responsible for one's actions; impulse or bravado can often outweigh the carefully considered remark or action. I remember in a pub once a fight had broken out, and one of the protagonists was lying on the floor with the other standing over him. The standing one picked up a chair and was about to hit the other one over his unprotected head, and in the time he had raised the chair over his head, I had realised what was about to happen, leapt to my feet, grabbed the chair from the bloke and wrestled it out of his grip, threw it violently across the bar and was sitting back in my chair holding my drink.

So here I was and there she was, and there was no time to think. I walked right up to her and said, "Hello, you're Gill. I've seen you down at the Angel in Poole, you're a friend of Phil and Dick from the pad in the High Street, I'm staying there at the moment but I'm up here with some friends from Mitch— I mean London. Would you like to meet them?"

She smiled at me or maybe even laughed, but I was feeling faint and my heart had risen to my head and was beating to the tempo of *Tiger Rag*.

"You must be Ralph. I've heard about you, you play the guitar. Pep thinks you play well."

At that moment I couldn't have cared less what Pep thought; this beautiful girl knew my name and I was sure I was about to pass out. I found her walking with me the few hundred yards to where I'd last seen my mates; I must have said something, but by now the huge rush of adrenaline that had enabled me to make the initial move had deserted me, leaving only a rush of words and a tangle of tongue and lip sounds speaking biblical babble.

With trembling fingers I attempted a roll up. The paper stuck to my perspiring fingers and half the tobacco spilled on to the ground and when it was finally ready to light my beloved Zippo had run out. I dextrously pulled out the inner tank from the cover and blew down the end to force the remaining gas up to the wick. On the first flick of the wheel, it caught and lit the cigarette all down one side and the burning tobacco fell out over my shirt and the most beautiful girl in the world said, "Would you like one of these?" and offered me one of her 'tailor-mades'.

I remember nothing of the rest of the day except that after a fairly decent interval she left to rejoin her friends and I was left with only the sound of her voice and the helpless sense of loss and doubt as to whether I had impressed her at all and if she would be coming to Poole again.

Days passed and only the sound of Miles Davis with the Gil Evans arrangements filled the languid atmosphere of the pad as summer began to assert itself on the late spring. Now Francois was spending more time with George, and George seemed to be glad of a new audience. Francois was becoming interested in getting on a ship and maybe even a union card. George and he made frequent trips down to the harbour, and eventually George got him a boat. It was only a coastal run but, just like riding a bicycle down a road you always drive along, the world from Shoreham to Portland is full of sights, smells and sounds that seem entirely new.

Francois was black-haired, swarthy and foreign-looking, but his speech was like that of the aristocracy as far as I was concerned. He too spoke thurbish, and that would have to go if he was going to make his way as a seaman. When we next saw him, he was a different bloke; the accent was the same but his manner had undergone a huge transformation. Most of those on board his vessel were foreign so they did not notice his upper-class speech, and he was able to help the ship's master with translations. The crew all thought him the bee's knees and that was the last time I ever saw him.

Once while I was at Croydon Tech I had all but enlisted in the Merchant Navy, until someone asked incredulously, "What do you want to join up with that bunch of poofs for?"

The very thought of Paul Potter or Harry Barnet (my neighbours from Croydon) having anything to do with poofs was absolutely unthinkable. But here it was again—the rumour that homosexuals were attracted to the Merchant Navy. It was enough to put me off and it did. I told George that I nearly signed up and asked him his opinion as to whether it was true.

He said nothing for a while, and proceeded to roll a cigarette.

"Yeah, it's true," he sighed after a while and blew a stream of blue smoke from his nostrils. "You mainly get them on the ocean-going boats but there are some on these inshore runs, you see no-one bothers them and they've got their own little scene going, they've got their pubs and so on and they don't bother straight people that much when they know you ain't bent."

"Have you ever come across them?" I asked.

"Oh yeah, oh yeah I have, Ralph, and I hate them bastard nancy boys. It ain't in my nature any of that old game but we'd been out at sea for weeks and I got pissed up one time and a couple of them come on to me and I never realised what was going on till it was you know like and I ain't proud of it and I try to keep away from them bastards now."

I felt a little nauseous at the thought of it and when I looked back at him there was a tear of regret—or was it a fonder memory? I would never know.

Then with a "hrumpf!" and a cough he changed the subject slightly: "Anyhow, how's your luck? I hope it's better than mine—I made a pass at that Anna and she's gone all tearful on me. I think you're a fuckin' jinx on my love life, Ralph."

Well, I've just met the most beautiful girl in the world, I nearly said. But thankfully it came out as: "I met this girl at the jazz festival and she's from round here, so I'm hopeful if you get my meaning."

"Well good luck to you, mate. I hope I get to meet her when she stays over."

When she stays over? Christ, I hadn't even got that far in my mind. I was still wondering if she had wings. Gill did not have wings, but she did have a Lambretta motor scooter, and a few days later she paid a visit to the pad and took me out on the back.

I was totally besotted with her, and she must have found me amusing as she didn't seem to mind making the journey over from Bournemouth, where she lived, to see me.

I was deeply jealous of everyone who said "Hello Gill" to her, and there were lots of them, mostly boys so much more sophisticated than me that they failed to walk out of the room backwards when in her company. Some of them were even able to speak to her without getting tongue-tied or sweaty. Many were clean and had some money; none of them paid much attention to the brooding obsessed skinny Brando/Dean figure that skulked in her shadow. They obviously failed to recognise the Brando/Dean reference, and in fact barely observed the scruffy skinny kid acutely aware of his own insecurities and lack of money, transport and confidence.

Gill was the second daughter of a clerk at the local family allowance office. Her mother was a little stuck up, not to say snooty. She had her father's small features and long limbs, while her elder sister looked like their mother. Gill was not very academic, but she loved horses and was a good rider; I suppose she was barely out of that schoolgirl crush some young girls have with horses when I met her. Men would fight for her attention, and even be prepared to kidnap her from me. Looking back, I probably rushed things, but at the time I felt I was playing it as slow as I dared. Luckily for me she responded to my attentions and we became a couple.

Back at the pad things were changing too. Sad to say, Phil was becoming odder, Dick seemed to want to move on elsewhere, and Pep was the father of a little girl with Anna, who was still crazy. Francois was at sea on a coastal steamer and looking like something out of a fifties black and white movie, and George had got lucky at last (not Anna of course, but allegedly someone we all knew—I suspect it was Mrs. Dawes[4]).

Before the pad broke up entirely, Pep's relationship with Anna was floundering and he was flirting with heroin. Tony had made up his mind

---

[4] Some years later my attention was drawn to a piece in a newspaper about a family called Dawes who had found a way into an old crypt. The kids kept bringing artefacts to school and it's doubtful that the teachers' suspicions would have been aroused if it hadn't been that one of the boys overstepped the mark when he brought a human skull into the class for the nature table. These days George seemed to have money on him and none of us knew where it came from. Some alleged that he and Mrs. Dawes had gone into partnership as a couple of middle-aged burglars but the whole idea seemed preposterous. They did however go exploring deserted houses for 'left-behinds' and perhaps that's where the confusion arose.

to become a vibes player, and as soon as he had the money he bought a set which were installed at his family's home. He dedicated himself to learning this instrument and indeed became very proficient, though he never gained any real recognition. He started to wear three button suits and slim ties and the distance between us grew until I eventually lost contact with him.

A couple of years ago I was walking down Northcote Road market when I bumped into Judy, a girl I'd not seen for years. As we talked of the old days we both agreed how sad it was about Les and Beau dying, and then she mentioned Tony's suicide. I nearly passed out with shock; Tony, it transpired, had been gay, and when his lover had found religion and abandoned their relationship, Tony had found the future too awful to face alone and hanged himself. Once the enormity of this story had sunk in, I found myself trawling the past for clues as to any of this. I did remember once talking to him in the pad and closely questioning him about motives for what he was doing. Really I suppose I was asking him if he thought his work was any good, and probably I was trying to help him grow up and realise that just because you want to be a writer or musician, the intent doesn't necessarily make you one.

He laughed, and then, his eyes full of compassion and the beginnings of tears, turned round to me and said, "You don't understand, do you Ralph?" His eyes now overflowed with tears and all the time he was smiling as he spoke.

There was no hint of anger in his accusation and I thought little at the time beyond being sorry if I had hurt him. Now as his words came back to me, I wondered if he was seeking to confirm something of deeper significance. I never saw Tony with a girlfriend and in those days before gay lib, his life must often have been lonely. Perhaps his dedication to the vibraphone was made easier to understand in this context.

Ever since the army, I had always been either with a girl or after a girl, and though not yet completely au fait with all the mechanics of sex and its delicate relations, I was doing a lot better than most of my friends. My technique was simple: someone would tell me so and so liked me, and if I liked her too I would ask her out. I think Gill was the first girl I had boldly gone after. With the others I'd had a start. Fortunately for me Gill was on the phone, and when I was unable to see her at least I could talk to her, which I did every day. I was desperate to make love to her but she made me wait a long time. I know she had been badly hurt by some arsehole from the college who tried to worm his way back to her once word got out that she was seeing this skinny proto-Beat character 'from London', and I often dreamt of avenging her pain in a fist fight.

There was a lightness and romance to this part of my life that was not to come again until Paris. All sensations were exaggerated by my circumstance and freedom away from home, and the fact that we did not actually sleep overnight with each other until some time later. In the meantime there was still some order in our lives, as she had to be in at her parents' house in Cranleigh Gardens by a certain time most nights. Though I don't think she got on that well with her folks, she was wise enough not to make waves. We saw a great deal of each other.

She taught me to drive her scooter and, helmetless with her hair in our faces, we zipped all over Bournemouth and the roads to Poole. I would have been the happiest kid in the world if only I hadn't needed reassurance in just about everything to do with her. Bournemouth is home to countless foreign students, all of whom fancied Gill. She was known to most of the kids at the college as a part time model; all the musicians knew her because pretty girls always get to meet musicians; people on motorbikes waved to her, and it was clear to me I was going to have to make our own story if I was to lose my doubts or jealousy.

I resolved to go abroad the following summer, earn my keep through busking and take Gill with me. I only achieved two out of the three.

GILL

97

shiver

After the pad at Poole broke up, I moved into a house on Southbourne High Street which Henry was renting with Beau.

The house was owned originally by the Lady of Brownsea Island, who had it built as her chauffeur's residence. It comprised a cellar, kitchen, lounge and bathroom and two bedrooms upstairs. The whole place was fixed to the garage, which was big enough to hold three cars at least; it was empty but locked and off limits. The house was within a few yards of the beach, but the sea held few attractions for us, especially under the moody skies and the cold wind which should have warned us of the harshness of the time to come.

By the time I arrived at the place, Beau had already split, owing Henry money for rent, and Pep, who was working with Henry as a train washer, suggested Keith, a potter from Lytchett Matravers, as a reliable and steady subtenant. 'Irish Mick' and I arrived with a handful of belongings and my by now well-travelled guitar.

Henry was genuinely pleased to see us and was more effusive than usual in his introduction of both of us to Keith. A friendly face means a lot when you are broke and a bit scared as to where the next bit of food is going to come from, and so it was with Henry at our meeting. Keith was a smashing bloke and a genuine artist; he already knew Gill from the art college, and as well as being a good potter he was immensely practical and was in charge of glueing all the bits and pieces of electrical sound systems together. He'd even fixed up a speaker in the kitchen so that we could have sounds on when it was our turn to do the washing up. This order was achieved by means of a rota and it worked surprisingly well, the only problem being that there was hardly anything to wash up—Henry was out of work, Keith ate at the college and Mick and I had neither work nor money.

I had met Irish Mick in Croydon. His surname was Doyle, and he was a Dublin man. Mick wore his curly black hair in an elaborate Tony Curtis. He had the gap between the front teeth and walked with a slight swagger which did not denote any overbearing, just a confidence in himself that was both casual and reassuring. We were an unlikely pair of mates in many ways; he laughed a great deal and he just made me feel good. How I wished I could be so light of heart; Mick worried about nothing at all, and if there was any *craic* to be had out of a situation he would find it. Nothing daunted him and he was practical if not always morally sound as far as I was concerned. We all had reason to be grateful for his amorality before very long.

Henry showed us up to our room, which overlooked part of the garage. We found two beds on opposite sides of the room but no bedclothes; there were a pair of floral curtains forlornly hanging from the window and a bit of carpet on the floor.

I dropped my bag of belongings on the floor and said, "I'll take this one then."

"Okay," said Mick, "and I'll take this one so." We looked at each other and burst out laughing.

"We're going to be feckin' comfortable tonight all right," said Mick. I was almost at the point when I would laugh at anything, and that sort of near hysteria has always made everything else seem even more ridiculous. Mick, momentarily gaining control of himself, said, "It's going to be feckin' freezin' up here tonight."

"I know," I responded and then burst out laughing again. This only made Mick start again and by the time we wandered back downstairs to the other lads it looked as if both of us had been crying.

"Now lads, have ye anytin' to eat?" asked Mick boldly.

"I was afraid you might ask that," said Henry.

"All we got is some potatoes," offered Keith and for the first time I noticed his rich Dorset accent.

"Right," said Mick, going into the kitchen, "let's have some potatoes." By making use of just about everything that was left in the cupboard—salt, pepper, tomato sauce, a bit of milk and the last of the Echo margarine—he produced a meal of mashed potato that whetted everyone's appetite for more. Unfortunately there was no more.

The place was getting colder by the hour, and then by the minute, and we were all moving about and looking at the two-bar electric fire that was the only visible form of heating in the room.

"When does the feckin' heat come on then?" asked Mick.

"Not yet," came the curt reply from Henry. "It's on a meter and we've only got a shilling so we're saving it till it gets really cold."

"Well I'm really cold now and I still have a shillin' so if one of youse fellows will show me the meter I'll be glad to share me bob wid ya," said Mick.

Henry took Mick out of the room and showed him where the slot machine was, and within a few seconds they were back downstairs and all four of us sat huddled round the one bar.

"It lasts twice as long," observed Henry cleverly.

"Yeah, but two bars would be twice as warm," reasoned Mick. We all ignored this wisdom and started smoking and chatting about this and that and the price of potatoes and where we were likely to get a job.

Most of us would convince ourselves we were warm if some part of us was heated; perhaps a warm thigh or shin would be enough to make us ignore the north wind at our backs or the draft blowing up a trouser leg. Indeed some of the women on the estate back in Croydon had burn marks on their legs from sitting so close to the fire. All was merry and the pain of hunger began to dwindle in the glow of the electric fire and the banter, when suddenly the bar went off with a click.

"Is that it?" demanded Mick. "Jesus we're only after sitting here a feckin' minute or two."

The remaining shilling was reluctantly inserted in the meter. Keith put on some Woody Guthrie, and we smoked some more cigarettes and when the last shillingsworth ran out we stayed up until our teeth were nearly chattering with tiredness, hunger and cold. I said my goodnights and went upstairs to the dreaded bed. I emptied out my bag of bits, put most of them on and spread the rest over me and lay there shivering wondering what the hell Mick was going to do. All he had were the clothes he stood up in, and there was nothing I could see in the house that could possibly have helped to keep him warm.

A few minutes elapsed before Mick entered the room with much blowing and bustle. With the enterprise we would come to expect from the man, he had purloined all the towels from the bathroom and stuffed them inside his corduroy jacket and had swathed around his shoulders the carpet runner from the landing.

"Jesus it's feckin' cold wha' boy?" He spoke loudly to himself, but it was also a check to see if I was listening and still awake. I said nothing. From the corner of my eye I could see him scouring the room for more comfort materials, and finding none, resignedly sighed. He turned off the light and fell into the bedsprings with a chorus of pings and boings that started me silently chuckling in synchronicity with my shivers. There was a great deal of tossing about with musical accompaniment before, with a huge groan, Mick got out of the bed, threw on the light and threw off his carpet. He walked over to the window and proceeded to tear at the curtains, ripping them from the rail.

At this point I could hold in my laughter no longer and burst out, "For Christ sake Mick hold on, I'll give you a hand with that." Having more carefully removed the curtains, which were only of light summer material, the only thing to do with them was to wrap them around ourselves and climb back into our respective instruments of torture.

It was obvious that we were not likely to get any sleep like this, and during a brief pause in the giggles Mick said, "Look Ralph don't get me wrong but why don't I get into your bed? We'd both be better off with the warmth of our bodies being shared."

I was so surprised that I stopped laughing, then the silence was broken by a huge guffaw from both of us at the same time as we realised the absurdity, and soon the two of us were lying, albeit uneasily, back to back on the one bed, each hardly daring to move for fear of giving out the wrong message to the other, before sleep eventually came and we were woken by the light pouring in from the curtainless window. Somehow during the day we managed to obtain some sleeping materials and we slept separately from then on.

Henry hated his job as it started so early at 5 am, and Pep, who was by now sharing the work, was also getting ready to quit. The search for work was desperate and we combed the paper nightly looking for jobs. I got a job as a tyre fitter, but on reflection decided that it was not a good idea as a budding guitarist, so I never turned up for the first day. Both Mick and I were putting off the start as we just wanted to hang out and have some fun.

The evenings were best; someone would turn up with some food or cigarettes or a new record, and we would sit around talking and joking. A girl called Barbara came to see us quite a lot. She desperately wanted to be part of the group, but was so far removed from us by class and culture that she was tolerated only out of kindness by the boys; her parents were horrified at her association with us. She used to cycle over to hang out, and looking back she probably fancied one of the boys, but which one I've no idea even now. She had been told that any foodstuffs would be appreciated, and usually obliged with sausages or some potatoes or cigarettes. One night Mick and I managed to hang her bike up a telegraph pole, but the sight of her tears of desperation took all the fun out of it, and to make it up to her I let her buy me a Rev. Gary Davis album from a shop in Bournemouth. She really tried to get into the music contained in those grooves, but I think it was all a bit beyond her. Some of it was beyond me too.

I wonder sometimes if we feel as intensely about music as we get older. In this place music was played constantly and all of it was different and all of it was good. I was heavily into the mysteries of Blind Boy Fuller, and Mick had become fascinated by an album of Woody Guthrie and Cisco Houston—especially a track not penned by Guthrie called *The Bold Philadelphia Lawyer*, which he tunelessly warbled around the house. Keith loved Jimmy Reed and John Lee Hooker, and Henry was seriously into Charles Mingus and an album containing the track *Oh Lord Don't Let Them Drop That Atomic Bomb On Me*. At the time, I found Mingus pretentious and unmusical but I/we had to tolerate it for fear of being shown up as musically inferior to Henry's advanced appreciation. Only Mick had the honesty to tell Henry what he thought of the strange sounds from this record.

The weather grew worse and the house grew even colder. Money got scarcer and the battle for the chair nearest the electric fire became intense. The shilling per night frugality finally became intolerable and one night Mick snapped.

"I have an idea about how to get more from the meter," he said confidently, and walked out of the room and up to the loft. There followed a couple of loud bangs and then like a miracle the fire suddenly came back on.

"How did you manage that?" we chorused in admiration as he came back into the room.

"It's just a little trick I learned in my last place," said Mick. We all were massively impressed as Mick climbed over the chair and sat warming his hands and grinning at us all whilst basking in our amazement. I was first up to my room that night and on the way I decided to take a look at Mick's engineering skills as I passed the loft door. I pulled it open and looked at the meter and there with the shattered padlock lying on the floor lay a hammer and screwdriver, the tray containing one solitary shilling was pulled open and I wandered dismayed down stairs to confront Mick.

"Ah, don't be givin' out to me," he chuckled, reading the expression on my face. "We're all feckin' freezin' to death here and when we get a job we'll soon make it up and pay back what we owe and at least we'll have some warmth."

For once his laugh did not amuse me.

"Where's all the money from the meter, Mick?" I accused.

"Oh Jesus, you don't think I'd steal the money do you? I put it in the shilling jar in the kitchen. I thought we could buy sometin' to eat with it tomorrow. After all it's our money and we're only borrowing it till we get fixed up."

I bought breasts of lamb for a shilling and Mick came back from the grocery simply laden with stuff: vegetables and spaghetti in a carrier bag but, more worrying, other items like sweets appeared unwrapped from his pockets. The others declined to notice and nothing was said. That night we let Barbara come round and had a great feast, except Barbara left most of hers so Mick ate it as he took away the dishes. I caught him gnawing on the bones as he walked to the kitchen.

"Wha?" he laughed as we walked past each other in the hall. Mick put on his Woody record and stood humming tunelessly along with the speaker on the wall as he swilled the kettle full of water round the greasy dishes in the sink. We sat in the other room smoking tailor-mades and thinking things weren't too bad after all. I pondered the morality of what we were doing but only for a little while.

Snow fell in the next few days, and a few days after that it settled and stayed the whole winter long. Henry didn't even try to get up for the train coach washing job. The house got even colder and some of the pipes froze. Then one evening I had a great idea. There were radiators all over the house, and in the cellar I had discovered behind some rubble an old boiler, so all we had to do was get some fuel and surely we would be warm as bugs in a rug. The only trouble was that we had no money to buy any with. Mick decided we should 'borrow' some coal.

There was an old portable toilet down in the cellar with a huge handle, and it seemed perfect for the job in hand. Although I knew that what we intended was wrong, I found myself enormously attracted to the idea of nicking a little heat; like stealing food for one's babies, it did not seem such a crime.

That night Mick and I ventured down the quiet suburban streets of Southbourne armed with a hand shovel and the toilet-sized bucket. We were leaving fresh tracks in the snow wherever we walked, but the cold made us reckless and when we were a good few streets away from home, we crept up our first garden path. Having made our way round the back we searched for the coal bunker. It was situated just past the back door, and suddenly as we crept nearer to it there was the most unbelievable crash. A dog the size of a polar bear had thrown its body against the back door and commenced a terrible deep barking.

"Feck!" said Mick.

"Shit!" I agreed, and we turned and ran slithering down the path dragging the toilet behind us, over the front lawn, straight down the street and round the corner. Finally we stopped, about a hundred yards from the foiled attempt, and collapsed into a privet hedge in fits of frightened laughter.

"What in the name of Jesus was that feckin' thing?" said Mick. I blew on my frozen fingers and wiped away the laughter tears that were already beginning to freeze on my face. We were luckier with our next attempt, as we seemed to have found an empty place, and once we had knocked the frozen chunks of coal apart, we shovelled away uninterrupted until the bucket was full. Warmed from our efforts but covered with snow and coal dust, we stood up and made to leave, but now the toilet was so heavy we could hardly move it. A car went past and we instinctively ducked down behind the bunker.

"We're going to have to empty some of it out," observed Mick.

I really couldn't believe what we were doing. We left about half of the coal by the back door and resolved to come back the next day and collect it.

"What are we going to say if someone stops us?" I asked Mick, but he said nothing. We staggered off down the path, leaving even deeper footprints in the snow that continued to fall. We had to rest every few yards as the thin metal handle cut into already painful fingers, and the trail we left behind became even more intriguing as the pairs of footprints were accompanied by a circle every so often as we set down our stolen burden. We were within sight of home when I saw the lights of a car approaching on our side of the road.

"Just act natural," said Mick.

"Natural? What's natural about two blokes walking out in the coldest night of the year dragging a portable toilet between them half full of stolen coal?"

As the car approached, Mick moved in front of it and adopted a pose of studied nonchalance; leaning in an unnatural bent-kneed crouch with one elbow on the rim, he took out a packet of Park Drive and offered me a smoke. The car drove past and I nearly fell on the floor. I was still chuckling as we dragged the bucket into the house to the not too admiring glances of Henry and Keith.

"That's not much, is it ?" said Henry.

"You try feckin' haulin' this stuff!" said Mick, not really angry. "Have ye prepared the fire in the boiler?"

Henry and Keith had, and after two or three attempts at rebuilding it we got a burn going. Keith checked outside and reported that smoke could be seen coming from the chimney, and we began placing lumps of coal on the fire. There was a series of different stopcocks connected to various pipes, and Keith, being the most technical, thought it best to open them all so that the water would have free passage all around. Once the fire was well and truly going, we all ran round the house feeling the pipes for any change of temperature.

From downstairs I heard Mick's voice shouting, "This one's warming up!" and after a minute, "I'm having the first bath!"

The very prospect of heat started to warm me. Suddenly there was a huge bang and then a crash which emanated from the bathroom downstairs. When I got there, the others were standing dismayed as they surveyed the scene. A pipe in the wall had exploded and blown plaster and brick work into the bath. The place was a mess and we just looked disbelievingly at each other. Fortunately we had Keith, who immediately went and turned off various stopcocks and valves, preventing the heating system from adding flood to our lists of woes.

Henry looked close to tears as he wondered what we would tell the landlord. That night as once again I lay shivering in my bed smelling comfortingly of coal dust, my thoughts turned towards home; the meagre comforts there seemed luxurious in comparison to what we had to contend with in freezing Hampshire. When we awoke next day to cold, hunger, penury, something akin to bomb damage, and partial flood, we could now add drought.

That night, the temperature dropped dramatically. When we arrived downstairs in the morning one by one, we checked the toilet and bathroom, hoping that by some miracle the wall would have righted itself and the damage repaired. But of course it had not and there was more to come. During the night someone had got up and had a crap, and though they may have flushed the toilet, the biggest turd in the world had not gone away and was lying there in a few inches of frozen water. Worse still, the toilet could no longer be flushed as the water in the earthenware cistern had frozen and the expansion had cracked it. All the water pipes inside were frozen and we didn't even have enough in the system to make a cup of tea. We all stood around wondering what to do next, half amused and half amazed that whoever had dropped that log in the drain could still walk unaided, let alone keep a straight face in denial.

I wandered out into the garden and filled the kettle and a saucepan with snow—about a foot had fallen overnight—and by this means we were able to get something hot to drink. Then we tried to flush the toilet by pouring boiling water down the loo, attempting both to disperse the turd and to defrost the bend. We were only half successful and the thing stayed with us for several days, which meant number twos had to be taken in the public toilets down on the wintry sea front until lots were drawn—which I lost—and the offending article was fished out and buried in the garden. From then on we had to flush the toilet with melted snow because when Keith did eventually get our water supply back, there was still no way we had money to repair the cistern.

Somehow we soldiered on and Mick kept us going with an assortment of items from the corner shop. The old bloke in the shop was very slow and would take forever to find things. By now Mick knew where everything was kept, so he would send the old chap across to one side of the shop and liberate an item from where he was standing. Then he would do the same in reverse and something else would vanish under his brown cord jacket. Afterwards I remonstrated with Mick that this was stealing and that he would probably put the old guy out of business. As usual Mick's defence was laughter and he pointed out that I had been enjoying the fruits of his providence on several occasions already. I protested that I had done this only because I didn't know they were nicked and swore never to eat any of Mick's supplies again.

That night as the boys tucked into a bowl of cornflakes and watered down milk, I sat smoking my dog-end mixture and thought how good it felt taking the moral high ground. Then I recalled something that had come up in conversation with George Foulser in the pad at Poole. One night the subject of the new trend towards supermarkets had come up and George had talked of how the system should have been adapted to the socialist ethic, where huge outlets could provide food at low cost for the masses.

To make conversation and to show concern for the well-being of my fellow man, I had said, "What will happen to the little corner shop keeper?"

"What will happen to the little corner shop keeper? Fuck the little corner shop keeper! Some of them are the biggest thieves going, selling stuff that's gone off and short measures! They're bigger robbers than the bastards who run the supermarkets, and most of them these days won't give any tick," George had stated calmly, making me feel like a naive twit.

As soon as I thought about it I knew he was right and I ought to make up for all the times I had been gypped over the years. I walked into the freezing kitchen and casually asked the lads if there was anything left in the packet, but of course there wasn't and so I made the tea and glanced into the cupboard in the vague hope that there would be a few scraps of something left—but of course there wasn't, except for about a dozen bits of old spaghetti in a blue packet. I made tea and poured myself a cup.

"Go easy on the milk!" the other three chorused, and I wandered off to sip the brew in the room with the two bar fire. As I sat there warming my hands round the mug I was joined by Henry and Keith, each with a tea.

"That's the last of the sugar gone," said Henry smugly.

"We're going to have to get some money somehow," we all agreed.

"Where's Mick?" I asked and Keith told me that he was doing the washing up.

"But it's not his turn," I protested (we had a strict rota and no-one ever volunteered out of hand).

Perhaps he feels guilty, I reasoned to myself, about stealing or eating all the cornflakes. Anyway, it meant that it would be another day before I would have to do it and that suited me as I have always hated getting my hands in water too long, for the feeling you get afterwards always makes my teeth go on edge. At that point Mick came into the room and put on his favourite Woody record and pressed the switch that sent the signal to the kitchen.

"Jest a bit of music while I work," he explained. I picked up the guitar and strummed along to the songs and soon we were treated to Mick's tuneless warbling from the kitchen and my accompaniment from the living room.

Henry started to chuckle. "Hark at that, that's the worst singing I've ever heard."

Suddenly Keith said, "I have an idea, maybe we can record him by using the speakers in the kitchen as microphones."

"How would that work?" I asked, relishing the prospect of hearing Mick on tape and seeing his embarrassment.

"Well you see a speaker is only a mike in reverse," said Keith, "so in theory if you shout into a speaker that is connected to a mike input you should be able to get enough signal to record."

"Oh go on do it do it," I implored.

As soon as Keith turned off the record player, Mick shouted from the kitchen, "Oi, turn it on lads."

"We will as soon as I've fixed it," said Keith. "Something's gone wrong but it won't take a minute."

"Good," said Mick, "it's just coming up to me favourite, the *Bold Philadelphia Lawyer.*"

Keith started unscrewing things and taping bits of wire and cable together, and of course without any music Mick stopped singing. After a few minutes Keith announced that the job was done and we listened anxiously to see if we could hear anything. Keith turned up the volume on the tape recorder and sure enough we could hear Mick banging about in the kitchen; we looked at each other with wonder and back at Keith with admiration.

Amongst the sound of plates and knives and forks we could just make out a low tuneless hum which suddenly broke out into, *"...two shadows he saw on that wall..."* out of tune and with gusto. There then followed a bit more tuneless humming, and then, *"...one less Philadelphia lawyer in old Philadelphia tonight..."*

"Quick quick, record him," I shouted urgently at Keith.

"I am already," said Keith, and Henry and I sat there relishing every out of tune moment as Mick went through his repertoire of song and hits of the day accompanied only by the clatter of pots and pans and the sound of kitchen work going on.

I suppose we had recorded some ten minutes of these sounds when I suddenly said, "How long does it take to wash up three bowls and a couple of cups? He's taking a long time to do such a little bit of work."

We all stopped to listen and all we could hear this time was the clatter of a spoon and bowl.

"He's eating something," said Henry.

"Don't be daft," I said, "there's nothing to eat."

"Let's take a look," suggested Keith and the three of us carefully opened the door to the living room and crept up the darkened hallway to the closed door of the kitchen. The three of us started to sniff the air. There was definitely something cooking. I grabbed the door handle and like the three musketeers we burst into the kitchen together. Mick was standing over the draining board with a bowl held almost Chinese style to his lips, and a fork cramming a few strands of spaghetti into his mouth. It is hard now to communicate the gravity with which we viewed this situation; our friend and colleague was cheating on us and had kept back some food for himself.

All laughter had ceased and we stood frozen like statues in the doorway with our mouths gaping open like fledglings in nest waiting to be fed. It is a wonder that Mick didn't walk over to us and drop a worm of spaghetti into each incredulous mouth. Instead he just stood there frozen like us, except he was in mid-mouthful. At last he could suppress the comedy of the scene no longer and sprayed us all with the contents of his mouth as he collapsed into a great wail of released guilt and laughter. "Jesus lads I was so feckin' hungry, I can't sleep at night with the hunger on me, Jesus lads I'm sorry." He set the bowl down on the draining board.

"Where did you find anything to eat?" asked Henry as we all moved closer to inspect the remains of his bowl. As hungry as I was, I have to confess that Mick's snack looked distinctly unappetising. He had taken the remaining twelve strands of spaghetti and boiled them up quickly in a solution of watered milk and a spoonful of marmalade that he'd scraped from a jar that had been 'finished' that morning. None of us wanted the ancient pasta and now Mick was unable to finish the few seriously *al dente* bits left in the bowl.

"Look lads, I'll make it up to you," he offered, and we knew he would. Nevertheless we let him stew in his guilt for about ten minutes before we remembered that the whole scene was being recorded in the front room. We hurried inside to rewind it and play it back to an incredulous Mick, who was still standing by the draining board as the awful strains of *The Bold Philadelphia Lawyer* reversed out of the speakers to an utterly amazed Irishman.

"YOU feckin'... How the feck?... is dat me you feckin'... Jesus that sounds feckin' terrible turn it off... you bastards!"

Soon we were all in hysterics as we relived the entire experience again; at that moment in that freezing house we were warmed by laughter and companionship. The next day Henry and I got jobs, and a few days later so did Mick, and naturally our fortunes changed.

∽

SUMMER LIGHTNING

robbery

H enry's job was as a trainee Hoffman presser in a laundry; I became a kitchen porter in a hotel in Bournemouth. We both had early starts and, of the two jobs, mine was the easiest, because after the breakfast rush there was a great meal for the staff. Then after lunch I was left alone to wash all the pots and I usually made myself a huge ice-cream sundae. I managed to find my father figure in Len, the sous chef. He was about forty and from Lancashire. He taught me how to wash pots properly and how to make new potatoes out of old ones. He covered for me when I was late in and said I could do better for myself than being a KP.

This taking of lowly jobs on my part was quite deliberate; I had become fascinated by the life of Woody and his praise of the working man and, in order to rightfully claim my place alongside all working heroes, I felt it necessary to try as many different jobs as I could. Later on, when I read George Orwell's account of life as a plongeur in Paris, I realised I was not the only one who had slightly patronised the workers by accepting menial jobs below his ability. Truth to tell, with my qualifications I think my only options would have been office trainee, but I loved manual work and I still do; anyway I suspect Orwell of having masochistic tendencies.

My work at the hotel was boring in the extreme, but the lads at the house were grateful for any little bits I could manage to bring home. Len, realising our predicament, often gave me the nod to take an odd bit of chicken or a bit of leftover bacon. This of course was added to with a few sausages that were never missed.

My wages were £6 per week and I suppose all I could eat. Henry's wage as a trainee Hoffman presser was five pounds a week, but this rose to seven pounds after training. This was a con as it turned out, as anyone with a little sense could learn the game in a day or so. Henry taught Mick how to do it by demonstrating using the kitchen table as a press, and we thought very little of Mick's interest in the art until he turned up one day at the depot posing as a trained presser. He'd blagged his way in and explained discrepancies in style as having learned the trade in Ireland; as a skilled man his wage was seven pounds a week.

After two or three weeks I jacked in the KP job and signed on with the two other lads as a trainee, and we were all united once more. Bollom's had shops all over the county; vans collected the gear and cleaned it in a central place, and then it was given to us to press and bag up before returning. Some of the poor bastards were on piece work and worked like machines. Mick was pretty quick, but refused to go on bonus, while Henry and I just plodded along and did enough not to be sacked.

I was the only one in a relationship; with the late hours and lovemaking, I was very tired during the day and needed a lot of stimulus and conversation to keep me awake. Because of the subterfuge regarding Mick, Henry and I had to pretend to get to know him, and we had a foreman who did not allow idle chat between pressers. Anyway Mick was on the other side of the building to me, so I had to be content with Peter, who was very strange.

He was thirtyish, with curly hair and the thickest glasses I'd ever seen. It's awful how you suspect anyone with a slight affliction of being odd or unsavoury, but the truth is wherever I have worked in places that are cut off from the chance of social interaction, be it a warehouse or packing department or dispatch office, I've come across weird people.

There was a bloke at Philips who only went with whores and admitted he detested women and anyone who drove cars; if some poor unfortunate ever stopped him to ask directions it was his pleasure to misdirect them. He was an unsightly man with uneven teeth and a very upright posture with splayed feet. He reminded me of Trotsky with his tiny glasses, and although he had no beard there was always the hint of one as he was never able to shave himself properly; it was as if he shaved parts of his face leaving patches completely alone. As we worked together loading TVs, I would sometimes hear him muttering horrible threats to the women he could see in his mind. There was a time that I felt he was ready to kill, and I spent long hours promising him that there was a woman out there who would love him for who he was and that they weren't all bad. When he asked me how I thought anyone would ever fall for someone who looked like him, I was stumped for a minute. Then I said, "Perhaps you could find a blind girl?"

Another time, I came across an anarchist who was so withdrawn that it broke my heart, and I really worked on him to win his confidence. When he trusted me completely, he revealed that his main ambition in life was to get a machine gun and go out into some crowded place and mow down as many people as he could before they got him. As he told me his plan, his colour changed and little foam clusters formed at the side of his mouth; his eyes widened and he positively seethed hatred.

My pressing partner Peter was not as mad as these two, but he was very withdrawn and strange, and the worst thing was that he never wanted to talk. This was torture to me, as I needed some human communication to lift me above the drudgery of the work and the constant hiss from the presses that makes you think you've lost the top end of your hearing. I was convinced I was sounding like old Mr. Cox, the husband of our landlady at the Waldrons, who was so deaf he never pronounced his 'S's and neglected most of his 'T's too.

As well as the noise there was the smell, for even after the garments have been washed/cleaned with carbon tetrachloride and dried so that there are no dirt deposits, they still smell of their owner's sweat. If you've ever walked into an charity clothes shop, you will be aware of that smell. Now if you imagine that warmed up and add humidity, you will understand what I'm talking about. We all looked forward to tea breaks and there were two a day; each lasted ten minutes, which was just time for tea and a fag. The company was so mean that they only supplied the tea on a subsidised basis, and we had to buy our own sugar.

It was Mick (of course) who noticed that our sugar was going down a lot faster than the others. He suspected that the tea lady, who was also Irish, was doling it out to her favourite lads; she made no secret that she did not like any of us. To catch her, Mick devised a simple plan. The next day after the afternoon break, he produced a small bag from his pocket and emptied the contents into our sugar bag before returning it to the counter in the canteen for safe keeping. The next day we were all deliberately late for morning tea break and none of us took our sugar; we just sat down and waited for the fun to start. One by one people began to gag on their teas; some spat it out, swearing, and others sniffed their brew or tried stirring it more vigorously, to no effect. Blokes started to go back to the counter to complain and Mick, Henry and I were there to hear them.

"There's salt in this tea!" was the universal charge, and indeed there was.

"Now then missus," says Mick, "Do you still say that you're not puttin our sugar in their teas?"

"No, no, it wasn't me," she denied, but of course it was, and everyone knew it. But still she persisted in her innocence. It was the first time I'd ever seen anyone caught in a flagrant lie and deny it, and it confused me greatly. Mick just laughed as usual, but our fate was sealed and it was not long before I'd had enough and quit the pressing game, and the others followed suit as the atmosphere in the place deteriorated. Soon we were all broke again like before, but spring was with us and optimism was in the air. Gill and I were making plans to travel abroad and we had the freedom of the scooter and each other. An easy camaraderie prevailed in the house. Then Norman arrived.

Norman's crimes were that he was one year younger than all of us, had very frizzy hair, couldn't say his 'R's properly, had too much confidence, and was from a different class than the rest of us. Henry had persuaded us to allow him to join us because the extra rent money would help out. We tolerated him, but he was always questioning everything we did and trying to find more sensible ways of doing things when he should have been more respectful. No-one got on with him and he failed to notice.

The business of rent was a sore point, as Mick and I continued to pay whenever we could, but unfortunately Henry forgot to pay the landlord. Norman soon got a job and was not really much trouble, and anyway he would share his fags with us, which at least took away the necessity of delving into the stinking dog-end jar. One night, Keith happened to mention that he'd got a job as a steward at a country point-to-point meeting. He explained about how everyone was so trusting and that money was left lying about for anyone to pick up once they were inside the compound. Mick's ears pricked up immediately.

"Is there money really lyin' about?" he asked quietly.

"Well you know it's not locked away or anything," said Keith, a little more cautiously.

"Well where is it then?"

"It's kept in the steward's hut. It's like the money from the betting tote. It's just sort of left in a cardboard box on the table," said Keith, beginning to look worried.

"Can you get into the hut?" asked Mick, his voice steady but insistent.

"Course I can," said Keith, "that's my job—I go in and put the money in the box and generally help around the site."

"Could we get into the compound?"

Keith bent his head low to the table and said in a relieved tone, "No, only people with an official sort of badge can get in." He looked round at us two for support before saying, "So whatever you were thinking you can put it out of your mind."

Mick was insistent. It would be easy to pull this one off, he said. I was grinning, allowing this fantasy to continue for as long as it lasted, knowing full well that we would never attempt a robbery in real life. Henry looked bemused, and with nostrils flared to suppress his bemusement sent glances back and forth between Mick, Keith and me. Norman's eyes were like saucers.

Keith drew a sketch of the area, the approach roads, and the outline of the low security fence where the bookies were, and in a few moments Mick seemed to have come up with a plan. The important thing was that no-one should actually be able to connect the theft to Keith, and this could be accomplished by all of us arriving at different times wearing clothes that we didn't usually wear. Each one of us would handle the money for a short time as links in a chain that would culminate in him (Mick) getting on the back of Keith's motorbike and being driven away steadily by Henry, who had a licence.

I was to act as lookout and receive the stolen cash from Keith over the fence. I was then to move quickly up the hill to where the bookies were all positioned and hand the dough to Mick, who only had a short walk to the motorbike. I was to return to hanging about down at the compound so as not to arouse suspicion, and after a discreet time leave for home, discarding my disguise before catching the bus. By this time, Henry and Mick would be home, and after Keith had spoken to the police, he would get a lift to his girlfriend's place before taking the bus back to the house. It all sounded so simple and professional. There was to be no job, however, for Norman.

"Oh go on, let me do something, please," begged Norman.

"No," we chorused.

"You're fuckin' mad," said Henry.

"Now come on lads, what could be simpler?" demanded Mick.

"Sounds a doddle," said I, still believing that reason would prevail. "How much do you think would be in the kitty, Keith?"

"About two hundred pounds."

"You wouldn't, would you Ralph?" asked Henry, his eyes wide with incredulity.

"How much, two hundred quid? Sure, why not?"

"Two hundred, you could do a lot with two hundred couldn't you eh wha'?" chuckled Mick.

"Well if Ralph's in, then I'm in," said Henry loyally.

"That only leaves you, Keith. Are you with us or against us?" demanded Mick. We all looked at Keith.

"Oh all right then," Keith agreed.

I couldn't believe what was going on—they actually intended to go through with it. There was no going back even if I'd wanted to, because waiting in the wings was bloody Norman, and anyway the others were already discussing their ideas of what we would wear.

That night I hardly slept with the anxiety of it all, and the next day it was the only topic of conversation. We rehearsed our moves around the house and garden and kept on trying to anticipate problems which we solved on the spot, and then we'd talk about what we'd spend it on or go all mysterious on poor old Norman, who had been totally frozen out of the plans. It didn't stop him, however, asking if we would give him some of the loot if and when we'd pulled it off. Perhaps it was my time in the army, but I insisted that we practise our routines properly, and came up with a really original hiding place for the money: we would secrete the notes inside the lining of the fridge door. Perfect! I was almost beginning to look forward to the caper.

On the actual day I got up early to find Henry and Keith making Marmite sandwiches without margarine, and I joined them for a cup of black tea, sweetened with jam, as we were once again without milk or sugar.

"We're still going through with this then?" was about all I could manage. Henry gave me one of his withering looks, which were always the more withering in the morning as his wayward eye looked vaguely up at the ceiling, giving him a look of exasperation and disgust.

"Just remember the plan and don't screw it up," he intoned with a dark authority. Keith busied himself with his final preparations and hardly looked at me.

I watched the two of them leave, and heard them kicking over the motorbike a couple of times before it started. The two friends climbed aboard and drove off down the road into the fine spring Saturday morning to commit a robbery. I felt sick.

Henry dropped Keith some way from the course and went and hid both bike and himself in a field. Keith walked the last distance by himself. When pressed as to where his machine was, he would later explain that he had hitchhiked to the course. Mick and I took a bus, talking all the way in our disguises. The clothes were not that different to what we might have worn anyway, but I had parted my hair in the middle and had, by listening to Keith, perfected—or so I thought—a pretty passable Dorset accent.

My whole subterfuge was set off by a brown tweed jacket borrowed from Alan, a kindly friend of Gill's. Mick had borrowed a pair of someone's prescription glasses, though I suspect just to satisfy me that he was trying. His late Tony Curtis hairstyle had been lapped down, but he still looked different to most people in the area. The glasses made him look ridiculous. A lad that wore his clothes like that would not have been seen dead in specs like those.

We tried not to let others know we were together, but the journey was a long one. We were nervous and were soon laughing at things that weren't even funny, becoming highly conspicuous.

"Well I'll be seein' yez all later," said Mick in a huge Irish accent in the middle of darkest Dorset as he climbed off the bus some way from the ground.

"So long Fred," he shouted pointedly at me, before nearly missing his footing as he half fell off the bus.

The point to point itself was a colourful affair, but I was so nervous by now I didn't take a lot of it in. Sure enough, everything was laid out pretty much as Keith had described it, although it was smaller than I had imagined. Bookmakers were setting up shop, and horses were everywhere; people walked in and out of the compound below with no checks, and cars arrived all the time. By now I was hungry, and to my deep disappointment I realised I had no money to buy anything. From the top of the bank I saw Keith in the compound, and he gave a sly signal that he wanted me to come down to meet him.

"Oh no," I thought, "he's already done it," but I realised he only wanted to give me some instructions. Before I slithered down to the fence, my heart pounding, I signalled that I understood, and by pointing to my mouth and rubbing my stomach managed to infer that I was both hungry and nonchalant. It is hard to limp when sliding down a grassy bank, and my gait must have looked more like a man suffering from St. Vitus' Dance than a crippled local. I wondered if my act might be a little over the top.

Keith said nothing, but as I drew near, he bent down to do up his shoelace and left an envelope on the grass at the foot of the fence, then turned and walked briskly away. My heart was banging away so fiercely I thought I might pass out as I picked up the package and commenced to try and run up the still dewy bank. But something told me that this was not the right envelope as it was not full enough, and as soon as I could, I opened it to find a steward's badge and a hastily scrawled note from Keith to the effect that the badge would get me into the enclosure. Therefore I wouldn't have to hang about the perimeter drawing attention to myself. When the time was right, he would signal me to move outside and take up the prearranged position.

I didn't like this. Already the plan was changing, but I put on the badge and as my heartbeat returned to somewhere near normal, I affected my limp and stumbled off with my centre parting and my Dorset accent at the ready in case anyone should talk to me, praying that no-one would, and wondering if everyone else was as scared as I was.

When your intent is criminal, it seems as though everyone is looking at you suspiciously, like when you walk through Customs and you feel as if you might as well have a pound of heroin secreted about your person. I limped around the paddock trying to look as if I knew what I was doing. It was odd passing by Keith all the time and not being able to say anything. Once or twice I nearly blurted out something as my tension rose. Surely it was time to move: our deadline was the three o'clock race. Keith walked past me once more, and as he did so he raised his eyebrows in an inquiring manner which suggested 'are you ready?' He mouthed something which I couldn't interpret and suddenly we were on.

As quickly as seemed reasonable, I limped off in the direction of the rendezvous by the fence and was halfway across when I realised I was limping on the wrong leg. I quickly changed over, looking round to see if anyone was noticing, but they paid me no attention. Over my shoulder, I saw Keith purposefully entering the shed where the money was, and I felt sick again. As I rounded the corner of the paddock, I saw Keith lay a package down on the grass between the fence and, as planned, he walked over to another official and started conversing with him. This was it.

My limp had acquired manic exaggeration as I raced round to the pickup point. I stooped down and gave the brown paper an instinctive squeeze. It was money all right. Stuffing the parcel down my shirt, I once again slid and slithered up the bank, and with a strange music and drumming in my ears, hurtled through the crowds sometimes forgetting my disability but managing not to hit anyone either. Up past the bookies I went and towards the car park. There was no sign of anyone.

Oh Christ, I prayed, where the fuck is everyone? Then I saw Mick over by one of the bookies studying the form.

"Jim," I shouted (it was his agreed alias). There was no response.

"Jim!" I bellowed. Again, nothing.

"JIM!!" I screamed like a soul demented, and the sheer desperation in my voice made almost the entire course turn round in my direction. This time he noticed me and as surreptitiously as he could ambled over to me.

"What's the matter with you Mick, you were supposed to be here," I wailed, close to tears.

"Ah come on, we're all right. Have ye got it?"

"Yes," I said as we exchanged jackets out of sight of the main throng.

Mick grabbed the package and was just about to unwrap it when I almost screamed at him, "For Christ's sake get going you idiot!" Stuffing it in his shirt, he raced across the car park to the spot where Henry had been revving the bike for nearly ten minutes, attracting comments from other racegoers about noisy yobbos.

Mick flew through the punters and leaped onto the back of the bike, which caused Henry to let out the clutch too quickly and the engine stalled. Henry then flooded the carburettor and it was some little while before the two of them actually got away. I was oblivious to this as, my limp now miraculously cured, I took myself off to join the racegoers. I saw the end of the four o'clock race before I casually left the course and aimed for the Bournemouth road.

At six o'clock I was still walking. I got my first brief lift at around seven, and walked the last six or seven miles home to the house, my stomach roaring with hunger but the pain tempered by the warmth of the spring evening, the birds singing, and the certain knowledge that the raid had been a success. Me and the boys would be on easy street. My steps quickened as I neared the front door, where I could see Keith's motorbike leaning against the wall. Unusually the door was closed and I had to ring the bell. Keith answered, saw it was me, turned, and walked into the kitchen. His lack of greeting took me aback. After a second I stepped inside, slammed the door and hurried into the room where the three of them were sitting.

"Well?" I said beaming, but just my first glance told me there was something wrong.

"Well what?" said Henry, giving me his world-weary look.

"Where's the money?"

"Oh, the money," said Henry, faking surprise. "He wants to know where the money is." Then, looking round at me, he said slowly, "There ain't no bleedin' money. Tell him, Keith."

Poor Keith, he looked so downhearted, though slightly flushed with the wind and sun.

"They didn't do what they normally do. They had a safe in one of the caravans and only the race marshals were allowed in there and even if I could have got in there I couldn't have got it out without the combination." He looked close to tears as his voice droned on in more detailed description, but I heard no more of what he said as a peculiar humming had begun between my ears and my legs had suddenly began to ache severely. I began to feel dizzy and angry and I did not believe a word of it.

"You're kidding me!" I looked imploringly from one to another as I reached for a chair and collapsed down into it. "Please tell me you're making it up," I tried again.

Suddenly Mick, who had been avoiding my gaze, burst out into one of his huge guffaws.

"So you were kidding!" I smiled with relief.

"Ah no," said Mick, "I just can't look at your face without laughin'.

We didn't get a thing."

"But what about the package?" I persisted.

At this Henry reached over to the draining board and picked up my prize and gently dropped it on the table. "Have a little look."

I picked up the brown paper parcel and gently opened it to find... two soggy Marmite sandwiches!

"You signalled to me that you were hungry," offered Keith, "so I dropped the packet by the fence for you. The next time I looked round all I could see was you disappearing above the bank and on your way. There was nothing I could do to stop you, so when I was finished I just picked up me money and came straight back here."

Slowly and with great deliberation I picked up the first sandwich and started to eat it, and in a couple of seconds I had demolished the second one too and I sat there with crumbs falling out of my mouth with my three friends in hysterics and soon I was laughing with the rest of them. Then I had an idea. Norman had not yet come in from work. I couldn't bear the thought of giving him the satisfaction of knowing we'd screwed up.

"How much have we got between us?" I asked.

Someone answered, "Not as much as we had this morning."

Of course Keith had his thirty bob for the job, and when I explained my plan they all prevailed upon the uncertain Keith to lend us his money. By the time an excited Norman arrived back from work, Mick and I had been to the shop and bought five mannequin cigars, ten Woodbines, a large bottle of cider and a few cheap candy bars. Back at the house we gently prised open the lining of the fridge and inserted a ten shilling note so that the corner just stuck out enough to reveal what it was. We put on the music, turned up the volume, filled the room with cigar smoke and dealt out the playing cards, and with the aid of matches were to be found gambling away our ill-gotten gains at three-card brag.

Norman threw open the door took in the scene and yelled, "You did it you bastards you bloody did it! How much did you get?"

"Two hundred and seventy quid," said Henry casually.

"TWO HUNDRED AND SEVENTY QUID?"

"Keep it down!" we cautioned.

"Where is it?"

"In the fridge," said Mick. "Where else would you keep hot money?"

Norman leaped to the fridge and yanked open the door.

"Where in the fridge?" he asked disbelievingly.

"In the door," I said.

"Christ there's a note sticking out," he said. "Can I have it?" But before there was time for any of us to say no, Mick had leaped to the door and plucked it from the lining and stuffed it in his own pocket.

"Have a cigar, Norman," he offered magnanimously, and he lobbed the last cheroot in Norman's direction. It was like having pulled off the perfect crime. The only trouble was that we were still broke.

By now the backlog of owed rent was insurmountable, and one night Henry's dear old dad drove down to Southbourne, threw everything in the car that he could and whisked Mick and Henry back to Mitcham.

I had already left for a short stay at home as Gill and I had definitely decided to hitch to Spain. Keith was getting a place in Bournemouth, Mick got a job in Thornton Heath as a Hoffman presser and eventually Henry did the same and even got to manage a few shops. I started working in one of them as well, before my bad timekeeping forced the other workers to get Henry to ask me to leave. That was fine with me; I had other plans anyway. The summer was on us and the road was calling me again, and this time it would be great.

olé

Terry and Mandy were the first of our friends to get married, but to be fair they were older than us. Terry Atkinson was two years older than me, and Mandy was two years older than him. No-one was surprised—and anyway, lots of working class kids got married in their early twenties. However, the first to get engaged was Les. Whatever was between him and my cousin Chris had not been possible to maintain for reasons of distance and other diversions, and slowly but surely a deep friendship and then love built up between him and Margot Rossario. She was of Indian background, but as Croydon as the rest of us, and her two friends Cathy and Pat were part of our coterie of friends from the Whitgift Arms. All three of them were very pretty and Margot had the added attraction of being the tiniest and most exotic.

For the life of me I cannot think what brought them to the place, but they were happy to spend many evenings there. Cathy soon fell in with a nice bloke called John, who was from Northern Ireland and a scaffolding ganger, and they became inseparable. Pat started to go out with Steve, and I was deeply in love with Gill but she lived in Bournemouth and I only saw her on certain weekends when she hitched up to London to be with me.

There was now nothing in the way of our plans to hitch around Spain, and with a few possessions and a determination that this time I would be able to make my way with the guitar, we left for France.

Popular knowledge warned about trying to get a lift from Calais to Paris, so we took the train and arrived in the Gare du Nord. We ate a *sandwich jambon* as I now knew not to have egg and chips, and after a coffee and my first Gauloise we walked right through Paris with our bags and my guitar.

Somewhere near the start of Route National Seven we stopped a car. It was a Citroen Big Six and I fell in love with it and knew that one day I would have to own one of them. In my halting schoolboy French I told our driver how much I admired his *voiture*. He was only a young man and he beamed at my compliments. We had travelled quite a distance before we realised that the N7 is not the best way to go to Spain and that we needed to be much further over, but I was so delighted with the short wait that I hadn't really thought about direction.

Gill was an incredible asset. Drivers nearly caused accidents whilst attempting sidelong glances at her. We slept out in the open and ate little. Gill was optimistic and confident, while I was excited and so happy to have her with me all the time that at first I didn't worry about the attention she was getting.

The weather was warm and the scents of the countryside intoxicating. Even hanging around for lifts was not a problem, as we had each other and cigarettes. And because she was so stunning, I didn't even have to hide in the hedgerows.

Each time we got on board a lorry, I glowed with the solidarity of the working class; to travel this way was truly in the socialist spirit and all truck drivers were comrades. We were stranded for some time on the Spanish border, and I discovered some old ruins and had a scout about whilst Gill sat on the roadside above the bank. After a good look round, I climbed back up the bank and sat with my arm around Gill listening to the birds and looking back up the road towards the border with France. Here we were in Franco's Spain armed only with optimism, a few quid and a handful of Woody Guthrie songs. As the shadows lengthened, I took out the guitar and sang for the pleasure of being part of the picture we were both in.

There were very few cars or trucks at this time and I began to wonder if we should stay where we were, just off the road. Then I heard the slow clop of a horse's hooves, and from round a little side turning appeared a cart pulled by a very elderly horse. The cart was built round an X frame and was not able to carry very much, which was fortunate as I don't think the old horse could have hauled much more than he had already. It was such a picturesque sight that both of us smiled at the old boy sitting up the front with a big yellow cigarette stuck in his face. He gestured at the back of his wagon. We looked at each other for a moment, then grabbing our stuff, threw it on the back and climbed up. The old horse did not even break step, and we rolled through the Pyrenees on a bed of newly cut grass, with the sounds of the day giving way to those of the evening as cicadas and crickets took over from the birds and the sun slipped behind the mountains.

We eventually arrived in Barcelona's outskirts and saw the sea. Lifts had been regular and easy, but our overall progress was slow. We had no destination in mind; just being together and travelling was all we wanted. Again I hadn't bothered with money as I was confident that I would be able to earn it by playing. I had the experience of Germany behind me, so why not? Between us I think we may have had as much as twenty pounds when we started out.

I wrote to Woody Guthrie from Fascist Spain, telling my dying hero that I was playing his songs to the working people. Which I was, in a way, sitting by the side of the road waiting for rides, but also in towns and villages whenever we stopped.

Somehow, though, I always managed to find a reason not to go busking. Gill did her best to give me confidence, but it seemed that I needed more reassurance than she was able to provide. I ate very little and Gill had no great appetite; the weather was beautiful and the heat of the noonday sun hotter than anything either of us had experienced before. We thriftily inched along the coast road towards Valencia, Gill a cheerful counter to my worries about everything from money to food to where we were heading. She was happy and beautiful and we were very much in love. We tanned by the roadsides, and her hair if anything became even blonder.

One day, high up in the hills where we had been trying for a lift for hours, we heard the slow grind of a lorry steadily climbing below us and I knew that this would be the one that was going to stop. As it hove into sight round a curve, I could see that it was painted sky blue and carried the biggest load of hay I had ever seen. The driver, who had plenty of time to take us in as he approached, leaned over to the passenger side. Without stopping, he threw open the door and motioned us to hop aboard.

Lifting Gill up first and then running alongside the cab backwards and forwards to where our little heap of stuff lay on the side of the road, I managed to get it all on. I scrambled, sweating, on to my seat next to Gill, who squeezed my arm happily. If you have never hitched a lift, it is difficult to communicate the feeling of those first few seconds, as with relief you climb into the cab. You start off by thanking your driver and then begin to work him out. Ours was a small thickset man in his forties. His name was Alphonso and he was going all the way to Valencia.

Gill sat between the driver and me. The truck had about thirty gears and in spite of this was terribly slow. I was nevertheless content to lean with one arm on the open window, taking in all the countryside and delighting in the lumbering progress of the huge *camion*. Neither of us spoke Spanish, but with my smattering of French I was able to convey our gratitude, which became greater when Alphonso stopped and bought us little snacks on the way.

Conversation was inane and minimal given my weak vocabulary and the thunderous noise from the engine, but gestures and smiles and affectionate looks from this benevolent driver were reciprocated by me as far as possible. It took us a couple of days to get to Valencia. The first night Alphonso slept in the cab while we slept outside. We lay in our two separate sleeping bags but in each other's arms under the stars, and wondered what it would be like in Valencia.

As we moved further south the sun got hotter and my right arm was as brown as a nut by the time we arrived in the city. Alphonso drove us around the city to the football stadium. I was not the least bit interested in football but I had to admit the place was impressive. He was obviously proud, strutting about gesticulating at the pitch and the goalposts and the vastness of the place. He spoke incomprehensibly fast to his friend who had allowed us to look inside, and I could see that he admired Gill by the way he kept shooting glances at her. It was the colour of the stadium's grass that I found striking. I wondered if it was it as green as that back home. Spain was all brown and greyish-green, bleached like a workman's shirt by the sun, but this was so vivid it almost hurt my eyes.

Later he took us to a restaurant and bought us a dish made from mussels in a black sauce. The nearest thing to this sort of food I had eaten was fish and chips. Perhaps it was the wine that Alphonso was pouring for me so profusely, or maybe the strange clear liquid that he insisted I try, but suddenly I felt bewildered and very sick. Time after time I threw up, and eventually Gill came and found me outside the restaurant. When she had cleaned me up a bit, she ran over to the lorry and took our little pile of stuff out.

She indicated urgently that she had to get away from our driver, and after staggering down some back streets she stopped, held on to me and burst into tears.

"What's the matter?" I wanted to know.

"It's Alphonso, Ralph, you don't know what he's been like," she said, her voice trembling. "Every time you got out of the cab, even for a pee, he was all over me trying to get me to leave you and go with him, and every time you nodded off in the cab he tried to touch me."

By now the tears were running down her face, and I was struck dumb. All the time I was talking to him about the working people and how we must all stick together, he was trying to stick it to my girl. I knew immediately what to do, but threw up again instead. My head was spinning and I was becoming delirious; my legs wouldn't work and sweat was pouring off me. Finally I passed out.

I awoke in a small room that apparently I had managed to walk to. A kind passer-by had directed us to a pension. The tiny room had a sink and a tap, so I cleaned myself up as best I could and went through all the facts of last night. My feelings of betrayal and stupidity hurt me deeply, and I begged Gill to let me know if it ever happened again and we would live with the consequences.

The room was cheap but still I was anxious to get out of it and back on the road. However, neither of us cared to venture further south. Instead I suggested that we try the South of France as we knew that there would be opportunity to make some money there. We started to retrace our steps back up the coast. We blagged our way into a Youth Hostel and sat drinking a mixture of cognac and coke until we got quite silly. We watched the sun go down in a dusty square sitting on the edge of a fountain.

We still had little inclination to eat much and got by on tomatoes and bread, with sometimes a little cheese washed down with *Gassos*, a primitive but delicious lemonade that was about a penny a litre. Our journey was positively speedy in sleek DS Citroens, swaying 2CVs, huge lorries with chain smoking drivers and, on one occasion, the back of a tractor.

One of the large Citroen vans that were never imported to Britain pulled up and a youngish chap with a huge moustache leant over and invited us in. There was a seat for him and part of a seat for Gill, but I had to crawl into the back amongst piles of disorganised angle iron and roof supports, so that I was coiled through the parts like a snake. If he'd had to stop—indeed if he *could* have stopped suddenly—I would have been chopped in half, as the soft parts of my body were pressed up against sharp metal. The journey was slow and noisy as night descended and the difference in the countryside reminded me how far from home I was.

Every so often the guy glanced back to me as I lay amongst the twisted metal like some crash victim and yelled, *"Ça va?"* and I would yell back, *"Oui!"*

As the light faded and the roads grew smaller it seemed our journey would never end but at last we arrived at a little house in a village somewhere and I was able, just, to uncoil myself and climb out of the van. We were invited into the driver's home and introduced to his pretty wife, who could not seem to work out what we were doing or why we were doing it. As if we knew! She attempted to talk with Gill, who could not speak any French, and eventually took her to wash while the guy poured me a glass of wine. Later he showed us up to a room where they had made up a bed for us. I was quite overwhelmed by this hospitality. He then asked if we were married. I tried to say that we were engaged, but that failed to ease the situation, and with much consternation he consulted his wife, who made some suggestion. He seemed pleased with the proposed compromise and came again upstairs with a pillow, explaining that because I was not married Gill should have the bed and I was to sleep on the floor. Then he bid us *"Bonne nuit,"* and left, only to return again a few minutes later with a metal bucket and a toilet roll.

"Bonne nuit!" he said again, and Gill got the giggles at the sight of the bucket.

That night, in spite of the nearness of Gill, I did indeed sleep on the floor.

riviera

Lorries, cars, hunger and tiredness, dust and thirst, insects singing loudly at the sides of roads, us getting confused and wandering down wrong turnings, complaints and blame all fuelled our long journey back towards the Mediterranean.

We arrived in Fréjus on a beautiful sunny day and bought bread and tomatoes. Someone had told us that you could get a night's stay in the local hostel for a few francs and we were ready to have a bed for the night. I was generally opposed to Youth Hostels as I thought them soft, but I became increasingly appreciative of them. Although I never joined up, I was grateful for the few nights I managed to blag my way in.

Gill and I were separated. I slept fitfully dreaming that I was in a series of car crashes; Gill was being bitten by mosquitoes. Perhaps because of my darker complexion I had been spared, and though Gill was a mite sorry for herself, her feelings soon changed to pity for a poor girl we met later on the road to Cannes. She too had spent the night in the hostel and the result was like nothing I have seen before or since. One side of the poor girl's face was as big and swollen as a football, her eye was barely visible with the swelling, and her neck was covered with infected bites.

The two of us on the French Riviera was a joke. I made the mistake of buying an orange juice that cost as much as a night's rest in a hostel, and took my shirt off, exposing my body for the first time in years. I resembled a neopolitan ice cream, my body all differing shades of red, pink and brown. I don't think I removed my shirt in public for the next six years. The contrast between us and the people that moved around the place we were in was huge. My resentment was growing, for if we had parity with the poor people of Spain, here we could just about afford a glass of water. I wondered how anyone acquired such wealth; they couldn't all be bank robbers.

All I wanted to do was get the hell out of there, and that is what we did. The next lift we got was with an Italian dentist who nearly crashed his DS several times from staring at Gill and muttering, *"Bella, bella."*

In French he asked me if all English girls were as beautiful as her?

"Yes," I lied, "there are many beautiful girls like her in England." He might have had a lovely car but I had Gill. I still had not found the courage to play in public.

Charlie was a very experienced hitchhiker, having travelled all over the States. Charlie explained that he felt the reason most hitchers take so long to get lifts is that their appearance puts other people off.

First of all, he reasoned, never carry a rucksack, as it suggests camping; wherever possible use a suitcase instead as it implies that you are only resorting to this method of transport because of an emergency. Secondly, be clean shaven (how much is a razor blade?) and keep your hair short. Next, avoid jeans and wear a pair of plain grey trousers or slacks that you hang up each night to keep the creases in. Wear a white nylon shirt that you can rinse through and have dry by the morning. If you are carrying a coat, drape it over your arm: the whole effect will make you look like this is something you don't normally do and the rides will come effortlessly.

I could find no fault with this logic, but for me the whole point of travelling was that it was a part of self-expression, and what I wore was part of that. If I had to wait twice as long as he did, I at least was a true martyr to my own style. In fact I had to wait more than twice as long as Charlie. I know this, for we met up several times along the Côte d'Azur and he was always there days before me even though I was travelling with the beautiful blonde-haired girl.

We arrived in Cannes and it was raining. Not unpleasant cold rain, but big warm dollops of it. It was getting dark, and for once we were both hungry. We found ourselves in an area where there had been an open air market of some kind. Still determined to hold on to the little money we had, I started looking for fruit and stuff that had rolled on to the floor under the stalls, while Gill sat at a small pavement café having a coffee. Looking up, I saw her being approached by two men.

As I walked over to where they were talking, Gill was just uttering her standard response to allcomers, *"Je ne parle pas francais."*

"Qu'est-ce que vous voulez m'sieurs?" I asked in as friendly tone as I could manage. The two turned around and I saw that they were both North African. The younger one was only three or four years older than me and thin, with quick nervous eyes, black tight curly hair, shabby sports jacket, slacks and sandals. The elder of the two was scary; in his late thirties, and taller than his friend, with a hideous scar that ran from somewhere near the top of his head across his right eye and down under his ear. His right eye had been removed—that is to say, most of it had been removed, because underneath the lid that would not quite close there was something floating about. I didn't look too closely.

They were alarmed to see such a pretty young thing sitting on her own, and wondered if they might assist her to her accommodation, or perhaps keep her company. In spite of my fear at the sight of them I used the sign that seems to be understood throughout Europe to indicate when two people are together: I extended my two first fingers and, holding my hands out with palms down and thumbs tucked in, brought my hands together three times. The older one nodded his understanding. The younger one of the two just stared at Gill. Good manners have led me into some dreadful predicaments and here I was not only getting myself into hot water but possibly dragging Gill with me.

Whilst the younger one stared with open admiration at my girl, the older one asked if we had eaten anything. When I said that we were about to eat he insisted, much to my horror, that he would join us and that he would pay for us all. Gill looked at me incredulously as they joined us at her table.

"Don't worry," I breathed, "we'll have plenty of time to slip away." We ate a thin steak and chips which was delicious, and as the warming effect of the wine took hold—and neither man was drinking—I began to wonder if my judgement was a bit hasty. The younger of the two continued to gaze at Gill while the older one told us of his life. He was a soldier, and I told him that I had been in the army too. He was impressed by this and after we had taken coffee he asked where we were staying that night. It was hopeless—I had not yet had time to figure that one out, so I just said that we would find somewhere. Of course he would have none of that and insisted that we stay at his home.

"Where are we going?" Gill asked.

"He is going to find us a room," I said, half truthfully.

We crossed the road and after about two minutes' stroll we turned into a little courtyard. We were bidden upstairs to an old door which was unlocked and walked into a tiny room. All that was in there was a table with a bowl and two army style beds with a mattress on one and a few blankets on the other. The elder one gestured to the beds and indicated that we should take them.

"But what about you?" I asked as Gill looked at me with widening eyes.

With a sweep of his hand he indicated the floor. I told Gill to get into her sleeping bag and pretend to fall asleep while me and the old soldier talked. He reached behind the table, pulled out a bottle of cognac, and poured out a glass for me and a monstrous one for himself. The younger one just stared at the sleeping form of Gill as I sipped at the spirit. The half blind one warmed to the drink, and when he checked that she was asleep he decided to show me his battle scars. He pulled off his shirt. Oh my God, I thought, we're both going to get it.

I was wrong. The old soldier went on to explain that most of his injuries had been caused fighting in Algeria and he had been caught in the tail blast of a grenade that had pierced his back and gone through his lung. The eye had been mostly lost in some other skirmish, and the drink (which was against his religion) was to relieve the pain in his shoulder. He was an awesome sight, a big man covered with campaign scars like a sailor would pick up tattoos.

I noticed the young one was yawning and was slowly leaning more and more towards the floor, then taking off his coat, he rolled it up, said something in Arabic to his friend and adopted a sleeping position. The old soldier gallantly did the same and lay down in front of the door. Within a few minutes he began to snore, at first softly then louder, so that I had confidence to lean across and whisper to Gill, "Are you OK?"

"Yes, are you?" she answered softly.

"Christ I'm tired," I said, and Gill told me to get to sleep. I tried but I couldn't really go under. Some time in the night, between sleep and dreams, she shook me gently and whispered, "He's trying to get into my sleeping bag."

I quickly realised it must be the younger one because the elder was still snoring.

"Just tap my shoulder next time he does it," I whispered back. I contrived a view of him by twisting my head and looking slightly over my raised left shoulder. I saw him move to climb on to her bed at exactly the same time as she tapped my shoulder and, with a gigantic stage movement and a roar like an animal in pain, I swung over on to my left side as if tormented in some terrible nightmare and caught him a fearful slap across his face.

I have never seen a reaction like what happened next outside of a cartoon. He leapt into the air like a cat, clearing the bed entirely and landing back in the corner from whence he had begun his stealthy encroachment.

The rest of the night slipped by without incident—I know because I was awake all night, even after I heard the steady snores of the younger one joining the sleepy sounds of my exhausted partner.

If I had been surprised at the opulence of Cannes, I was appalled at the excess in Nice. We could not afford to have any luxuries in cafés and I began to get angry. I suspect that my mood was as much affected by my inability to play the guitar in public as my inability to provide anything but the most meagre support for my girlfriend. Gill still did not complain. Further into the town I found a little grocery and bought one or two bits. It was cool in the narrow lane and shadowy light, and holding my purchases behind my back I walked up to Gill and said in a hammy actor's tone, "Lush and ripe fruit from the orient I bring!"

Then with a flourish I whipped the paper bag off the biggest tomato that either of us had ever seen. She laughed so much, I just loved her even more. All the time I was conscious of how inadequate I was. Around this time I wrote home to Henry, and wondered if he might be planning to come out to France on his scooter. I remember saying that if I saw his face sticking out of the crowd I would surely have the confidence to perform. Although this was for the sake of both Gill and me, it made her really sad. She told me that she wanted to be the one who could give me the confidence, and that we should not need Henry, even though she was as fond of him as I was. Her sadness made me feel even more useless. Of course she was right. Soon, I assured her, I would be ready to go to work.

Work, however, was to come from another source. Someone in the place we were staying told us about a little engineering store in some tiny back street that needed stock takers for a couple of days. The old guy that owned the place was glad of our cheap labour and we were really happy to get two days' money each from the incredibly boring work. There were several other kids there from the Youth Hostel and the atmosphere was light and friendly. Predictably it was me who got restless soonest and with our funds replenished somewhat, decided that as we were so near we would go to Italy. Because we had money now, I decided that we could be separated for the night and we'd stay at the hostel that was perched high above the town in a small house facing the line of the incoming sea.

There was an incredible view from the top, but after climbing the steep hill we found that there was a huge queue of kids waiting to get in, and by the time we got to the door, it was full. Night had fallen and we were too tired to return to the town. Instead, we walked some way up the road, and in amongst some trees we found a concrete platform with a wall round it. As we unrolled our bags, we could see the odd car headlights way off through the trees. Behind where we lay was the hill, below us the town , and above us the stars as bright as a Van Gogh painting. The concrete was still warm from the day's sunshine, and although the ground was hard on my boney body, I drifted off into fitful sleep.

I was awakened by a gentle tugging on my sleeping bag which at first I ignored, then I became aware of being almost bodily moved and my eyes blearily opened to see in the still starry night two shadowy male figures carrying a sack away from me. From out of the sack a slim arm was hanging on to my sleeping bag and that arm was attached to my Gill. I was always scared of losing her, but I never imagined that she would be physically dragged away. In the darkness all I could see were her eyes, full of fear, and her lips moving with no sound coming out. I was wide awake. I knew not to make any sudden movements. I took in my surroundings whilst my mind worked at what my alternatives were. Yes I had got it. After thinking through all the options, I had worked out that our situation was hopeless: I would be killed and she would be raped and then killed.

Slowly, very slowly, I raised my torso off the ground, and addressing the man holding her feet I cleverly came up with, "What the fuck are you doing, what's going on?" and then, *"Je m'excuse, qu'est-ce qui passe?"*

At this burst of English and schoolboy French, the one who had her arms let her go and jumped over to me pressing his knees into my neck as the only thing appearing from my sleeping bag was my head. I was still trying to get my arms out of the bag. In retrospect this was the best thing that could have happened. The one who still held her feet had to put her down and he moved away from her and spoke something in Arabic to his accomplice. Gill was by now shaking uncontrollably at my side and slowly I reached out one hand showing it to be empty and reached out to comfort her. The guy behind me was scared, I could feel that as his knees started to tremble fiercely in my back and his hand went to grab my forehead.

I shook my head and in a loud voice spoke to the other one, *"Nous sommes Anglais. Voulez vous voire nos passeports?"*

I don't know where this came from but it seemed to work. It suggested that we might have been in the wrong by being there and that they were there in some official capacity.

"Oui, vos passeports?" the one at Gill's feet ordered.

Easing my other hand slowly towards my back pocket, I allowed the sleeping bag to fall from my shoulder till I was half clear. As I handed the man my passport, I hooked the bag so that I was sitting on it and now I was halfway out of it. With both hands free, I motioned towards my scruffy white holdall and implied that I was getting Gill's passport. The one behind, whose knees were almost knocking, moved away from me and spoke agitatedly in Arabic to his friend.

Feigning some trouble with the zip on the bag, I managed to get right out of my bag and with the confidence that gave me I demanded, *"Votre pass!"*

"Nous sommes agents du police," he declared and entering the double bluff pulled out an identity card.

I leaped to my feet and yelled, *"C'est une carte d'identé! Vous n'etes pas des agents!"* Then, in a huge roar as if I had only just worked out what they were attempting, "You bastards! I'm calling the police!"

At this bellowing, the nervous one shot off in the direction of the road beyond the trees whilst the other one muttered something about radioing the police station and walked, altogether more steadily, towards the direction his friend had disappeared.

"You bastards!" I screamed after them as we heard a Deux Chevaux start up and putter off as fast as it could back down the road. For a long time Gill was unable to speak, and after she had stopped shaking we sat holding on to each other.

"Ralph," she said, "I was so scared. That guy, the one who stood behind you, had a huge knife. He was holding it just above your neck. I thought you would be killed."

"Don't worry," I said, "This is the last night we sleep outside. We'll go to Italy tomorrow. Things will be different there."

∽

returns

We crossed into Italy via Menton. It was exciting to be visiting another country; the people seemed friendlier, and not so many quizzical glances came our way.

We soon learned to say, *"Due cappuccini, prego?"* and I delighted in repeating the magic number *cinque cent cinquante cinque* just for the sound of it.

Our few francs translated into massive amounts of lire, and some of the notes were the size of newspapers and had to be folded several times in order to be pushed into wallets. Unfortunately not *our* wallets. There was a note of optimism in the air as we worked our way down to Genoa, where we had been told about an inexpensive youth hostel. Once we arrived we instantly felt at home in the place: a rambling villa with floors on different levels and a large communal dining room. There was somewhere to shower and it was easy-going and kindly. We washed our clothes and at least they smelled cleaner for being washed in Wright's Coal Tar soap.

We did not leave the place for the first day and just sort of recovered from our travelling. For a hundred lire you were provided with a meal of spaghetti and tomato sauce with a little cheese on top that was absolutely delicious. It was my first real taste of Italian cooking and I was totally captivated by it. Along with a salad and a little cheap red wine we thought we had arrived in heaven. Of all the places I went in those days, I can still recall that food the best. Every so often I might be eating a spaghetti and something about it will remind me of that taste and I'm back in Genoa and it's 1963.

Sometime in the evening, showered, shaved and with clean pants, socks and shirt, I brought my guitar into the garden. There were some steps and big evergreen conifers dotted about and old stone walls and carved banisters around what must have been a beautiful family villa. Groups of kids lounged about, some writing postcards or reading, some chatting animatedly in groups. Most of them were not English and all of them seemed young and immature. In the warm evening watching the shadows grow longer, I became aware of the sweet smell of marijuana floating on the breeze. I continued to strum away—maybe just a little louder in the hope that the smoker might declare himself.

We did not have long to wait. I pretended not to be aware as from behind a wall at the end of the courtyard appeared the blondest bloke I'd seen since my brother's hair darkened to yellow when he was about ten years old. He was a couple of years older than Gill and me, and walked with a slow, bowlegged gait; he wore a white shirt and white trousers with the kind of Indian sandals you still see in Kensington market, and his skin was the shade of brown that only Scandinavian skin seems to go. He was bearded, with piercing grey blue eyes, and because he was smiling as he listened to the music, I could see that his front tooth was slightly crooked. He looked a little out of it.

"Hey man, you play nice guitar," he said.

"Thanks," I responded.

He went and fetched a little red wine from the canteen and soon we were talking. He was a bit stoned, and we started to feel the effects of the wine. It soon emerged that we had no money, and he said that if I could play like that it would be easy. Gill confirmed that she had been telling me the same thing, and after a few more swigs of wine our new friend suggested we went down to the harbour.

"Bring your guitar man," he ordered, so I did.

His name was Olaf. He was Norwegian, and an ex-merchant sailor. I knew about Norwegian sailors from old George Foulser down at Poole and whilst checking him out, it was clear to me that he had joined as a career move and not because he was in need of an enclosed environment in which to express himself. This was further reinforced by the way he kept looking at my Gill. Christ he was a handsome confident sunburnt experienced exotic Scandinavian bastard. I liked him, and off we set for the harbour.

It was early evening when we arrived and the local population were on their promenade. Europeans go out for evening walks for the sheer pleasure of looking at each other or trying out new clothes, to improve their appetite for their evening meal, or to walk their dinner off. It was all new to us and pleasant to see all the sights and the general buzz around the harbour. Every now and then I saw old ladies selling loose tobacco and cigarette papers, so in the end I bought some. It was very cheap and I was happy to have saved some money. It smoked alright too. I had my guitar in its case and Gill was holding my other arm.

Suddenly Olaf walked up to some poor geezer who was transfixed staring at Gill and demanded in English, "Do you want to hear some music?"

The bemused Italian signalled that he did not understand, so Olaf signalled back that he would get me to play if the man so wished.

"*Si Si,*" said the bloke, who probably was relieved that he was not about to be stabbed by this jealous Norwegian with the piercing eyes.

Olaf turned to me and ordered in a loud voice, "Play!"

So that is what I did. I took out the guitar, played a chord of C and launched into a passable version of *Guitar Shuffle*. The Italian looked bemused and seemed to enjoy this entertainment just for him and at the end he sweetly gave me a round of applause.

"*Cento lire!*" ordered Olaf and after just a moment's quizzical glance at me. who was just as surprised, the 'audient' handed over one hundred lire.

"*Grazie,*" said Olaf taking it, and immediately handed it to me.

"Easy isn't it," he smiled, showing his crooked front tooth again.

Gill was positively beaming, for she was sure that now I had broken my nervousness, and as the prospect of a measure of financial independence grew, we three breezed about the market area and bought some more cheap wine.

The following day Gill and I wandered about and talked about our new acquaintance. We agreed he was likeable but a bit domineering, but what I was really interested in was whether Gill fancied him. The more we travelled, the more I realised how scared I was of the responsibility of caring for us both, and on several occasions I was glad to be in the company of blokes.

In most of these youth hostels there were boys and girls our age. Unlike us, they were protected with money, monster rucksacks and good walking boots. The worst of these organised travellers were the Germans, who were always complaining if anyone was in late and then proceeded to be the first up singing what sounded to me like marching songs to the tuneless drones of their accursed electric razors. We usually bought the roll and jam that was on offer before wandering downtown to meet up with Olaf and to maybe try a little busking. Usually my nerve failed but we made a bit of money before I felt we should move on. I noticed that the cigarettes I was making were giving me a cough.

You cannot be in Italy and not see Rome, so one hot and humid morning Gill and I said our goodbyes and hit the road south. When we arrived at the hostel, in the hottest weather I have ever experienced, we were told that there was no room—but because Gill was a girl they let her in. I slept outside. The air did not move that night and I didn't even have enough money to buy an ice cream. I was getting resentful of these kids who seemed to have so much more than us, and as for the Italian boys, well my temper was always on edge because everywhere we went there were whistles and comments and I could only guess at their meanings.

I finally cracked one day on the road when a group of them were calling after Gill as if I was not even there. There were at least six of them. Tired, hungry, and now totally pissed off, I dropped my bag, put down the guitar and raced across the road towards them. God knows what I would have done if they'd turned to face me, but to a man they turned tail and ran away.

I'd had enough; the heat was formidable and the city moved at breathtaking speed. I had no money for any accommodation and would have had to sleep outside, so without so much as a glance at a Roman ruin, I declared that we were leaving. We headed back north to France. Once again my confidence had failed me and I became morose and difficult.

It didn't help when I found out how the old ladies could sell their loose tobacco so cheaply. One day I saw some poor old thing picking up dog-ends from the gutter and generously offered her one of my loose tobacco rollups. This simple gesture between two souls with a mutual need united by common poverty was met by a very odd look and then a gesture to her bag which rested by the side of the road. Sitting alongside of her dog end bag was a tray of the type that the old ladies used to display their wares. Then it dawned on me. This was what I was smoking. These old girls collected cigarette ends and nipped off the ends and then opened the stubs and recycled the remains. What some old boys referred to back home as 'roadside returns'. I was pretty choked off by this realisation but such was our condition that I refused to throw my stash away and smoked it all until it was gone and then I switched to another workman's brand called 'Nazionale'. Faced with the choice of food or fags I would take the smokes every time.

By now we were both flat broke, and with my depression creeping up on me, my attitude towards Gill became strange. All the time she tried to reassure me, but it was no good and somehow our desultory travelling led us far away from the south of France and back towards Paris. One night we were travelling across the *Massif Central*; my mood was as dark as the hills that I could not see, Gill was asleep with her head resting on my shoulder and the driver and I were filling up the cab with Gauloise smoke. Thankfully he did not want to talk and I was content to stare out at the murk.

Suddenly there was a flash of lightning and for a second the whole countryside was as clear as day. You could clearly see trees and even animals in fields, mountain peaks and roads. The only strange thing was the colour of the sky which was a sort of yellow, then pitch darkness again. I gently shook Gill from her sleep just as a mighty thunderclap began and then shortly afterwards another flash of lightning.

When we reached Lyon, there was a fair going on. The whole city seemed to be celebrating and once again the opportunity to play presented itself. There was the smell of chocolate and hot dogs in the air, and in the evening the sight of people out to enjoy themselves with money to spend. My morale, however, was so low and we were so broke and hungry that I knew what we had to do. Gill was all for heading south again back to Spain where she thought we might get a job. She may well have been right, or perhaps the thought of being back with her family was even worse than the situation that faced us. I only blamed myself, for she was optimistic to the last, but she was my responsibility and I'd had enough.

With our very last centimes we bought some grapes and a piece of bread. I made some enquiries and found the British consulate in Lyon, and it wasn't difficult to convince one of the officials there that we were in need of some help. They provided us with a travel document to get us back to England and stigmatised our passports with an official stamp in the back to the effect that the British consular office had advanced us ten pounds to repatriate us. More importantly, we were given a little money to buy some food. I don't think we ate egg and chips.

I was a cowboy
out on the prairie
Life sure is easier
back home in the alley

PART THREE

BUILDING

podger

I felt totally miserable on my return to England with Gill. With just a little more confidence—actually confidence raised to the power of ten—we could have been in Morocco, or anywhere but bloody Croydon. Not only that, I had a repatriation stamp in my passport. This was the worst aspect because I knew that Woody would never have gone cap in hand to his embassy to get home. He would have got a job on a Liberty ship washing dishes, kept his dignity, and written another 58 songs about it.

Gill had tried so hard to reassure me that we would be OK, and she was more than prepared for whatever was to come our way. The truth was that I had found myself lacking when it came to my responsibility towards Gill and her safety on the road. It should have been fun—and often it was—but we had no safety net as we had no money, except what I could earn by playing. I think that would have been tough for just one person—but two?

Gill was beautiful even before the sun had made her hair stunningly blonder and turned her skin to an irresistible golden tan. It had become a battle to keep drivers' eyes on the road and their hands to themselves. And I had no plan whatsoever—all I wanted was not to stand still. My life was all musical discovery and Gill. We had sort of agreed to be engaged before we left on the trip, but I found I was faltering on this commitment too. Gill seemed to understand, and lightened of my burden of travel bag and guitar, along with our 'understanding', life returned to some semblance of normality.

Gill returned to Bournemouth, and later that year I got a job as a storeman-cum-checker at the Philips electric factory across the Purley Way in Croydon. Gill hitchhiked up to be with me every week, to the amazement of my mates. As I recall, Gill had no trouble hitching in England. She never waited at the roadside for more than four minutes and she could time her journeys to the half hour.

Naturally these forced breaks between us meant that every reunion was consummated at the first opportunity—given that I was back home with Mum and Bruce at Miller Road. Our outings were mainly confined to the Whitgift pub and friends' homes, where we would listen to music or play guitars. I was now totally obsessed with the guitar. If it was not in my arms then Gill was, or at least by my side. Parting was misery, and queuing at the end of the road for the public phone brought only temporary relief from the torture of separation. My wages precluded moving into a flat, and besides I was still wary of deeper commitment.

The job at Philips was a nightmare of boredom. It consisted mostly of weighing the contents of boxes and stocktaking, with a little dispatch work. Old Bob, the foreman, was deeply suspicious of my career intentions, deducing correctly that I was the student type and had no real interest in the wacky world of grommets and screws. I became quite fond of him; he was a kindly and gentle man who had been there since the factory opened. He always wore the same brown overall and was completely content in his work. I started to bring the guitar into work so that I could play it in the lunch break. Above the noise of the factory floor we bellowed pleasantries to each other and he often covered for me although I was perpetually being docked wages for poor timekeeping. I hated the clock which we had to use to punch our times in and out of work. Woody Guthrie once made a drawing of a fist smashing into the face of a time clock as a reward for its passive tyranny. That's what I felt like doing.

Part of my job was to collect huge pallets of television sets or boxes of Lord knows what, and this we did with the aid of a clever piece of equipment that levered the pallet off the floor just a few inches and then locked it into position so that we could drag it to the next storage area. I discovered that if I lifted the handle to an upright position and stood on the chassis, by rocking from side to side I could create a forward motion and soon I was able to get the jacking trolley up to quite alarming speeds. The wheels were metal, and there was no need to alert fellow workers that I was on my way as you could hear me coming from all over the place. Soon other lads were travelling down the vast wide corridors in the same fashion. Perhaps because it raised morale nothing was said against it.

Every afternoon the dreaded 'Music While You Work' used to come on the Light Programme on the radio. This was a show that was originally broadcast to help keep up spirits during the war effort. Old Bob used to whistle away contentedly to every tune, and it was only after several weeks that I noticed the same songs were played every day. I couldn't believe that no-one had noticed or seemed to care. Old Bob didn't seem to mind. I thought it was grounds for a general strike.

It certainly hastened my need to depart. Through Cathy down at the Whitgift, I got a job with John, her boyfriend from Northern Ireland, as a scaffolder's labourer.

My life as a scaffolder was short. You seldom see scaffolders over the age of thirty five anyway; I was nineteen when I started and nineteen when I quit. You have to know when it's time to hang up your podger when you do this job and I found out quickly that it was not for me. Like most young men I was greedy for experience, but the only competition I wanted was with myself. I ran everywhere. Walking was too slow and after the army I ran even more. I was so fit compared to my mates back home that on several occasions I found myself running on in front and then walking back to them because I couldn't stand their slow pace. As a kid I loved to climb trees though I remember once not being able to get back down and having a hell of a job convincing my mum that I needed help.

One of my recurring nightmares is that of being stranded on a high functionless building with only the faintest hand hold and no earthly means of escape: my hands tire, my anguish increases, I am too far beyond human contact to be heard if I cry for help, and finally I fall.

I do not like heights, yet I am obsessed with tall buildings and have dragged unwilling friends up all the classic skyscrapers in the world, from the monument in Billingsgate when it was sixpence to the CN tower in

Toronto with a hungover Bert Jansch and Martin Jenkins.

In Croydon, the dominating presence at the end of the street was the old gasholder and I knew that one day I would climb it—and I did, several times. And when the new Greyhound building was almost completed, Colin (Dan) Archer and I climbed up the inside until the stairs ran out and from there up the outside scaffold till we were on the top. From twenty-three storeys up I took a pee off the top as I gazed down at the buses the size of matchboxes passing below. Dan had to relieve himself in a different way (and left his mark covered by his flat cap... I often wondered what the men returning to work must have made of that).

Even though we had both had a few ciders from the Whitgift, the fear was not really diminished as we walked across narrow walls and hauled ourselves to the top, but the sweaty palms and thumping heart were all part of the thrill. I was so high on it that I had to do it again and I was almost sorry when it was possible to climb all the way to the top via the stairs.

I was telling someone about my adventure down at the Whitgift when I was overheard by John, a scaffolding ganger, and he asked me if I wanted a job, as he was short of a labourer. What could I say? I had to accept, and so with trembling hands and thumping heart I turned up at Robstart Street in Streatham to begin work.

A scaffold gang comprises three men: a ganger, a fixer and a labourer. It was a lovely sunny, frosty morning but as I looked up at the proposed eleven storey building that was already up six floors, my heart sank. John introduced me to the other member of the gang, Marty, and suggested that I try bringing up five by five tubes, that is to say five tubes that were five feet long to where the two of them were working.

Even though the sun had been on the pipes for a couple of hours they were still frozen together and had to be prised apart and loaded on to my shoulder. The method is simple and obvious—but I had to be shown as each of the ice cold pipes wrestled and squirmed over my boney, ill-clad shoulder. John showed me how to load three on first and two to bind them. Then, raising my arm higher than looked casual, in order to raise the muscle to a height to cushion the weight, I would advance towards the almost vertical ladder rungs that ran to the sixth floor.

My progress must have been hilarious. For a start you only have one hand to grab at the ladder, so you have to develop a rhythm that allows you to throw yourself lightly at the rungs as you step. At first you take a step, then bring your other foot on to the same rung, then move your hand, then your leading foot, then bring your other foot on to the same rung, and so on. You can always spot the new boy on the job.

By the time I got to the top I was sweating and hot, though my hands were numb with the cold and my legs were shaking with exertion and fear. Suddenly there I was on a two plank platform six storeys up with no hand rail. I was carrying the hand rail. I lowered my frozen burden and Marty grabbed one and expertly fixed it to two of the uprights and then connected a larger tube to it and I felt a little more secure. I had been much higher before, yet it was more scary being up these mere six flights than climbing twenty three after the pub. It was a good view from where we were. Once I realised that neither of the guys were showing off and that they were only trying to help me, my nerve improved, and by the end of the day I was quite getting the hang of it. By the time I got back to my place, though, I was completely shattered. Dreams of wet planks and skidding off open ended platforms kept me twitching and hopping all night but I was there again the next day on time and we had tea in the hut before starting work.

By my third day, I had worked out that John was mature beyond his years, patient and kind, and that Marty was mad. Why else would he wear plimsolls in the middle of winter and refuse to use the ladders, preferring to climb up the outside tubing? He might have been older than John but he didn't act it. I asked about falling and John told me that he had fallen four times; the greatest distance was thirty feet and he survived it with just a broken leg.

"In those days we weren't obliged to build traps to stop falls like we are now," he said, motioning below us to where corrugated iron sheets leaned out at a reassuring angle a couple of floors beneath. "The biggest danger is not from falling off but from letting things fall off, like joints that are heavier than a house brick or the odd time you let go a tube. If that happens you just have to shout as loud as you can and pray there's no-one underneath. When I started, my ganger dropped a twenty-one foot tube from the top to show me what happened to it. Believe me, it looked like a hairpin by the time it hit the bottom."

I shuddered inwardly and hoped that I would never let go of a tube. The weather was good and I improved a little, though to be fair I wasn't really tested. While I was with them we never 'struck' a building, and that requires real teamwork as anyone who has had the time to observe a good gang at work dismantling a scaffold would agree. The labourer stands at the bottom of the building with a short hessian sack between his hands and catches the heavy joints in its cradle soundlessly, whilst in between drops he receives the tubes and slides them on to the lorry. Up top, the fixer moves along the boards with podger in hand twirling the joints apart and passing them to the ganger who drops them below.

The biggest test of bottle comes when you are fixing the big twenty one foot verticals in place; John let me practise this on the ground. The technique was as follows: first you balance the tube on its end and then, lifting it clear of the ground, you lean it back slightly over your right shoulder at a very slight angle. Keeping your left hand under your right and about a metre apart, you pull the bottom of the pole and push the top, and this way you and the pole are stable. Once the pole is completely at the right height to drop on to the spigot, you advance to the edge of the board and place your tube on to the waiting spigot. You then change hand position so that your left hand steadies the pole and quickly tighten up the spigot with your podger. Sounds easy enough until you find yourself on a wet plank six storeys up in the pouring rain moving steadily forward to the edge of an unprotected drop with fifty pounds of freezing cold steel at least twenty five feet over your right shoulder waving about in the air. John only allowed me to attempt it with the smaller tubes, which is probably why I am still here and able to write these lines.

Our principal job was the one in Streatham but we moved about a bit; mostly small jobs because basically all the scaffolder has to do is stay in front of the brickies, especially if they're on piece work. Halfway through the third week we moved to another job on top of a block of flats where we were to build a hanging scaffold to affix a cradle for some window cleaners. That was where I decided that I would prefer to donate one of my kidneys to science without anaesthetic than to continue my career as a scaffolder's labourer. The weather had got worse and we were slipping about on a wet flat roof, dangling tubes over the edge as John designed and made instructions for the support system for the cradle that the men would use. The whole process terrified me. I wasn't getting on with Marty particularly, and when there's only three of you, any lack of enthusiasm or lack of weight pulling is felt immediately. All I needed was a reason to leave that didn't smack of cowardice.

Fortunately I picked up a minor lesion on the site. My leg swelled up and became red hot and I could not put any weight on it. There was no centre to the swelling and it just got bigger and angrier. Because of my presumed allergy to penicillin, I was only taking mild antibiotics and the leg just got worse. The only thing to do was to rest and not go out until it got better. So I went out every night as usual and walked through the pain. Finally my mum suggested that she should try to draw the infection with one of her father's old cures. I remember her telling me of things he did for carbuncles and warts with bits of raw meat, pieces of cardboard and knitting needles, and the thought that I might have to spend the next week or so with a dead rabbit tied around my knee and an onion in each sock would normally have put me off, but something had to be done.

On the Sunday afternoon Mum prepared a poultice of bread and a bowl of scalding water; there was no sign of an onion or dead rabbit so I sat down and she worked on the leg. First the poultice, then the hot water and so on until the water cooled, and then repeat. The infection was localising; she said she could feel it, but it was too painful to touch and she would have to let me do it myself. So it was that, gritting my teeth with the pain, I finally managed to exert enough pressure to express the poison.

If it had not been my own leg and my own poison that I was working on, I would definitely have passed out. As it was I felt faint with the sight of it, but almost at once the pain vanished and I began to feel better. Mum just took it in her stride; no wonder half the street came to her if anyone was injured, bleeding or otherwise.

John was kind enough to collect my money and deliver it to my house on the Sunday evening. The money was the most I had earned to date: it worked out to a little under £17 a week.

❧

engaged

Gill got an interview and then a job at Bourne and Hollingsworth's department store in Oxford Street, in London. Along with the job came residency at the store's own hostel for its female employees in Gower Street. This of course meant that we could be together more, although there was a strict 'no men' policy in force at the hostel. So we met and walked the streets and alleys of the West End every Wednesday night, and Gill came down to Croydon on the weekends.

She seemed to enjoy the job and I was scared that I might lose her to the temptations of London life. In this mood we once again became engaged. This time it was official, and Gill found a little gold ring in a jewellers in Goodge Street. It was shaped like a tiny flower in turquoise and it cost £5.

Since Southbourne we had never been able to spend a whole night together. While we were travelling, the people who kindly sheltered us expected us to stay celibate until we were married, and the hostels were separated anyway. Somehow we kept up the torture of pretence that we were waiting to be married whilst making love at each and every opportunity. When I heard Robin Williamson's *The First Girl I Loved*, with the line "never slept with you though we must have made love a thousand times", it was reassuring that another young couple were forced into that.

We found little places for intimacy everywhere. Although there was room at home in Miller Road, the idea of staying overnight would have been an impossible suggestion. One day in November 1963 we were walking down Charlotte Street talking about what we were going to do about setting up together—or was it setting off on another trip to Europe that summer—and wandered into a small coffee bar. We were the only ones in the place and the radio was playing quietly in the background as we sat down with two instant coffees in glass cups and saucers to extend our goodnights.

Suddenly an announcer interrupted the music with the message that President Kennedy had been shot. Gill reached for my hand and we stared at each other. The woman behind the counter looked at us kids and then back to the radio.

"What did they say?" I asked. I looked back at Gill and her tears splashed down on the table.

I was aware of the politics of the blues and the early songs of Bob Dylan which were related to the civil rights movement, but my own politics were unfocused and slightly patronising—if a nineteen year old could be patronising. Kennedy was youthful and smiling. He was one of us somehow; we sensed that he understood that we were going to change the world for the better. I was aware of the Bay of Pigs debacle but had not disentangled the Cuban situation from my general idealism, which was still loosely rooted in the rights of man and a folksy Woody Guthrie philosophy of the left, without actually embracing communism (unlike many of my friends).

It was like discovering there was no Santa Claus. Idealism could be blown away by an assassin's bullet. Just as the civil rights marchers had been disposed of and union leaders in the states, now it seemed even the president could be dispatched at a whim of a madman. The prospect was numbing.

As I wandered home it was like being stoned yet angry—there was nothing to grab hold of to steady oneself. People were bewildered and silent on the tube and train home. I still did not abandon some belief in man's greater goodness, but the seeds of cynicism and doubt were planted that evening and nothing would ever be quite the same again.

Going down the Whitgift was becoming a nightly habit. I would run all the way there and stumble back. Small dramas unfolded and relationships floundered and flourished, all accompanied by a cider-induced late-teenage beatnik logic. Songs were sung, pianos played, gropings rebuffed, undying friendships confirmed. Les finally cemented his relationship with tiny Margot and they were married at Croydon Registry Office.

Les and I had become a little estranged, but so much drink was taken on the night before the wedding that I was only a little hurt when Les asked that Steve should take care of him. Steve failed to live up to the challenge and Les rebuffed all offers of help to get home. Somewhere up Scarborough Road, he fell into a hole being dug for the gas board. After several attempts to get out he decided to stay overnight.

He barely had time to get home in the early morning to don his suit and stumble back to the Whitgift where Maurice the landlord lent him a tie. After the brief ceremony they were driven off by Max in his ancient Morris 8 convertible. There was a rather drunken reception paid for and attended by Margot's family and some of Les's. Margot's dad made a speech in which, in an almost stage Indian accent, he told several jokes which he then explained. Les's huge sobbing guffaws got the whole place rocking—which Mr. Rossario found encouraging and set him off on even more banal stories.

In the photo that exists of the event, Gill and I are standing apart. I am wearing the suit that Steve would wear to Court and Tony would wear to a job interview. I would get married in it, but not to Gill.

Henry had started to organise some Sunday afternoon sessions at the Olive Tree coffee bar where my brother Bruce worked, which had a tiny stage and dance floor downstairs. They were loosely-run affairs, but people came along. Phil Allacker and I put together a few tunes and played there as residents, and I loved it, though it wasn't so good for Phil; he would throw up before going onstage. Poor Phil, he suffered a lot; I was nervous but he made me look positively devil-may-care.

Whilst we were probably awful, people continued to fill that little downstairs area to hear us and Jacqui McShee with Little Chris Aldous and the other aspiring players. This was also the second time I saw Wizz Jones playing to the small but enthusiastic crowd.

Others who performed there included Davy Graham and Alex Campbell, who gave me my biggest compliment by inviting me to join him as his accompanist. Of course we neither expected, deserved or were paid for these sessions, but it was great to get applause and I loved the guitar so much that friends said I was practically welded to it.[5]

I would never be over my nerves before playing, but I was improving; and some people even seemed to like my singing, which really surprised me as I never even thought about that side of things. I needed work if Gill and I were going to have another attempt at travel; this time we thought India would be a good idea; after all, Stan was doing it and he couldn't even play an instrument.

After jacking in the scaffolding job, I applied for work on the building site on a Tuesday and got an immediate start for the Wednesday. It was a very odd feeling going back to my old school—only this time wearing old jeans and a tattered shirt.

The job was to build a school for girls. It was the re-siting of the Coloma Grammar School for Girls, a catholic school. The firm was an outfit from Crawley. They seemed too small for the job, and definitely short of hard-bitten labourers. There were two or three sikhs, a handful of Irish lads, a pipe layer called Les, a student called Andy, an Aussie called Pete, a site foreman called Fred, another guy called Fred, a Liverpudlian ganger called Ron, an old labourer called Bob—and me.

It was a grey miserable morning in January 1964 as I stumbled out of bed much earlier than I had been accustomed to of late. It had been raining for several days. I had to run for the bus as usual and joined the coughing chorus upstairs on the 130 to New Addington. I wiped a hole in the steamed up window and looked out over the familiar suburbs printed in my mind from schooldays, as the bus was joined by some early kids on their way to my old school. I jumped off the bus at the old familiar stop and, with just a glance at the old building, turned right through the gate and made my way to the site office.

"You're late lad," said a Liverpool accent in a cloth cap pulled over one eye. "If I say eight o'clock I don't mean ten past. If you're late tomorrow

---

[5] I incidentally picked up my first media mention at this gig, playing with Phil in support of Wizz. It was in the Croydon Advertiser in a review written by a young Robin Denselow. I also remember Sandy Jones, Wizz's wife, sitting somewhere behind the stage with the dribblingest baby I had ever seen, Simeon, now a very accomplished sax player, university graduate and father of two.

you'll be docked half an hour. OK, pick up a shovel from the store and come with me." I followed him out of the shed and across the upturned ground that resembled a bomb site, as all newly-begun jobs do.

Ron the ganger pointed to a pile of earth that was about as big as the shed we had just left and said, "I want tha' lorra 'oggin over there purover there an there's a barra so get shovellin'!" Loosely translated this meant take that lot of whatever it was over there and put it over there. For a brief moment I was glad of my time in the army where I learned how to understand dialects.

Andy was a middle class boy waiting to go to university. He worked like two men, but had the piss taken out of him unmercifully by some of the blokes because of his accent. Sometimes when he was addressed by our ganger, he looked around to the rest of us for help, as his ear never really got tuned to Liverpudlian. In the end this became a source of amusement to Ron himself, watching Andy's brow furrowing in consternation as he wrestled to interpret his wishes.

Over my shoulder and to my right was the outline of a building. The area had been filled with hardcore and was now awaiting a layer of hoggin to be compressed by means of the whacker which would provide a more level surface for the first skim of concrete. Hoggin is a mixture of clay and pebbles, and it is always tricky to shovel as you are never able to get a clean sweep at it without your shovel stroke being brought up sharp by hitting a pebble or two. Manipulating the substance is further complicated by its stickiness, and to relieve the shovel of its load you are often forced to bang it on the side of the wheelbarrow. Add to this the frost factor, making the heap almost as hard as concrete.

I hadn't done much manual work recently and handling scaffold tubes had not hardened up the skin very much. I tried to remember the tips I had learned as a gardener for the Tickle family: not to hold the shovel too tightly, to spit on my hands, and to get into a proper position and have the wheelbarrow in the right place. Once lined up correctly, I took a swing at the pile, only to watch my shovel bounce right off with an ear-piercing clang and an impact that hurt my elbows and rattled my fillings. Like all new boys I was convinced all were watching me, so I redoubled my effort and with my second swing managed to collect two pebbles and three heaped tablespoons of clay, which I tapped into the waiting barrow (which suddenly seemed huge).

I then decided to attack the heap from nearer the top and succeeded in dislodging almost half a shovelful and so proceeded in this manner wandering up and down the heap until after about fifteen minutes, I had managed about half a barrow load. Then in order to make some impression on my ganger, I went to wheel my tiny load across to the hardcore. Unfortunately my efforts had made me very sweaty and out of breath and by suddenly standing up from the semi-crouched position needed for shovelling, I had become dizzy and slipped sideways causing my barrow to empty half its contents on the ground. The rest stuck obstinately to the side of the barrow.

I righted it and was scooping up the spillage with my bare hands when Ron said helpfully, "We normally find it's a bit quicker to use the shovel, lad." He walked past with his big wellington boots turned down pirate-style.

Over the next hour I had managed three respectable loads. I had acquired two fairly substantial blisters on one hand and a spectacular one on the other. My limbs were trembling uncontrollably and I was feeling faint. I realised that I was not going to last until lunchtime unless I improved my technique.

Help came in the form of a short man in a cap and an orange sweater, his trousers tucked into his boots. His name was Gupta Singh; he was a Sikh but had cut his hair. Without patronising me he showed me how I was wasting energy and how by using the inside of my knee against the top of my forearm, I could increase my leverage and double my strength so that I no longer sounded like a demented woodpecker tapping away ineffectually on my hill of stones. He then showed me that I should dig from the bottom of the pile so that any stones dislodged higher up fell loosely on to the ground to be retrieved on the next shovel load, and to get round the uneven surface on which I was digging he produced an old piece of once corrugated iron which we ran into the heap at ground level and as I cleared each section I replaced up against the pile. By lunch break I had hit rhythm, but was incredibly tired and very shaky as I sat down with a cheese roll and huge mug of tea. Peter, the Aussie, sidled over and asked me how it was going. I lied that everything was all right and then he noticed the blisters on my hands.

"Shit mate, you better piss on them."

"Yeah," I said, nodding in agreement but not knowing why.

I looked out of the window at the shed-high heap that awaited me and considered creeping out of the gate and catching the bus home.

Then a Liverpool accent bellowed through the door, "All right lads let's be havin' you," and as we piled out from the tea hut, "Well done there lad, you're getting the hang of it, now get stuck in and shift that stuff."

There was just the right amount of encouragement in his expression to lift my spirit, but the shovel felt twice as heavy as I went out to resume the attack on the hill. A soft drizzle had continued all through the day and in spite of the waterproof jacket that I had worn all afternoon, I was still damp when I arrived home. It was a tired boy indeed who met his friends down at the pub that night.

I was awoken the next morning at seven in order to get to work on time, and as I tried to lift my head off the pillow, I became aware that I had become an invalid overnight. There was an excruciating pain in my neck and shoulders and my back had locked in the position that I had fallen asleep in. My hands were too feeble to grip anything without aching and my thighs felt as if they had been run over by a lorry. My stomach muscles were inflamed and I was unable to bend my body in any direction without agony. I was not so much in panic as in a quandary as to how to go about getting out of my bed. In the end I managed to roll out on to the floor and from this position ease myself into a half crouch and from there on to my feet. I limped into the bathroom and washed carefully, then into the kitchen where I ate some cereal.

Getting dressed was painful. Going down the stairs to the front door had to be done by resting on each step as I had done on the scaffolding ladder on the first day. Even Mum laughed as I limped up the path to the gate and hobbled down to the bus stop. The step up to the bus platform nearly had to be abandoned and if it hadn't been for the general crush of people getting aboard I would not have made it to work. Getting off was just as painful and once again I was late.

"You'll be stopped half an hour for that," said Ron, "an' fer Chris' sake liven yourself up a bit lad. That's the trouble with you young lads, up all night shaggin'."

I picked up my shovel and staggered over to my heap. It had grown during the night and as my shovel chipped away at the first barrow load I wondered if an office job might be more suitable.

By tea break I thought I would have to quit, but as our ten minutes ended a brick lorry arrived and I was diverted from working on the hoggin to unloading. This made for a change, and I was put in with the other lads. We were issued with strong rubber gloves, and hopped on to the stack which was already about six feet high and therefore at a good height to walk off the bricks from the lorry. By watching and trying you learned how to pick up and catch the bricks in groups of five and soon your judgement enabled you to throw them in line and tight up against other bricks. It was labour intensive work as each brick was handled several times, but before pallet loading, every brick on a building site was handled at least eight times before the mason actually laid it in a wall.

It was not unpleasant work because of the banter and craic from the other lads. There was also the element of competition, as boys used to see how many bricks they could hold together in a line. One lad managed fifteen before the middle three dropped out like a sagging piano accordion. Working through the pain eased my aching muscles, and I felt a lot better at the end of the delivery than I did at the start. Working as hard as this was a buzz and a new experience. I took delight in performing on terms with the other lads, and keeping my eyes and ears open, learned quickly the skills and knacks that you need to get you through even the simplest tasks.

As the last few bricks were put into place one of the boys said to me, "Now smell your gloves."

I slipped them off to see my blisters had burst and the skin was all soft with the sweat that had accumulated through the loading. My hands smelled just like a pair of sweaty feet and as I recoiled, a couple of the others smiled and I began to feel all right about my new job.

The banter in the tea hut was louder than the previous day, partly because I was now part of it. I sat opposite old Bob, the head labourer who entertained us with jokes and ribald comments.

As I finished my cheese roll, he grabbed one of my hands and turned it over to where my blisters were shredded and new ones forming and remarked, "You better piss on them boy before they get worse. And don't wash either."

"Yeah too right," I agreed, still not comprehending what on earth this instruction could mean. Then I was back to my heap and Pete was assigned to help me. We worked an arrangement so that sometimes he filled and I wheeled and vice versa, and the afternoon sped by more quickly. As I climbed aboard the bus home, I began to feel like I belonged and looked forward to the next day.

I woke up the next morning, convinced I was paralysed. Once more I was reduced to rolling out of bed and climbing to an upright position like an evolving species of man ape. I swallowed down some tea and a piece of toast and sort of lowered myself down the stairs leaning heavily on the banister before limping up the road and clawing my way on to the bus platform. I could not face the climb upstairs and so spent the entire journey on the lower deck. At the site I sort of fell off the platform and staggered through the gate.

"Don't try to amuse me with them funny walks lad, you only just made it in time," said the dry voice of my ganger. "Get over on that 'oggin now." I grinned at his sarcasm, and though painful, my back soon felt better than when I got up.

∾

'oggin

The days began to fall into a pattern of work where we continued with whatever we had been doing the day before, to be interrupted by the arrival of lorries carrying materials that had to be unloaded by hand. Although this was hard work, it provided a break in the monotony, and all the labourers got to have some fun together and talk about the weekend or last night. As the sweat got up with the increase in effort, the temptation was to take off the gloves and this proved to be very unwise especially with the arrival of a load of flittens. These are bricks cast from very rough moulds and when they have been fired and turned out, there are sharp edges of terracotta sticking out from every edge. By letting them slip through your hands and into place on the stack, these sharp bits slice into your skin and cover your hands with minute razor scratches. After my first load, both my hands were bleeding from cuts and one of the Irish lads said to me that I ought to piss on them. Blisters from my first day had not healed up and now there were new ones and cuts and slices across my palms as well.

At last my pile of hoggin disappeared and was laid in position for the hardcore, which was a lot easier to handle. Broken bricks and old concrete were run from a huge heap across barrow runs of boards and offloaded in heaps that, once levelled out, would be compressed into the hoggin by means of the whacker.

The whacker was operated by Sid, a powerful but simple lad of twenty two with piercing blue eyes and a shock of black curly hair that was kept under a red and black striped cap, with a tiny ornamental buckle at the back. He wore a scarf throughout the time that I knew him, and in winter and summer his nose ran constantly. He was given undemanding tasks by the ganger, who understood that there were many elements to keep together for a site to remain happy, and one of those elements was to have a lad like Sid about. When it came to unloading a brick lorry you could never find him, but he would miraculously appear with a broom once the work was done to sweep the lorry of dust before it left the site. And when it came to being in the front of the queue for tea, he was always there.

The chaps on site had fun with Sid, but there was always someone to make sure that things never got out of hand. Ron decided as a reward to let Sid operate the whacker. Sid was always fascinated by this piece of machinery and it would be impossible for any harm to come to it, or Sid, because it was only propelled by its own vibration and was only operated within the confines of the room about to be hardcored. I was working some way off when I heard the cries of panic and saw a very distressed Sid wringing his hands and looking around desperately for help. I dropped the shovel and ran over.

"Oh Ralph, the fuckin' thing's gone mad!" he wailed.

I looked over at the machine and you could just about see the piston pot above the hoggin as the whacker had vibrated itself deeper and deeper into the earth. Obviously as usual, Sid had become distracted by something he had seen and paused to watch, The machine, sensing its chance, had whacked itself into the ground and like a struggling man in quicksand, wedged its way further down into the ground with each vibration. I leaned over and switched the engine off and looked at him. The poor lad started to cry.

"Don't worry, we'll soon have it out of there," I told him, and ran over to get one or two of the other lads. As if a life depended on it we freed the machine and replaced the hoggin after telling him that he had to keep it moving from now on and no dreaming. We cleaned it up and got it going again and before anyone had noticed, he was back at work with a big grin on his snotty face. At tea break I tried to avoid sitting with him but he always found me; the thought of him drinking his tea with a good portion of what was coming out of his nose filled me with revulsion.

I was not the only one who felt this way, and one lunch time things came to a head when one of the blokes burst out with, "For fuck's sake wipe your bleedin' nose Sid," and in the general agreement from the others that he should do something about it, old Bob popped out his top set of false teeth and dropped them in Sid's teacup. I just sat there in amazement and looked around at the others, most of whom were either stunned to silence or collapsing with laughter in anticipation. For some reason Sid did not slurp his tea down in the normal fashion, instead he kept turning his head to try and focus on where the seat of the fun was coming from. Sid always ate with his mouth wide open so that food fell all over the table, and his ability with liquids was not much better. At last the moment of truth arrived and Bob's false teeth slid to the mouth of the cup and lay grinning at the drinker, who unable to believe his eyes at first, pulled the cup away from himself, the better to focus. As he did so, the teeth once more vanished from view.

Sid then plunged a pair of mud-stained digits into the brew and after a second or two's groping, fished out the top set. By now the whole tea hut was in uproar and even old Jack, the oldest tea boy in the world, was smiling. Sid held the teeth between thumb and finger and just stared at them as if unable to recognise what they were. The laughter in the hut grew even louder at his bewilderment, and then suddenly the penny dropped and the horror hit him. With a demented scream he flung them without aim as far from him as he could.

"Oi," shouted Bob, "careful, thaths my thmile you've got there thun," and rushed to retrieve his teeth from the floor. After giving them a quick rinse in his tea cup, he popped them back in his mouth. The merriment in the tea hut was enormous but Sid came close to having a fit; he was screaming and shouting and crying all at the same time and it took a little while for anyone to realise just how serious the situation had become. Even old Bob, who Sid normally worshipped, could not calm him, and it was only when Ron the ganger came in that order was restored. The way Ron handled it was to severely reprimand old Bob in front of all of us so that Sid became open-mouthed and calm as he listened to the dressing down the old labourer got. There was much winking and knowing looks exchanged and eventually Sid and Bob went out to the site together and Bob minded the boy for the rest of that day.

Old Bob was an extraordinary man. He had been a gunner in the war and lost one eye and the hearing in one ear for his pains. He was forty seven when I joined the job and had a birthday in the time I was still working there. He looked about ten years older and had not an ounce of fat on him. He was incredibly strong and uncomplaining about any job that was assigned to him; he was also an alcoholic. At the time I joined he was already subbed a week in advance and this was against any builders' policy as it meant that the firm had no security against you leaving.

By the time I left, Bob was subbed ten days in advance and every penny was spent on beer and whiskey. When he lost his digs, they let him stay in the tea hut where he ate the stale rolls from the day before. As far as I'm aware, that was all he ate, except on Saturdays, when someone would treat him to a hot pie in the pub up the road. Every now and then, he would claw back a bit of his debt by doing a bit of unpaid overtime, but by Monday he would sub it back again and so it went on. Ron assigned me to work with Bob on some trench work for the pipe layer, as the latter had complained about my meagre allowance of room for him to work and the fact that like most new boys, my trench always tapered as it got deeper and made work more difficult.

Bob was a terrific trench digger and he taught me how to do them properly, using a fork held at a forty-five degree angle and thrown down the sides to loosen the material before using the shovel to throw out the debris. Soon I could make them as straight as Bob and what is more, I enjoyed doing it. Even now, I get quite pedantic about the right and wrong way to build a trench.

When two men are working together, the subjects discussed are usually quite wide-ranging. Not so with Bob, who only wanted to talk about drink or how to get his hands on some money for drink.

One day he came out with, "You know, sometimes I get a bit of luck, it ain't always good luck though! I remember a time someone put me on to a soft touch and I got a tenner out of him straight away and fuck me when I went back for more he gave me more as well, I took him for another tenner. He was some kind of religious nut and as long as you promised to try and reform he gave you money."

"Where was this, Bob?" I asked, thinking I had heard this story somewhere before.

"Miles from here, in a place called Thornton Heath," said Bob, without breaking stroke in his digging.

I waited a moment carrying on shovelling and then asked, "It wasn't a bloke called Waters in Whilkes chemist was it?"

There was a sudden silence as Bob stopped forking down the sides of the trench and the fork fell from his grasp. He turned to face me, his face pale.

"Me and my fuckin' big mouth, do you know him then?"

"Yeah, my mum worked there for years[6]."

"You ain't going to tell him about me are you?"

"No, I just guessed that it must be him. How much did you get from him in the end?"

"Over ninety quid. I had digs there then, I was pissed for two weeks."

Just up the road from the site was a pub, and a few lads used it at lunchtimes particularly on Saturdays when we finished at around one o'clock. Whenever Bob had some change, he would go up for a pint or two. There was a very well defined hierarchy to the site. Ron, for example, would not have drunk with the boys, and the big boss would not have drunk with Ron, and yet there was a happy atmosphere on site which was due to several factors: the mixture of different types; Sid; tough but honourable conditions, and not least our ganger Ron.

Rather like a good publican, Ron wandered round the site telling a joke here or repeating one he'd heard from someone else. Occasionally he reprimanded someone for not pulling their weight or winding someone up if they had become too familiar. In this way he was everybody's mate, yet they were still eager to impress, and this made a perfect combination for work and respect. He clearly had his favourites, and amongst the young lads it would have been Pete, who looked like a young Tyrone Power and worked uncomplainingly on whatever job was assigned to him. He worked as hard as the Irish gang who kept themselves very much to themselves, and even they showed a grudging respect for his

---

[6] I later asked my mother if she remembered him, and she did.
"But his name wasn't Bob Wesson then," she recalled.
"What was it?"
"I think he said it was Bob Jamieson," she answered. From then on I always referred to Bob as Mr. Jamieson. The other lads assumed it was a reference to his preference for Irish whiskey, and in a way of course it was.

strength and commitment. He even played the guitar, and once on a Saturday I brought mine in and he played an extremely intricate version of *Deep Purple* from the sheet music.

Whenever we worked together, I found myself upping my rate to keep up and stay the distance. As the months went by, my strength improved, and work that would have crippled me earlier I could now take in my stride. Ron would share a joke with me and treat me like an old soldier and that made me feel good. I don't know if they were paying under scale on this job as there was a low turnover in labourers and once on the site most were content to stay for about five shillings an hour.

In that part of Croydon working up to the Shirley hills, the soil is waterlogged and of very thick clay. We were told that machines to dig would be inefficient and so there were several gangs working on the 'footings' around the many outlines of buildings that made up the school. The Irish lads worked on part of the project; their leader was a hard farm boy from Kerry, who had a difficult accent and a manner to match. I was at the concrete mixer one day when he approached the site hut with his band of five other lads and asked to see the foreman. These six great slabs of men stood lined up with their forks and turned down boots and when the bewildered face of the kindly Fred came to the doorway, Ron announced that they wanted a few words with him. Clearing his throat and banging his fork on the ground for emphasis whilst raising his voice to be heard over the roar of the clattering mixer he spoke.

"Me and the lads are not satisfied that this job is paying what it ought to. We're here sloggin' away in this clay for five and two an hour and the job has to be worth five and six and in any case they're payin' five and six an hour for diggin' in chalk over at Riddlesdown and there'd be more satisfaction there although it's hard enough on the wrists and shoulders but here it's frustratin' pulling out clay like toffee from off your fork and five and six an hour would be barely enough but we'd take it if you'd offer it, now."

This speech was offered at breakneck speed and was completely misunderstood by Fred, who looked forlornly at Ron and asked, "What did he say?"

"They want a raise," explained Ron.

"How much?" asked Fred.

"Five and six an hour," translated Ron.

"Well, I'm afraid that's impossible."

"Right then lads, we're off then," said Liam the spokesman.

And without an attempt at negotiation, they shouldered their forks, shovels and bits and bobs and like a small army of mercenaries, trooped off the site and off to Riddlesdown and were never seen again.

I stood there open-mouthed. Ron lifted his cap from his head and at the same time scratched his head, not because it itched but because he needed a second to think.

"Where are they going?" asked Fred staring after the little army.

"They've quit," explained Ron.

"But their cards and so on?" queried Fred in a tone that now sounded hurt.

"They'll send for them from Riddlesdown I expect. In the meantime we need some new lads." And turning to me he asked, "Have you got any pals need a start Ralph?"

I knew Stan my mate needed a job, but Ron was not so much requiring an answer as filling in a few seconds to gather himself for what to do next. There is always a deadline and these blokes would be hard to replace. They were on twopence an hour more than the rest of us, and they were asking for a paltry fourpence an hour more which would have cost the company about eight pounds a week. It sounds incredible today.

I got Stan the job, and around this time the labour force was augmented by several others, among them a short wiry Irish lad called Michael.

The weather was awful and we were often rained off, but unless it was hopeless, we worked through it. Digging was laborious and Ron would constantly rotate the lads so that they did not get too restless. On the major excavation, which was for the boiler house, the water was actually visible coming out of the sides of the area that had been dug. A pump was put in place, but it was like working in a quagmire, slippery and exhausting.

It was proposed to dig a sump hole and this was to be about four foot square by five foot deep. There was no problem with this, except the weather was so wet that the sides constantly fell in and work was abandoned until there was a dry spell. It never came. The rest of the job was going well and one day in the tea hut, Ron offered the proposition to all who could hear:

"Does anyone want to earn tuppence an hour more digging out the sump hole?" This was accompanied by a large stage wink delivered on Bob's blind side.

"I'll have that," said Bob immediately, and so it was agreed. On the strength of this arrangement, he conned a few bob out of one of the new boys and sloped off up the pub for lunch break and came back with at least four pints in him. Most alcoholics don't need much to get them going again and lunchtime drinking has a quicker effect than at other times. When Bob returned from the pub, he was pissed.

The rain was still steadily falling as Bob donned his waterproofs including a strange sou'wester hat, and along with his shovel, bucket and barrow, he gingerly climbed down the ladder and got ready to work. I was working alongside young Michael some way from the boiler room but I had to barrow run soil past where Bob was working and I could see Ron standing on top of the side walls looking down at him.

"Come on Bob lad, get stuck in!" he encouraged and then seeing me, he looked round and winked. Ron motioned to me to climb up the bank and join him. There below us was our man sliding about with barely a grip on the muddy surface, digging away at the sides of the sump hole and trying desperately to retrieve the mud and load it into his wheelbarrow, which tipped over, unloading its contents back into the hole.

Bob scrabbled about as if he had just strapped on ice skates for the first time. If it hadn't been for the shovel to support him, he would have gone over many more times than he did. I started to laugh at the sight of the scene below and soon I was joined by one or two others. Bob's usual pallid complexion was now quite red from the exertion, but he did not give up scooping the slurry in his bucket into the barrow, which kept tipping over with him sliding about getting more hot and bothered with each stroke.

"Come on Bob, keep it going!!" shouted Ron.

"I am keepin' it fuckin' going," called back Bob irritatedly. Ron called out again, "Come on Bob! It's started to rain a bit more and we've got to get the job done."

"What's the matter with ya, I'm going as fast as I can for fuck's sake," shouted the mud splattered veteran of a thousand trenches as he almost slithered over. Then with a comic's timing Ron delivered the killer blow.

"Look Bob, if you can't do better than that I'll 'ave to take you off and give the job to a younger bloke."

"What?" shouted Bob, looking up for the first time and seeing us all lined up at the top. He wiped a muddy hand across a sweating brow, blew snot from one nostril and hurling his shovel as far away from himself as he could, uttered the words I will remember to my dying day.

"Well fuck you and fuck the job an' all!" Then turning round on to his blind side, he took one slippery step and disappeared head first down the sump hole.

For a few seconds nobody could do anything but laugh, then we slid down the walls of the boiler room, grabbed the only visible sign of Bob (his legs) and hauled him to safety. After a cup of tea or two, Bob seemed to be relishing his new found status, and Ron got the company to pay up Bob's subs. Once again Bob had gone down the pan but come up smelling of roses.

❧

grapefruit

The relentless drizzle of winter gave way to early spring and the journey to work was made more pleasant by the cherry blossoms that filled the streets and suburban gardens. Gill had got digs in a terraced house in Broad Green, and although she was not allowed visitors to her room, we had other ways of spending time together. She had got a job at Allders in Croydon on the make-up counter. She was a Cyclax representative and she looked quite stunning.

We met most evenings, and either stayed in at 17a Miller Road or went down to the Whitgift to see friends and play music. I had recently come across the song *Dirty Old Town* and it could have been written for me: "I met my girl by the gasworks croft." Every evening we would walk past on our way to the pub that had become our second home. The words gave a dignity to both my roots and my aspirations. The cooling towers and gasholders were as monumental as cathedrals in the dark lane that led from our road to the brighter lights of the town.

Our plan at this time was to leave England with some money. I had tried travelling without money and it didn't work. I remembered a statement made by a bloke called Steve I met somewhere on the road. He had obtained a monkey in India. "Times were hard," he said, "and just when

I'd trained it to go without food, the fuckin' thing died on me!"

This time we would eat and stay overnight indoors, so we were saving as well. I was as happy as I'd ever been at this time; I liked my job, and with the warmer weather my spirits soared and the prospect of more adventure spurred me on.

With the approaching summer the job was coming on; although there was still digging to do, there were other jobs as well, like running hardcore, and now the laying of concrete on beds that we had so carefully prepared. Often the heat would allow us to strip down to our trousers and boots, and already we were getting weathered and sun-tanned. Add to this the fact that Stan had decided to bike to work on his old fishtail Velocette and the anticipation of summer was complete.

Stan and I were a good pairing when it came to rider and pillion, so much so that on more than one occasion I fell asleep on the back. The whole secret is trust, and acquiring that trust needs bravery, in particular leaning into corners at high speed. Stan had learned the hard way when he only had his old trials bike, a Greaves which he truly loved. With Linda on the back, he lost it on a bend when she had tried to correct a lean. When he saw Linda stagger to her feet unhurt he went to get up too, but his shin had broken and was poking through his leg so naturally he fell down. He always walked with a slight limp and had a foot that turned inwards after that, but he was gentleman enough never to have blamed her, and the hideous scar was a kind of masculine result of a rite of passage. Stan was the first bloke to come to work in shorts.

I had learned to ride Gill's scooter and felt ready to get a bike of my own. I heard about a Francis Barnett that was being sold by a friend of the family. I bought it for £65, and I loved it. Because Gill was qualified as a driver, I could travel with her and it was great spinning about the countryside with her on the back. She was pretty trusting, though you couldn't throw the thing about like a more powerful machine. It was only 175cc but it was fast enough for me. Especially when I came off it. In those days helmets were not compulsory and all I wore was a cloth cap like my brother, who had earned some respect in the neighbourhood when he bought an old 500cc Matchless.

The second time I came off, I hit my head on the road and was surprised at how hard it was. I was pretty impressed by my head as well. The third time Gill was on the back, and coming into a roundabout a bit too fast, I felt the bike going and her trying to right it. Somehow she managed to step off and was completely unhurt. I, on the other hand, broke the fall with my chin and eyebrow, which I left somewhere amongst the gravel with the bike on top of me, which rubbed a hole in my knee almost to the bone. Fortunately, I knew someone close to where the accident happened, and left the bike there along with my pride. I never went to pick it up again, and sold it for about the same as I paid for it, as I reasoned there might not be a fourth time I would walk away from a crash. From now on Stan would ride and I would partner him.

As the spring moved towards summer and our trip abroad grew nearer, so the shape of the job became more apparent. On one side of the building, a real stonemason was at work cutting and laying white Portland stone and all the shapes of things to come were clearly visible. There was still some digging to be done, and along with young Michael, I was working at the far end of the site. We were maybe twelve feet down and throwing up to six feet, and from there up to the top. At this depth the walls of a trench should be supported with boards and acrojacks, and were shored up as soon as was possible. Down at the bottom of the trench it was cool out of the sun.

It was hard getting any conversation out of Michael. He was a typical shy boy from the west of Ireland. I felt very sorry for him and persuaded him eventually to come out with us all for a drink at the Whitgift, which he was reluctant to do until he had some money for some clothes. I remember coming into the bar on the appointed Friday evening to see this young man, almost unrecognisable in an obviously new blue suit that was at least a size too big for him and a Windsor knot in his tie that was almost as big as his head. We of course looked little different to the way we went to work, except that we were marginally cleaner. Every time Gill or one of the girls tried to talk to him, he blushed so deep I thought he might blow a blood vessel. In spite of all efforts to relax him, he steadfastly refused to let go of his glass until it was reasonable for us all to disperse and go home. It was seeing him in the suit that I realised how young he must be. Barely a hair on his lip and hardly a teenage pimple on his clean skin.

"How old are you, Michael?" I queried the following Monday.

"I'm fifteen, but sure I work like a man and I'm entitled to me wage am'nt I?"

"Yes Michael, you certainly are," I agreed.

The final big trench progressed well and soon we were sent old Bob, who Michael liked. Bob's old body was showing signs of considerable wear and tear, though it never occurred to him that he might try something a bit easier. He was as hard as nails and to watch him go to work was an inspiration. Michael's hands were sore just as mine had been when Bob told him to piss on them.

Ron kept up his amiable rounds and as I had been on the site as long as most, he would relax a bit with me but at the same time make sure that Michael did not think he could get away with anything.

One day Michael was on the platform above me shovelling out, and I was down the bottom rolling a cigarette when Ron passed by and looking down called out, "I don't mind you smoking on the job but I do object to your manufacturing them when you're supposed to be workin'. Now get on with it Ralph!"

I lit up and smiled; it was a gentle reminder that he was paying us for our time. There were few idle breaks, but once I remember saying to Michael words to the effect that it must be strange for him to be working in a big city like this when it sounded so different to where he came from, and he answered, "Yeah, it's a long way from Clare to here."

Summer progressed, and our young bodies got deep brown tans, except Michael's whose remained obstinately pink. The *craic* was good and the ride home on the back of Stan's Velo a celebration of the day. We began stopping for a pint at the pub at the bottom of Sumner Road and we'd be the only two in the bar. From the window as we sipped a pint of Ind Coopes bitter, we could see the sun beginning to fall behind the gasometer: "Dirty Old Town, dirty old town..."

Gill and I had picked a departure date in the first week in July and if the weather in England was anything to go by, we were going to have a hot summer. A few changes had taken place on the job, but Bob was still there and Aussie Pete, although he had announced that he would be leaving soon. Stan was prepared to stay on for, like me, he was happy on this site and both he and I were as brown as Gupta Singh and his smiley slow fat mate, who had forsaken his turban and worked with his top knot showing. Stan and Gupta now worked the mixer between them. It had an automated shovel that hauled vast amounts of stone aggregate into the open upturned mouth of the drum and was controlled by hand levers; as to its voracity, that was controlled by its operator. Everyone was yelling for concrete and a big dumper truck had recently arrived on site to make things quicker than the barrow running that had been the norm.

There was still the last hand digging to be done and as it neared completion, young Michael, old Bob and I were allocated the deep trench. Things were going well enough; Bob and I were throwing the earth up six feet and Michael was clearing. The trench was half shuttered and we clambered out using the acrojacks. Bob was a little slower but managed well enough, so anxious was he not to be thought of as infirm in any way apart from disabilities earned in the defence of the realm. It was coming up to our lunch break and I could feel a cheese roll coming on.

I looked up to where Michael was shovelling and called, "What time is it?"

I never heard his reply for suddenly I saw the wall of one side of the trench move slightly and responded with, "Christ what's happening to the sides?"

"Jesus God the trench's collapsing! Quick get out!" shouted Michael.

"Quick Bob move!" I shouted. "The fuckin' trench is collapsing, get out of there!"

I was screaming at him as I grabbed at the acrojack in front of me and swung up to the next one. Michael was already on the top and grabbed my hand as I leapt over the side. Old Bob had at last responded to the cries and had got up to the first stage, but the earth was still moving and a huge part of the top of the trench was poised like a giant apple bite to fall in on top of him. Michael and I both knelt down over the trench and offered him our arms.

"Quick Bob, grab hold!" we shouted together. Bob grabbed Michael's arm but did not immediately see mine as it was on his blind side. At that moment the wall caved in. I got hold of the same arm as Michael and as the tons of soil collapsed we dragged the old boy as high as we could. He cried out with the pain as he took all his own body weight on the one arm but we hauled him up regardless. Nevertheless we couldn't clear him from the hole before he was held by the waist and screaming as his legs had been forced into crossing themselves and his balls were trapped between them. Michael and I tore at the earth with our shovels as near to the poor bastard as we dare; other lads had run over to us on hearing his cries, and for a while we all lost our colour as we worked away with only his whimpering to speed us on.

By the time we had freed him we were all shaking, pale and sweaty. We laid him out and called for help, but Bob insisted that no ambulance was called. The site foreman Fred agreed under sufferance not to call them after Bob whispered something in his ear. I can only guess that it was a deal he struck right there, where he waived all claims against the company or else he was shit scared that the authorities would be able to trace him over some misdemeanour or other. Whatever the reason, the poor man could not be persuaded to get any help, so we carried him carefully on a plank to the tea hut where he rested all that day and night.

In the morning he was much improved but only just able to walk, and according to Ron, "His balls are like two black grapefruit."

I was almost sick. We only saw the old fellow at tea break and as the days passed, he was seen to be making good and soon they got him on light work painting window frames and doors which had arrived recently. When I did manage to talk to him, he gave me a huge wink and said mysteriously, "Don't you worry about me son, I'm doing better than you think."

∾

dumper

Ｗith a week to go before our intended leave date, all the hand-digging was finished and most of us were concreting in gangs of three. I found this enormously satisfying once we had mastered the basic skills of levelling, agitating and tamping. We arrived each morning to find the work from the previous day set in stone, as it were. Barrow runs were constructed across walls and we literally did run them. I watched with admiration the subcontracted bricklayers hollering for more muck (cement) from their hod carrier, and marvelled at his dexterity and strength. He kept at least five men working and ran all day with a hod the size of a small shed.

Legends grow up around certain of the building trades. After the nutting up lump that roof tilers get on their chests, or the stamina required to be a plasterer's labourer, I guess that hod carrying comes next. There is always talk of legendary men at this trade and stories abound about the size of specially adapted hods that can carry twice as much as a normal one. All hod carriers have one shoulder bigger than the other and all have calluses where the little spur catches them as they offload the cement. All hod carriers file this spur off. So why do they have it there in the first place then? In spite of some considerable strength, by now I knew that I could not carry the hod on my skinny shoulders, although I would have loved the status and the money.

We were just finishing laying a concrete floor when Ron arrived and asked, "Can any of you lads drive?" No answer came. "We need a dumper driver," he explained.

"I can drive a motorbike, Ron," I offered.

"Go on then, see how you get on. Come with me." I followed him up to the mixer.

"Now, that there is yer clutch and you only need two gears, forward and reverse, the third gear is for if you have to go on the road and you won't be needin' that. Now the clutch is just on or off, you can't slip it, just give it some diesel and let it out and away you go. Try to see things in advance, as she steers from the rear wheels as you'll have seen, and when you're takin' a load put the brake on and don't overload the skip." I climbed up and perched on the metal saddle and engaged first gear.

"Away you go then lad," said Ron, and away I went, smoothly enough.

"Just like a real one," complimented Ron as I drew up cautiously to the mixer for my first load.

"Not too much Stan," cautioned Ron, "let him get used to it first." Stan filled up the skip on the front to about halfway.

"Right," said Ron, "take that down to where you were just workin' and yer mates'll be there to spread it when you unload."

I had never driven anything with four wheels before; it felt good and carried some kudos. I merrily chugged down to the lads and dumped the half skip and returned for more, giving the throttle just a little more this time now that I had the feel of it.

"Fill her up Stan!" I shouted with bravado, and Stan almost filled it to the brim. I made a bad reverse move and slopped a load of it out, but soon turned it round and headed off in the same direction just a little faster than the first trip. Suddenly there was a clank, and the steering wheel was wrenched from my grip as the back wheel hit a huge piece of rubble in the track. This caused the dumper to change direction, and as I panicked, I must have jabbed at the accelerator and the vehicle shot forward straight towards an unmanned trench that contained the upright metal rods which signify the steel fixers' craft. I was heading straight for it. It was time to abandon ship. I swung my left leg over the saddle and in one movement leaped from the machine only to slip on the dry dusty ground and the whole of the back wheel rolled over my left leg that was lying over my right.

It was maybe just a few seconds before the truck crashed into the trench and probably only a moment or two before someone found me lying on the ground, but the pain was immediate. I grabbed a couple of pebbles that were in the dust and just squeezed and pressed them into my palm to distract myself from the agony I felt in my leg. Although I had more experience of accidents than many, I knew there was something wrong. The pain was tempered by a feeling of stupidity as I could see the dumper nose down in the trench with one wheel spinning inanely, and though I told Ron (who had drained off at the sight of me on the ground) that I was all right, he insisted that I lay there till the ambulance arrived.

In a mixture of pain and shame and under the hot June sun, I went into a delirium, one that I have had on several occasions since: I am a first world war soldier in a shell hole in no man's land, and no-one can hear my cries for help.

Although someone was with me the whole time, when you are in pain I think you lock yourself into it to the exclusion of everything in order to cope. I have seen this manifested in others, especially in a woman who is in labour. The ambulance arrived, strangely out of place, so clean and scrubbed in the dust and rubble of the building site, and one of the men gave me a cursory examination. As, like most of the lads, I was wearing shorts and wellington boots turned down, this only took a glance. It was plain to see the wheel track over my calf as the tyre tread was perfectly reproduced on my skin in blues and mauves.

"You'll be all right son, we'll take you in for an X-ray but there's nothing broken."

I nodded with relief and thought at least I'll still be able to get on the road with Gill.

Seven hours later I was still sitting on a wheelchair in my work clothes in the casualty department of dear old Croydon General Hospital. The pain was greater than when the accident had happened, and here it was seven thirty, when a nurse who had been refusing me even an aspirin for the pain came up and breezily asked, "Right now what have you been up to?"

I told her and she told me to take off my wellington but I couldn't so she cut it off with a scalpel. There on the white part of my leg was the bruise where the tyre had gone over.

"Is this where the wheel went over you?" she asked.

"Yes."

"Well nothing seems to be broken, but we'll give you an X-ray and have a look at you. Take your sock off." Unfortunately this was not possible either so she cut it off too. What was revealed underneath it was not too pretty. My ankle was cut in two places although it had stopped bleeding, but it was now bigger than my knee and almost the size of my thigh and a horrible pink purple colour.

"Oh dear," I thought as I looked down at it.

"Oh dear," said the nurse. "That doesn't look so good. Let's get you off to X-ray."

The photo confirmed that the weight of the dumper had snapped the ankle bone where it took the weight of the back end of the vehicle as it was the only part of the leg that was in contact with the ground. Because I was young they had decided not to screw it back in place but would set it under anaesthetic. In six weeks I would be up and able to walk on crutches, and after about sixteen weeks I should be able to do everything I could do before.

"Now you will feel a little prick in the back of your hand." Not half as big a prick as I felt now as I lay there in pain and confusion.

"I want you to start to count backwards from ten," said the surgeon's voice.

"What will I say to Gill?" I wondered. "Ten nine eight seven six..."

I opened my eyes to find myself looking up at four or five people in masks and uniforms. I tried to raise myself up and started to speak but my brain did not properly oblige. However I did sort of sit up, and a man's voice shouted, "What the hell is he doing awake?" Someone forced me back down and placed a mask over my face and the lights faded and I came to again on the way to the ward kissing the hand of the nurse and swearing undying love. She was nice, though old enough to be my mother, and it was she who finally allowed me to have a drink of water. Once more I drifted off to sleep.

When I awoke and looked around me I was at the far end of a ward of about fourteen beds. Next to me was a gentle chap in his sixties. His right leg was in traction, and next to him there was a bloke in similar circumstances. Next to him someone was sleeping, then another leg case and I think someone recovering from an appendectomy. Across the other side was a very old man with cancer; next to him was a Scotsman who spent most of the day moving about the ward and bringing people tea; after him was another youngish fellow with an arm and leg injury, and opposite me there was an empty bed. I was wearing a hospital pyjama jacket and had a crate over my legs to stop the sheets from pressing on me. I had no trousers on and was conscious that the blokes opposite would by now know more about me than my own mother.

My left leg was encased in plaster up to the knee and the pain was excruciating. It was only the sight of the other poor sods that stopped me from bursting into tears, not from the pain so much as the realisation that I would not be going anywhere for a while.

I still had not been washed properly when Gill came to see me that first day. Her concern was obvious as she walked into the ward and hurried towards my bed. It is hard to convince anyone that you are in pain when you look well, and I don't think I have ever looked better or fitter. All winter and spring I had worked out of doors using muscles that had seldom been employed so rigorously. The sun had shone and all of us worked stripped to the waist and in cut off jeans so that all the labourers except some of the Irish lads were now tanned a deep rich brown down to the tops of our turned down boots. I lay there trying my best to look wounded and ill but the first thing she said after asking me how I was and me telling her, was that I looked so well. I showed her my cast and she asked where my trousers were. I had been promised a modesty sheet and we both laughed a bit and I felt so sad and soon her visit was over and she kissed me good-bye and I watched her slim frame in her blue flowered dress leave the ward.

I looked up and noticed that every other pair of eyes in the place had watched her leave too and I knew how lucky I was to have such a beautiful girlfriend and that they were all jealous and I loved her more at that moment than I had done for a long time. She visited every day and so did my friends and family and the sun shone outside of the window and the pain did not diminish and I began to think that they might have done something wrong in setting it. I felt so miserable, but eventually I began to study my fellow patients. I got a drawing book and wrote maudlin little notes to myself and bits of poems, and sketched the other blokes and drew pictures of my own foot.

There are some rituals to hospital life for the bed-bound that tend to strip one's dignity, particularly the morning ablutions. For supplying and removing bedpans, nurses should get immediate access to Paradise. The morning began with being woken, if you had managed to get any sleep amongst the groans, grunts, talking, muttering, screams, shouts, snoring and other sounds of the night, by a nurse with a bowl of water and some soap and towel. This all happened at about eight, after which breakfast would arrive and little Eddie the Scotsman would shuffle round with the papers. This would be followed by the arrival of bedpans to those who called for them, and there was no escape because in the afternoons on doctor's round or Sister's you would always be asked that ominous question, "Have you opened your bowels today?"

Once the pan has been delivered, there is the problem for some as to how to get on the thing unaided, which is further exacerbated if you are in pain. For those same unfortunate souls, there is the assisted dismount, from which there is no escape.

As the screens were drawn around various beds, the true morning chorus began: audible straining grunts and farts echoing into the metallic echo chamber beneath them. Men struggled to retain dignity and balance in equal measure in the knowledge that everything could be heard by everyone else. I resolved then and there never to use one. But to no avail. I was forced to break my resolution on the second day and join the rest in the morning ritual.

There was safety in numbers, and as sure as what goes up must come down, so what goes in must come out. I still had not discovered the joys of food. Helped by what was on offer at hospital, I hardly ate at all, so I was never on the pan very long and soon had the screens pulled and continued reading the paper as the others surrendered their offerings to the wonderful nurses who had to deal with this part of all our days.

My tension was relieved every morning by a loudly-spoken bloke whose bed was second from the end; he was always addressed as Mr. Evans and I never knew his first name. He always called for the pan a good half hour after everyone else. Like Old King Cole he would call for his bowl and with the assistance of two nurses be hoist up on to it behind the screens. The rest of us would be tackling the crosswords when from the second to end bed would emanate the sounds of an elephant greeting the dawn. Sometimes there would be a series of short sharp bursts like rubbing a wet finger on the side of a balloon, on other occasions there would be just a high pitched whistle as his anus imitated the embouchure of a trumpet player trying for a note higher than Maynard Ferguson. If we hadn't known better, we would have said that Mr. Evans was making the noises on purpose to entertain us. When he was finished, the two nurses would arrive to remove him, and the screens would go back. Without a hint of embarrassment, he would wash his hands and pick up his paper and the day would continue.

After a couple of days I still had traces of concrete on my legs, although I had tried to clean myself as best I could. I mentioned this fact to my kindly neighbour and he told me that I would probably have a blanket bath eventually.

I was always asking when I might be able to get out of bed. One afternoon the windows open to let in the warm summer air, two of the young nurses came up to my bed pushing a trolley. They both spoke with West Indian accents and had a delightful way of laughing after almost every statement.

"Well Mr. May, Sister has decided that you have to have a blanket bath and spirit rub down, so please take off your jacket. You can start by washing yourself on the top." She giggled and looked at the other girl. By now I had been given the 'modesty sheet', half a bed sheet that I was supposed to drape over my more private parts to shield them from the eyes that could see me through the tunnel over my legs. I carefully positioned it and removed my pyjama top. The water was warm and it was good to wash and towel myself down.

When I was finished, I handed them the towel and said, "Thank you very much," to which they replied, "You not finished yet, you got to roll over and we do your back."

More little giggles as my neighbour lightly snored beside me. Getting myself in the new position was not as easy as it sounds as my leg still hurt, but somehow I contrived to move my body over whilst attempting to cover my backside with the pathetic modesty sheet.

One of the nurses began to gently wash my back. It was a lovely feeling and very sensual. She seemed to be taking a long time over it and then she pulled down my sheet to expose my white bottom. Both of them giggled at the same time and I could feel myself blushing fiercely. Removing the wretched sheet altogether exposed my legs which were as brown as my torso, so that the effect was that I looked as if I was wearing a pair of white swimming shorts. This amused them even more and while one of them dried me the other one went to bring one of the other girls down. I was beginning to feel a mixture of freak and curiosity as there were now three of them looking at my bottom.

I tried laboriously to turn around when one of them ordered, "Lie still Mr. May, you got to get your spirit rub."

"What for?" I pleaded pathetically.

"So that you don't get any bed sores," the other explained, and one of them gently massaged some medicinal smelling spirit into my back, shoulders, and the top of my behind. Here I was, a fit and virile young nineteen year old, used to intimate relations with his girlfriend but now deprived of such pleasures, being gently massaged by one of three giggly girlish black nurses who were enjoying the effect they knew they were having on me.

"Right, now you can turn over," said the same voice.

"No, I think I'll just lay here for a minute," I said weakly. I was feeling a bit dizzy as the blood left my head and if I had turned over it would have been obvious as to where all the blood had gone.

"Come on now we'll help you," said another voice, and a hand reached for my shoulder.

"No," I cried out, and then more softly, "I'll turn myself round in a couple of minutes." They definitely knew the effect they were having on me. I knew some lads who would have certainly turned round if asked but I was not one of them. I waited several minutes before I felt able to resume my position and several minutes more before my composure returned. The thought that it would be weeks before I could resume normal relations with my girlfriend was depressing, and I wondered if she would mind the leg being in plaster. Well, it was something to look forward to.

Days passed, and then weeks. The pain I had was still great and I had to be reminded that others were suffering too. The old gent next to me had broken his thigh in two places and his shin in one place. He told me that as a boy he had been cycling past Allders department store in Croydon when his front wheel had got stuck in a tram line and he had been knocked off his machine by a tram and his leg received the multiple fractures. Being a young fellow, they had been able to fix him up with only a plate and two screws. I had never heard of screwing bones together and felt sick at the thought of it.

All had gone well until forty years later when he was leaving late from the office after attending to some paperwork. As he called goodnight to the cleaning lady, he slipped on her newly scrubbed floor and fell, popping out both screws and plate in his leg. He had been in hospital for nearly a year and things were not going well.

Each morning he luxuriated in the things he was able to do, like wet-shaving himself and carefully combing his hair. His wife brought in his own pyjamas, and he had more than one dressing gown which he would put on in the evening. He was pale from lack of sunlight and once a month received holy communion from a C of E vicar who did the rounds. We talked of all sorts of things from religion to politics, and though I did not always agree with him, I never really took him on about anything, as I wanted to be his friend. So the apprentice beatnik and the insurance executive became buddies and he talked of stocks and schemes and I talked of travelling.

Mr. Evans had broken his leg spectacularly in four places while out walking his dog, when his foot went down a rabbit hole. Scottish Eddie had been admitted with head injuries from falling in the street after drinking a copious amount. He had lost his false teeth somewhere that night, and although looking suspiciously healthy was able to convince the doctors that he was not ready to be discharged. He was a sweet guy and only too happy to do anything for you. I think he had an alcohol problem, but had weaned himself off whilst inside. Having the few jobs of bringing the tea and papers round had given him a purpose that might have been lacking elsewhere. His conversation was lacking in substance and unintelligible to many in the ward, but I could pass the time of day with him and I sometimes translated for the others.

Next to him was the most ill-looking person I had ever seen who could still talk. He was about forty, with prematurely grey hair and skin the colour of oven paper. Most of the day he lay with his eyes and mouth half open. Shortly before I got out, he was sent home to die with his family, although a month later I saw him in George Street when he should have been dead. I was going to speak but in the end I said nothing, though I see his face still, the clearest of them all.

Men came and went and we just stayed. I remember the first time someone died and there was an empty bed in the morning by the door. I was very shaken by this and realised the nearer to the door they put you, the sooner they expected you to leave. The shortest stay was an old man, who came in quite lucid if a little fearful. As the ward was full, his bed was placed lengthways down the middle of the ward. I could chat to him easily, and helped him with hospital routine. He ordered the *Daily Telegraph* for the first three days, but by the fifth day he was incontinent and placed in huge nappies. By the seventh he was demented, crying and shouting, and by the end of ten days he was dead. I found the loss of reason and dignity more frightening than the prospect of loss of life.

Shortly before I was allowed out of bed for the first time, I awoke from a fretful sleep to see a poor fellow being brought into the ward. It was in the small hours and although he was still under anaesthetic, he was moaning as the nurses fussed around him, wiring him up to some equipment and fitting a plasma bottle to his arm. I later learned that he had been run over by a fairground truck and had his hips smashed. He was in the most complicated traction that any of us had so far seen. As they worked away on him, he was coming to, and they still had one more job to do on him, the insertion of a catheter. I could not see what they were doing but I will never forget his cries as the pain brought him round. I could hear him whimpering for some time after the staff had gone. Eventually I fell asleep.

When I woke in the morning, little Eddie was chatting away to the new bloke, whose name was Jim, and had brought him some tea. He was a gypsy lad and over the next few days he provided a nice contrast to the dear old boy next to me. I don't think he could read or write but every morning he bought a paper, and to find out what was going on he would pick up on a photo illustrating a story and say something like, "Funny about that Princess Margaret."

I would ask, "What do you mean?" and then he would try and deduce what the picture was about to get a handle on the story. I soon figured this little ruse out and so often would start the conversation going from news in my paper, and in this way we would swap stories. If I couldn't work out what he was talking about, I would just say, "I don't think that's in my paper." I would then borrow his and explain what the essence was.

There was also a white West Indian boy from St. Lucia in my ward. I had seen him around the town; he had an accident to his arm that required pins and plates, and when they took it all down and removed the plaster, his arm had mended in a bent position. He freaked and had to be sedated as they had to break it and begin again. It was strange to hear the familiar litany of black curse words coming from his mouth, and his rage was scary. He threw punches at the nurses and succeeded in really hurting one of them before he was restrained.

My first steps out of bed were painful and they did not improve with time. My toes were always deep purple and after just a few steps I had to rest. When I was allowed to leave, the joy was tempered with sadness for my next door neighbour, who was still not out of bed and I think was sorry to see me go. I wrote to him once and got a letter back but I did not try to keep in touch after that. A camaraderie of 'bedfellows' builds up as you all become a team, but you quickly drift back into your old roles and underlined differences once you are free.

I know of no real friendships forged in hospital, although I assume they exist. It is just that we seek reassurance from each other when we are ill, so that together we can beat this thing and overcome our pain; often we complain about the food, or the attitude of those trying to help us, but it is only our determination to survive. We are united in our infirmity and vulnerability and our only way of showing any fight is through complaint. Later we can only marvel at our carers and the compassion, dedication and kindness we have been shown.

◆

reg

I was sixteen weeks on crutches after leaving hospital. The lads on the site had a whip-round and raised enough money for me to buy a cheap tape recorder, with which I made some recordings of my playing. The pain in my leg was still considerable and my toes a perpetual purple, sticking out of the cast. Gill had gone home to visit her family, and I decided to hitchhike down to see her. For some reason I decided to take my new tape recorder as well as my guitar. I felt confident that the sight of a crippled lad standing on the side of the road with these large and cumbersome objects would engender sympathy and kindness, and that I would be in with a chance of breaking my Croydon to Bournemouth record.

Well, I did break the record—it took me nine and three quarter hours to get there, and I was faint with tiredness and pain when I arrived. I stayed the night with Pep and his girlfriend, and I don't recall how we all got back to Croydon.

Once I could operate without sticks, I was invited back to the site and put on light duties, like sweeping. I was terribly weak and although Ron was still there, all of the lads I had worked with had moved on, the craic was missing. Already the air was alluding to autumn, and the drizzle of leaves and the slimy feel of waterproofs added to the gloom.

I was sweeping an area of concrete flooring when there was a cry and a thump. I looked over and a young brickie had fallen through a stairwell on to the floor. He survived the fall, but he was taken off the site.

"You're a fuckin jinx," joked Ron under his breath to me as he passed.

It was all the excuse I needed to leave the job. Bad luck follows you about, and once you get that kind of reputation, all misfortunes will be laid at your door. To be fair to the firm, they advised me to sue and I was awarded £100 compensation for my injury.

After a short time I got a job in the carpet department at Allders department store in Croydon.

I joined the department as a labourer and sometime van boy on deliveries, and once again was surrounded by a peculiar band of dropouts. It shocks me to think that I was one of them.

My boss was a slow old Welshman called Fred. His number two was an old asthmatic called Alf, who could sometimes be persuaded to tap dance in the arcade when we were loading carpets. Alf was a dear old bloke but his chest was awful. He wore a jacket and pullover over a shirt and vest, and in the stifling heat that helps lull shoppers into a trance as salesmen purr at them, the fluff and lint in the air conspired to induce the most awesome hacking.

After a particularly horrendous bout of handkerchief-filling expectoration, he would lean exhausted on the stacks of underfelt with sweat pouring off his forehead and mutter wheezily, "Phew, that's better, now you mind the shop while I go for a little smoke." Off he would totter a little drunkenly, and have a few pulls on a Woodbine to steady himself before coming back in to the store to breathe in more fluff.

There was another strange bloke there, a bit older than me, who used to wear Fair Isle pullovers and clonking leather shoes; he had dreadful teeth but a very posh accent. He was always complimenting me on my strength and telling me I looked like Michelangelo's David. I did not want to disappoint him so I kept my shirt on. Strong I might have been, but I was shamefully skinny. One day I heard him say the same thing to a new bloke and realised that he was queer. Without either of us acknowledging the fact we got on all right, but kept our distance.

The huge broadloom carpets were brought to the front of the store where the lorries parked on the High Street. We had special dollies that we put the rolls on and pushed them back to the store where they were fixed to the giant rollers from which lengths were cut. I must say I delighted in being able to throw these massive weights about, and with some bravado used to fly down the arcade, steering and scooting these massive lengths with some skill if not a little recklessness.

Department stores are like warehouses, in as much as they often house people who are only one step away from institutionalisation. In stockrooms and cubby holes lurk some very odd folk. I soon found some and as usual befriended them, even attempting to drag them down to the Whitgift and include them in my coterie of misfits, strummers, failed philosophers and political extremists.

It's as if in a big department store they are part of a family. There is a canteen and a simple hierarchy. The rules are simple and soon you can set your own agenda: best not to make waves, and no-one will really notice you. There were some very deep thinkers among many that I met in these places. Doing a mundane, undemanding job leaves your mind free to ramble and your thoughts roam in the delicious freedom of dreams.

People often asked me what I was doing with my life working in these places. I tried to explain that I knew what I was doing and that I was enjoying a kind of freedom of the soul. Also, I would like to have had as many jobs as Woody Guthrie. I even managed to get my guitar into work, and I would play round the back of the carpet stacks in my lunch breaks.

Occasionally I was seconded to help with the delivery of a particularly big carpet to the shop where they made up the fitted stuff. These were cut and sewn by a small group of ladies with an earthy sense of humour. I looked forward to these excursions as the old girls seemed to like me. The driver on these trips was Frank. He was from Dorset and had a great accent. When his van boy left I managed to get on the delivery rounds with him. This was terrific, as we went somewhere different every day. We would deliver mattresses and washing machines, carpets and lino, and I would have the map book. I still am tempted to turn the map round to face the direction I am going in, and Frank told me that was what girls did. I tried to read the thing like a man and that was why we ended up taking the long way around.

Frank couldn't read the map either without his glasses, and he could never find them anyway. He showed his displeasure by crashing through the gears of the various old trucks we had to use, and swearing the most incredible oaths at all and sundry. He was always in a state of sexual awareness, commenting constantly on every female on the street, making ribald comments the whole time and fantasising about the women who would open the doors in their night-dresses to welcome us in to deliver their mattresses that they would prevail upon him to try out. These little fantasies would calm him between gear crashings. On the longer journeys out to the suburbs of Croydon he would entertain me with tales of his youthful sexploits. Sometimes he would relish the telling so much that he would take his hands off the steering wheel for a moment and rub them together and utter the sound, "Ooooh..."

Sometimes he could be quite poetic. Once when talking about a particular girl from back in the mists of Dorset time he said, "'er little fanny was as soft as a mouse's earhole." He was big-hearted, bowlegged and bald with twinkling brown eyes. In spite of a slight limp from a dodgy knee he had an earthy spark and the ladies loved him.

Then there was Reg.

Reg was an absolute joy. He was lazy, fat, helpless and smiling. I had never met anyone like him and he fascinated me. He was always courteous and pleasant. His personal security systems were simple but had to be adhered to. Shaving every two days; highly polished shoes; and at tea break he went across the road to Lyons and had a pork pie, which he cut into several slices like a miniature birthday cake. He then smeared one side with English mustard and ate each portion, Oliver Hardy style, with the little finger held out. Whenever I eat a pork pie, I cut it this way and think of Reg.

Reg had suffered a nervous breakdown. This information was a long time coming and although I suspected something was wrong, it took him a while before he confided in me. My natural curiosity insisted on inquiring as to what made him tick, and what a revelation he turned out to be. He was about thirty five years old and rather tubby; his eyes were tiny and twinkling, he had a huge grin and walked in a quick energetic way, which implied more effort than he actually put in. When it was time to go home he donned a short blue raincoat and a small pork pie hat.

Reg liked music in general and was interested in my efforts, but his real love was jazz. His knowledge was extensive. He could name session and sidemen, chapter and verse, so long as the music was recorded after

1938. He favoured big band jazz, especially Duke Ellington, and had been to see Stan Kenton at the old Davis cinema in Croydon, and more recently Dave Brubeck at the Fairfield Halls. He and his brother, who he always referred to as Duke (he pronounced it Dook), went to see every visiting American musician they could, and Reg boasted how a certain bass player wanted to go off with his brother's wife and how they had all become great friends. Whenever he spoke about Americans (his interest spread to movie stars as well) his accent became more and more western until he sounded like a player from a cowboy film. I was careful not to take the piss but I did point it out to him eventually, by which time I had gained his confidence and he told me this story.

"I've always been a little overweight and as a result I had trouble with girls. Not talking to them, I never had trouble talking to them, but getting them close they always ran off like. My brother Dook was better looking than me but he wasn't so good at talking to them like I was if you understand my meaning. So we sort of became a double act, he usually got the best girls but at least I got a girl sometimes." He chuckled at the thought, his eyes flickering from side to side and only occasionally fixing on me.

"We would mostly work the weekends and bank holidays in the summers after I'd come out of the 'merchant'. What we used to do was to pretend to be Yanks. It was easy, I brought back a few suits from the States, big ties and them shiny black shoes that all the tourists have."

I knew what he meant; growing up after the war we became aware of these strangely garbed colourful people in powder blue suits and crew-cuts, their wives bedecked with huge sunglasses and accompanied by shrill voices with which they shrieked and bellowed at each other at close range. Draped with cameras and shoulder bags they trooped around London tipping cab drivers and photographing everything. Though hugely benevolent, they were still a bit resented from the war, when they were regarded as 'oversexed, overpaid and over here,' and I suspect there was the dawning realisation that in spite of Britain's enormous sacrifice, Blitz spirit and stoicism, we would not have won without them. Still we were happy to take their money, sell them Nelson's Column and Tower Bridge and were often bemused by their naïvety.

Reg and Dook turned that all around with their little subterfuge. Dressed up to the nines in powder blue and bright checked sports jackets, they cruised the sights where they knew the US visitors would be expected to be seen. Both sporting huge cameras (usually without film in them), dazzling, flat topped and gum chewing, they would engage young girls in conversation about everything and nothing in a loud mid-Atlantic drawl. By Reg's account it was flawless and foolproof.

In the early fifties before rock'n'roll, Britain was suffering all the benefits of a defeated nation: rationing, poor housing, shortages, grey buildings, grey skies, homes painted in browns and creams and kitchens in dark greens. Summers were yearned for whilst the melancholy of autumn tried to prepare us for winters that were cold, foggy and damp. The comedy shows on the radio helped to prop up spirits in the wartime manner of 'we can take it', but spring brought blessed relief as the daffodils and the Yanks arrived and colour was added to the monochrome. Reg and Dook must have looked like they had arrived from another planet.

"We'd stand outside Buckingham Palace like, and when we saw a couple of sorts who looked likely I would walk up to them and say something like, 'Say Miss, can you tell me who lives here?' and they might say, 'Why the King, of course,' and Dook might say, 'The King of England? You don't say. Hey Brad (that was my nickname) is that him looking out of the window?' and we'd all look up and Dook would pretend to take a photo or something and the girl might say, 'Don't be silly, he doesn't look out of the window,' and I might say, 'I thought I saw someone wearing a crown sweeping the steps earlier,' and one of them might laugh ("if you get them laughing you're on your way," Reg confided). Then Dook might ask something stupid like, 'Why do the guards wear those great big hats and what are they called?' And so on. It's good to ask questions that they would know the answers to, that way they think they're helping you and then the killer one is once you got them laughing, Dook would ask them to take a photo and hand them this camera and they wouldn't have a clue how to work it and then you can get close to them and help them to work it and stand behind them and lean over their shoulders and smell their perfume and their hair..."

At this point he trailed off and his eyes went glazed. Then with a shake of his head he came back to earth and chuckled, "And there you go!"

I stood staring at the little fat man in front of me, impressed by his elaborate subterfuge and preparation. To look at him now, his confidence shot, living at home with Mum and hardly venturing out. This man had been in the merchant navy, learned sophisticated manners as a steward and developed a taste for good films and jazz; now here he was, a porter in a department store, and this is where he would remain, ambition shot and insecure.

Could he have made all this up? I doubted it, and later he even produced a dog-eared photo of him and his brother fully attired as Americans in London to prove it. Taken in Leicester Square with Eros appropriately at their backs, it showed the two Croydon boys grinning from ear to ear with a couple of pretty girls on each side of them.

"They was from Yorkshire them two," said Reg distantly.

"Have you got any other pictures of girls you pulled?" I wanted to know.

"No," said Reg, "but they're all stored up here." He pointed to his head and one of his eyes produced a small tear which he brushed away immediately. I pretended not to notice.

"Do you ever get up West any more?" I asked after a while.

"My old stomping ground? No, only when I've saved up a bit, I sometimes go up for a brass," and his look signified that there were to be no more questions on this subject.

I persuaded him to come down to the Whitgift pub once or twice, and some years later when I met the Dook he told me that Reg had enjoyed these days but that he had been poorly of late and hardly went out at all any more.

Even the delivery men at Allders were characters. Quite early on, an old style three-wheeled Scammel British Rail tractor and trailer pulled up and the driver checked in to the carpet department to get us to come and unload. He was a bit odd-looking but not wild; he wore an old-fashioned train driver's hat and a waistcoat and seemed very old to me. He was probably in his mid-forties. He was either prematurely bald or else he shaved his head and eyebrows; perhaps he had been ill. We followed him out to the street and he began a running patter that he must have routined dozens of times before.

"Do you believe we have been visited from outer space?" he began. Reg said, "Oh sure."

"What about you?" he directed at me.

"I'm not sure," I responded cautiously.

"I can't see how anyone could doubt it," he went on. "Of course there is a conspiracy of silence—the Yanks have got dead aliens locked up in freezers over there. There have been loads of sightings."

"Have you seen one?" asked Reg.

"No, but there are lots of things I haven't seen but I believe they exist," he said. "Like, do you believe there's a God?"

"Yes," said Reg.

"Well have you seen him?" asked the driver.

"No," said Reg (at this point I was glad he didn't ask me because of course I had seen God, but I doubt if our descriptions of him would have tallied[7]).

"Well that's my point," insisted the driver. "I mean Jesus was a Venusian."

"What?" said Reg.

"He was from Venus," the driver said, warming to his theme. "You see all the world's great leaders come from outer space. Julius Caesar was a Martian, so was Alexander the Great. Mahatma Ghandi, he was a Venusian as well. I mean look at your bible, it's full of stories about visitors from outer space." Reg looked blank, but then he so often did.

"Take Ezekiel and the whirling wheel," he continued, "that was obviously a flying saucer." I remembered the story of Ezekiel and Woody had sung a song about it too. I said nothing.

"Moses was a Venusian as well. The Venusians had begun to colonise the earth and they designed the pyramids and they were going to guide us to better ways but they had an emergency back home and had to leave a few representatives here. Every now and then they return and bring us another leader to stop us killing ourselves and destroying the planet."

I was intrigued. I pushed the first great broadloom back to the store. When I got back to the truck he was still in full flow. Reg had climbed up on to the tailboard of the lorry and was listening intently (and resting at the same time).

"Take the three wise men, they knew that a great leader was going to be delivered to the world and they followed the space ship for days. It wasn't a star in the east it was a bleedin' flying saucer come to deliver the baby to Mary. No wonder the shepherds were scared. Bloody great space ship coming from outer space and frightening the sheep and all that."

"How can you tell a Martian from a Venusian?" Reg wanted to know.

"Your Venusian has a slightly higher forehead," the driver explained patiently.

---

[7] see *Angel Laughter,* page 30

I glanced at Reg and his receding hairline and just for a moment I wondered... no no, not Reg, although he might well have come from *somewhere* out in space. We hoisted the last broadloom on to the trolley and our ufologist hoisted up the tailgate.

"Keep your eyes on the skies," he advised, and we nodded and manoeuvred the heavy carpet up in the direction of the arcade.

"I think he was a bleedin' Martian," said Reg.

Gill had by now been working at Allders for a while. She had to wear a lilac-coloured uniform and wear her hair up. I thought she looked prettier with it down because this made her face seem smaller.

She was on her own on the counter and she was getting more and more unhappy. I am sure I was mostly to blame, as the feelings of freedom and possible adventure began to stir in me again. The spark between us had diminished and we talked of ways of restarting our adventure. Through a friend, she had heard about an opportunity to get to America, and Gill resolved to get a job there.

Within days, it seemed to me, she had found work as a children's nanny in Los Angeles. I failed to get the significance of this job at the time, and before I could take it all in Gill was off and I was on my own.

As soon as she had arrived in America I realised how deeply I loved her, but by now it was too late to get her back, and the deep ache I felt was only slightly alleviated by the letters she wrote to me twice weekly. All those soppy songs about waiting in agony for the postman now came to have tremendous significance. I know we had both been irresponsible in our relationship, but we were young and constantly in need to express our love physically (well, I certainly was: once we sent away for a trial contraceptive pill, but I became too impatient to wait the prescribed time for it to take effect and we both got the giggles and did it anyway). I realised the main part of the blame was mine and I determined to either get to the US as soon as I could, or to at least stay faithful to her until she was ready to return. I managed neither.

Gill seemed to settle in with her new family straight away and soon became very close to the two little girls that were her charges. The young couple who employed her were kind and considerate. Gill began to renew her confidence and I wrote long letters of longing for her to return. Gill did not respond to these entreaties and I applied for my American visa to go and meet her in California. One of the questions asked if my purpose for coming to America was to assassinate the president. After what seemed an age the visa was granted, but I was told that I would not be allowed to work. So, daunted once again, I continued the correspondence of hope for her return.

Although it surprised my mum when Gill left, I think she was relieved. She had guessed the depth of our relationship, and knew me well enough to know that I was a very long way from being ready to settle down, especially as a young father as well as a husband, but she said nothing.

amaranthus caudatus

It's not my arms, but my heart that aches.
Cradling this burden
Of emptiness.
Your look that said that
"This was done for us
This was meant to be."
That meeting, the concern that was
For you and me.

The neap tide that washed away
Our sand written future
With the turn of a wave
And hurled us with our makeshift plans
Into the undertow
And beached us on to separate shores.

I was always looking out to sea
Did you see it coming
At what cost, and what price?
For your decision and my backing.
And to show for it?
Nothing.
An emptiness, a crushing weight.
No towel round your shoulders
No shawl of comfort.

I wonder now
With the gap of time
If you were persuaded by our drifting?
Neither of us ready,
And even if you were, and I not,
We were not ready, us.
What we had made together, once destroyed
Would leave no claim from one
Upon the other;
Father, Mother.

No-one blames the honey bee
Lost in nectared ecstasy
For bringing pollen to the need
Of flower to gestate fruit or seed

He impregnates through innocence
Not by divine providence
Seduced by colour, movement, scent
It is design not accident

Who could deny the natural power
The wiles and ruses of the flower
To summon when and as they please
Helping intermediaries

And sometimes in their common names
We see reflected joy and pain
As if perceived humanity
Co-exists with mystery

By memory of old flames cheered
Jack by the Hedge, Old Man's Beard
Humour used against our fears
Love in a Mist and *Solomon's Tears*

Alice Sit by the Fire we're told
The warmest name for Marigold
Whilst *Crown of Thorns* and no *Heart's Ease*
Suits random dismal days like these

When petals blow across a lawn
Heaped in little drifts forlorn
No wicked truth or holy lies
Or mitigating alibis

For touch and reflex, fusion's spark
The bruised and fallen fruit is marked
Where autumn's drunken wasps are feeding
Spring's memory slowly receding
A dying sting for the unheeding
Forget-me-not, while
Love Lies Bleeding.

PART FOUR

MUSIC

harmony

Absence is always made harder when you wait for letters. If someone just goes away or you part under a cloud you just have to live with it, and eventually a day passes when you don't think about the one you are missing. Our situation was not like that; every day would start off with anticipation of some news, and if a letter had arrived, I would always feel there was not enough information. I would trawl each line for any indication of diminishing affection, and delve between the lines for a sign that there might be someone else. The pain of that doubt was so destructive. As a young man used to a full relationship, there was also the absence of sex; and as we had promised to stay faithful to each other, I took refuge in the Whitgift Arms.

Gill's letters were all about LA and the little girls that she was looking after and the young couple who were paying her wages. She missed me, she said, and indeed I missed her terribly. I poured out my heart in letters that I hope Gill destroyed: yards of soppy love letters full of doubt, insecurity and promises that I would be more understanding and would she please come back. This was all in the first two weeks.

As the weeks became months, my aching grew and I turned increasingly to drink for the sweet comfort of melancholy, and whilst sober felt lost, cowardly and miserable. Henry, my old friend, was a great comfort to me during this time and we often went out together in the old car that his Dad had taught him to drive in.

The pattern was established and gradually her letters spread out into the wider world of California. Her circle of friends grew and she mentioned some crazy girls who said things like "Far out" and "Out of sight". I thought to myself that it sounded a bit stupid, but before long we were using the same terms in England. It's funny how kids' slang changes. Our mob used a form of New York jazz slang mixed with more obscure cockney rhyming and other bits of patois from the street. A guitar was an axe; everyone was "man"; if someone was a good harp (mouth organ) player, his description might be, "He's terrible on the gob iron!" She still said she missed me and sent all her love.

My guitar and the admiration and encouragement of friends was a real stick to lean on during this time. I became bonded to my guitar in the way of a child with its comfort blanket; I doodled and played constantly and my fingers became calloused and strong in a way that has seldom been repeated. I often dragged the box into work or down the pub, shyly eager to share my new tunes with a few friends.

My obsession with the guitar had helped to introduce me to lots of other music lovers, and players too. Apart from Max there was Chris Ayliffe, Buck Polly and Pete Brown, and Little Chris Alldous, who accompanied Jacqui McShee (he was probably one of the best guitarists in our little circle) and could already penetrate the intricacies of the playing of Fuller and Broonzy. Jo-Ann Kelly had begun to play too, and her marvellously uninhibited voice was already showing the depth of tone and commitment that is thankfully preserved on record. Her brother Dave was also playing, and he too was blessed with a great blues voice from somewhere on the River Wandle delta.

Then there were the record buyers. I am grateful to Mick Hubbard ('M.B.') who lent me records and introduced me to other blues players and as this music filtered into our culture I was able to avail myself of dozens of LPs, which were avidly listened to on my Dansette, soon to be replaced by an Ultra.

"Listen to that bass," I would enthuse, as some thirties recording was played at maximum volume through the mighty six-inch elliptical speaker. One great record loaned to me by one of my brother Bruce's friends was called 'The Rural Blues', compiled by Sam Charters. All the songs were great, but one in particular leaped out at me: *Statesboro Blues* by Blind Willie McTell. The impact of this track on me was as great as Jack Elliott's *San Francisco Bay Blues* had been. The clear beautiful voice and intriguing lyric pulled me deeper into the tune, but above all it was the sound of that twelve-string guitar. I had to have a twelve! I found one advertised in the Melody Maker at Pan Music Studios in Wardour Street. It was another Harmony Sovereign and it was a bastard to play. All these extra strings and a high action, but it sounded wonderful to me. With my ear pressed up against the sides it sounded like an orchestra.

Once more I was in love. I played it until my fingers all but bled. The first tune I learned on it was *The Bells Of Rhymney*. I had heard Pete Seeger play this magnificent song somewhere, and I thought it the best British protest song I had ever heard for the miner. It uses a beguiling nursery rhyme format as the bells toll out their message. It was a poem written by a Welsh schoolmaster called Idris Davies, and underlined for me the importance of getting the lyric as near to a poem as possible before you add the tune, if indeed that is the order in which the components come. Seeger's tune remains I think his best, and the fact that he tuned the bass string down to D gave the whole song an unequalled majesty. I soon learned to play it and discovered that this was the same tuning that Blind Willie had used for *Statesboro Blues*. I was on my way.

Previously I had heard Buck Polly play his monster twelve string, and when he died from a heroin overdose, my friend Chris Ayliffe inherited his guitar and taught me the clawhammer lick (even the names of American guitar styles are cool). This opened up all sorts of possibilities for me. Soon I could make a passable stab at *Statesboro Blues*, and was beginning to get a minor rep as a picker. What a confidence booster this was, and some tiny compensation for the emptiness I felt in Gill's absence. So many songs seem to articulate my feelings, and I guess by standards set by a lot of the blokes that were playing, some of my preferences would have been considered soft. Because I could play fingerstyle and some blues tunes, and because at one time my right hand flat-picking was as fast as a bee's wing, I was judged OK with the chaps. Back home, though, I played Guy Carawan's adaptation of *I Love My Baby (and she's bound to love me some)* and I truly hoped that she did.

And the flimsy aerogramme letters kept arriving regularly from the

States and were eagerly opened with trembling hands. Sometimes longer letters arrived with accounts of people that she had met, but all I really needed was the signing off that she still loved me, because all the other news just made me ache. The shadow of the gasholder was over me; I relieved the pain of separation with music and cider, and tortured myself with thoughts of Gill falling for another.

The evenings in the Whitgift were now vital and I always drank too much. It was easy to get a bit of dope and I took to smoking it, only after a skinful the effects of this were fairly awful and I frequently experienced the 'swirling pit' sensation before passing out in some place or other. Some of our mates could be sick at will but ever since the times I was force fed at the nursery school and vomited when the spoon touched the back of my throat, I have had a dread of being sick. No, I always processed my alcohol and as a result built up quite a tolerance to it.

Bob Dylan's second album arrived, and already some of my mates who had disliked him from the first album were positively damning on this one. Commercial, sold out, crap, were just a few of the expressions used. I did not buy any of this, but I also did not buy the album. I loved his white boy interpretations of *Corrine Corrine* and the way he helped himself to old blues lyrics. He had adopted an Okie accent and talked and sang like some hillbilly and not a middle class boy from the mid-west. At the time I knew none of this and there was great cause for optimism through Bob's music. I could already play guitar better than him and I could certainly play the gob iron better. Now there were proper harmonica harnesses available and I guess there it ended.

I always loved Bob's voice. There was an energy and commitment to the interpretation of his own lyrics, and his vocal range is astounding as he can seamlessly soar from tenor to near falsetto with no crack in the voice as it moves from man to boy. Later on he astounded me with his baritone, and even in the hacked out rasp of recent albums there is a quality unequalled by any other singer. There are hundreds of singers now who have adopted his style based more on Jack Elliott than Woody Guthrie, but essentially Dylan invented modern rock singing and enabled a large number of people who cannot sing to make it, by adopting one or other of his styles.

Then there was the songwriting. I was already captivated by *Song to Woody* from his first album, which I would love to have written. Bob cleverly laced Woody's own words into a song of dedication. This could have been viewed as theft by some but in Bob's case it was respect and humility at source and the effect was profoundly moving to those who loved Woody's work and were growing to love Bob. Then there was *Girl From the North Country*. I was told that he had got the tune from Martin Carthy, but this is only half true. Sure it does have an English format to it, but it was the ambiguity of the chords around it and the straight declaration of the sentiment that bowled me over. It was of course about Gill. How did he know? How could he have understood every thought and doubt, each regret and uncertainty. How did he know her hair hung long? True, the rivers seldom freeze in California but I was prepared to overlook that. This was my song; I learned it straight away. Lots of other people learned it too and it seemed everyone played it slightly differently. However I was the only one I knew who did have a girl 'in a north country fair'—well, west actually, but the song was certainly the most powerful in my growing repertoire.

Other guitarists liked the contribution the sound of the twelve gave to their guitars, and I was often found playing guitar with other pickers. One of these was Eddie Parsloe, who had taken over Tubs' room at the Olive Tree (and, he alleges, some of Tubs' other diversions as well). He was singing with Jacqui McShee's sister, Pamela. She was slightly older than Jacqui and had an almost identical voice. I first heard them sing together at the Olive Tree, and they sang in unison with indistinguishable tonality. Pam was very pretty, with huge brown eyes, and quite one of the most gentle people I have ever met.

Soon the three of us were playing and singing together, and we even got a few gigs. Each Wednesday Pam would travel over from Merstham, and we would practice a repertoire that was more folky than bluesy, but nevertheless very enjoyable. Those evenings were a marker in my week, and it was also a night that I did not end up down at the Whitgift.

When Pam got married, Eddie and I motorbiked down to the church and formed a scruffy honour guard outside with our guitars, as she and her husband emerged. My Levis were a near-perfect washed-out blue, but they had also aged, and in getting on the bike they ripped from seam to seam at the knee. In the surviving photo you can clearly see a huge safety pin holding the trouser leg together.

One day Henry said to me, "Why don't you make a record?"

"Eh?" I responded.

"You can make a record at RG Jones Studio in Morden for ten quid. Little Chris has already made one."

Henry went on to explain that you simply went to the studio and they recorded up to four songs and then after about a week you got a record in the post. This sounded so exciting to me. Was I ready to record and more importantly did I deserve to record? We used to look at records as a sort of medal of musical achievement back then. Maybe I could send one to Gill and she would hear in my voice how much I missed her; maybe she would love me more. I resolved to make a recording. It was simplicity itself. They put two mikes in front of me and I recorded *I Love My Baby (and she's bound to love me some)*. I went into the control booth to listen. They played it back through their big speakers and added a little reverb.

I was so excited. I went out and recorded *Drybone Rag* as an instrumental and then *Girl From the North Country*. I finished up with *Bells of Rhymney* on the twelve and went in and had them play it all back to me. Christ it sounded all right. Of course I could not take the recordings home, but I was definitely encouraged by the sound I was making. A few days passed and then a small parcel arrived and inside were two single sized acetate EPs. I stuck one straight on the Dansette and out I came. It sounded nothing like as powerful as it did in the studio, but I was fascinated and called up Henry who came over and listened. He said little but grinned a lot at my obvious pleasure. I played it to Mum and Bruce and anyone who came by, and of course sent the other copy to Gill.

She wrote back as soon as it arrived. She made me feel so good about it. She still loved me, she said, and was so proud of me. I should have been very happy but there was a growing dilemma. Here was I promising to be true, and everywhere there were beautiful girls.

In our own little group I was aware that I would not have had to make much effort to have enjoyed female company, but to be honest I had that anyway. It was difficult to go without the sexual side of a relationship once you had become used to it. I drank enough in the evenings to lose my inhibitions, and by the reactions of some of the girls around in the company, I was able to guess who might be available. There was some sympathy with my condition from several of our girlfriends. I almost blew it on a number of occasions but I did remain faithful.

There were parties that we gatecrashed and this gave me more opportunities to get smashed and make passes that were never reciprocated. There seemed to be at least one every weekend. I don't know how we found out about them, but we ranged all over the place in a twenty mile radius and met all kinds of people who seemed to tolerate our raggedy appearance and bottles of rough cider.

I was still working at the store and it was full of pretty sales girls. One of them more striking than the rest. She was going out with a bloke from my old school who was a carpet salesman (from behind the broadlooms I would watch him and the other salesmen strutting about and a certain smugness used to creep up on me—this was their career, they were trapped, and soon I would be off on some other adventure). I did not have much to do with him. He was a little bloke and dangerous. He drove a Triumph 650 Bonneville with clip-on handlebars very fast, and was utterly fearless. He had fallen out with this girl and in the way that these things happen, the canteen rumours made it plain that she liked me. She was very attractive, and eventually I asked her out to the pictures.

She had a soft lisp and beautiful brown eyes. She was very gentle and sweet, and things could easily have gone further but there was nothing else there. She had nothing to talk about and no opinions on anything. She just faded out of the scene, and I don't even remember saying goodbye; she just seemed to disappear in front of me. All the other blokes thought I was mad to let the best girl in the place slip from my hands. I had no regrets. It was strange to be free of all the responsibility of a monogamous relationship and be unable to enjoy the freedom.

Around this time I was invited to join a great band who went under the name of the Hickory Nuts. They were three young, talented musicians from Dulwich, and I think they saved me from drowning in melancholy. We hit it off from the start and our rehearsals and get-togethers were bonded by laughter. I was never really sure about the politics of blue-grass music. I loved old-timey music, but bluegrass had the stigma of redneck right-wing connotations. My doubts were rapidly dispersed by these guys, who just loved the sound of clanking banjos and mandolins. Pete Chalkley was the leader on banjo, Ray Tassey played breathtaking mandolin, and Mick Lewis played the double bass. The boys had decided to go fully pro and had all abandoned their day jobs. They had clubbed together and with their entire savings had bought a brand new Morris

J2 van. A national tour was booked and we started to ramble. After two or three gigs which went down brilliantly, it was obvious that the agent was bent as we never got any money from the venues. We finished up in Birmingham busking in the Bullring to get enough money to buy our petrol back home.

We played a gig at the Accrington Stanley Supporters Club. It was a Wednesday and both supporters, enthusiastically playing the one-armed bandit and steadfastly ignoring the band. Within 45 minutes we had exhausted our repertoire, so I did a few tunes on my own. After an interval we played our whole set through again and no-one noticed the join.

Some time during the evening some other folks had dropped in and we were invited back to a pretty girl's house somewhere in the town. The streets were cobbled and the houses built with huge square pieces of brick made to look like stone. It was drizzling and the gas lamps threw muted reflections across the distorted surfaces of the streets. Somehow the girl and I dropped back from the others as we walked towards her house.

"You'll have to be quiet in case you wake me dad," she cautioned.

As she unlocked her front door I relayed the message to the rest of the lads. We walked into a two up two down, back to back cotton town house and immediately Pete and Mick almost blew it as they pointed at the wallpaper. It was imitation brick over real brick. I thought this a bit snobbish of them but I had to stifle laughter as well. The girl put her finger to her lips signalling us to be quiet whilst she went to the kitchen and put the kettle on. We tried to talk in low whispers and not to keep laughing.

Suddenly a voice boomed out from upstairs, "'ave you got someone down there Mary?"

"No Dad," said Mary, bringing in a tray with cups of instant coffee into the room. "I'm just 'avin' a coffee meself and then I'm goin' to bed."

"Right then. Don't be long," said dad.

More restrained laughter, then from above our heads we heard the sound of someone getting out of bed and the pling of elderly bedsprings. We all fell silent and looked at each other. Was he coming downstairs to check on Mary's honesty? We heard the footsteps across the room and the door open at the top of the stairs. All five of us were frozen in that moment when the silence was broken by the sound of a heavy tap being turned on and run into an amplified bath tub. We looked towards our hostess.

"Me dad's 'avin' a pee," she mouthed at us. The loo being outside, the old man was relieving himself into a bucket at the top of the stairs. Coffee cups jangled and spare hands were clapped over mouths as her dad enjoyed the longest pee in the history of the world.

At length there was a muttered, "You 'urry up and get to bed," and the footsteps returned to the plinky bedspring over our heads. It was no good, we couldn't stay; we were all nearly out of control. Leaving our coffees, we left as quietly as we could and ran down the road where we let out an explosion of suppressed laughter. I looked back up the road to see Mary under the gas lamp. She gave a little wave and we found our way back to the van.

∾

olaf

Hey man, what's happening? Why don't you come out to Italy, I'm high and stoned on grass at the moment. I am writing this to you from Genova. Come on out and we can make some music.

Love, Olaf

The address was 'Poste Restante Genova' and the writing scrawled by a stoned hand. I turned it over to see if there was any other information on the missive but that was all it said.

I turned over the short letter again and read the garbled message. How really uncool to tell me that he was stoned, I thought to myself. Did I really want to see this bigheaded bloke again? What had I got to lose, stuck in Croydon, with my girl in the States and a boring job? I handed in my notice and left the next day for France.

It was summer and once again the enforced solitude of the road gave me time for dark thoughts of how I could have let Gill and me drift apart. As usual my progress was pitifully slow, and in order to make some progress I took lifts in directions that were not exactly where I wanted to go. At least they were vaguely south, and I was at any rate on the move.

Over the two or three nights I slept out on the road a kind of acceptance crept over me and I fell asleep to the sound of rustling grasses and chirping insects, staring at the stars and dopily wondering what it was all about. I was terrible company for whoever picked me up. For a start my French was appalling. Expounding my 'philosophy' proved difficult for I had great problems explaining why, if I was headed to Genoa, I had arrived in the direction of Spain. Usually though, I was so tired from hanging about that within a few minutes, the rocking of the car or truck sent me off into deep and undignified sleep. I would frequently wake up with my head bouncing off the door window, mouth wide open and arms flailing, having been lost in a dream that we were hurtling into a brick wall.

As my terrified driver glanced over at me I would grin sheepishly, at the same time checking that I had no dribble down my chin, and as cheerfully as I could explain, *"Une rêve. Je rêve, je m'excuse."*

Once I actually slapped a driver on the ear and though he said it was all right, he told me that he was turning off the road and put me out only to continue in the direction I wanted to go. I couldn't blame him in all fairness.

This irregular sleeping meant that at night I was quite often awake and several times hitched through the night. One night, way off track I was in a huge *camion* and a huge moon low in the sky lit up the trees and bushes as we trundled happily through the countryside. As we slowed down to enter a small village, I saw in the truck's headlights what appeared to be a chicken sat in the middle of the road. I drew the driver's attention to it but he had already seen it and slowed down. We must have been nearly on top of it when the creature suddenly leaped up and hopped down the road in front of us. It was the biggest toad I have ever seen and once again I was reminded by this alien creature just how far away from home I was. Eventually after a few metres, the driver passed over it, between the wheels and as I looked back I could clearly see the creature still in the middle of the road until the next truck came by.

Over the next couple of days, I zigzagged my way in the approximate direction of Italy.

Somewhere still in France in the early evening by the side of a quiet country road, I had begun to look for a suitable place to sleep for the night when a 2CV pulled up. It was driven by a smart little bloke wearing white socks and beige leather shoes, pale trousers and a yellow sweater. As I gratefully jumped in he grinned at my enthusiasm. He asked me where I was going and when I explained that my eventual destination was Italy, he shrugged and mentioned a place that I had seen on a signpost which I knew was in the right direction. Off we lurched and as we drove, I realised that he was glancing at me over his shoulder. I also noticed that he had a ring with a jewel in it. This is not a bit unusual today but at that time it usually indicated a slightly effeminate man.

I remember an old guy that used to cruise the London to Brighton road looking for boys. His name was Wally, and when I told some friends of my meeting him, they all knew him and said what a nice bloke he was. One of my mates had even let him buy him a dinner and no favours asked. Once you had explained that you were not that way, he was fine. He still enjoyed the company of young men, but never tried anything on. On several occasions I'd got lifts with blokes looking for more than just company, and my usual way of dealing with unwanted attention was just to ask them to pull over and let me out, and that was all there was to it.

"*Quel age avez vous?*" he wanted to know. I told him.

"*Si jeune!*" he exclaimed, slapping himself gently on his right cheek.

"*Vous n'avez pas peur sur les chemins?*"

"*Non, pourquoi j'ai peur?*" I responded with bravado that I should know the meaning of fear, and I lowered my voice to an even more manly tone to indicate my lack of gayness.

"*Pourquois, alors les voleurs, bandits ou peut-être homosexuels!*" At this last word he turned and looked directly at me so that the car started to head for the other side before he corrected it with a quick "*Ooh la la.*"

I searched in vain for the words to indicate that I would be able to take care of all eventualities because I was strong and aggressive and a great and fearless fighter but I think it came out as, "*Je lui donne un coup de pied,*" and for emphasis, I slammed my fist into my hand with a crack that surprised us both.

My driver muttered something I couldn't understand but added "*si jeune*" once more before pulling up by the side of the road and telling me that this was as far as he was going. I'd only been in the car for a few minutes and he had stopped about a mile from the town in front of us. He then proceeded to drive off into the town that I was now obliged to walk through. Any hitchhiker will tell you that you can never get a lift before a town, you just have to walk through and out the other side.

However much I cursed that bastard, it was a lesson well learned, and next time I would keep them sweet at least until we got out the other side.

I walked right through the town and paused only for a coffee and some cigarettes. As long as I had a cigarette I was OK. That evening I slept all the way to Switzerland in the cab of a giant truck driven by a German who was surprised that I was English; he said that he thought by my colouring that I must be Spanish. I was pleased to be taken as exotically foreign, and by now my skin was quite tanned from all the standing around I had done. I can remember walking through Geneva and admiring the lake and by now being almost completely broke not daring to spend my last few coins, that were French in any case. I could not believe the price of everything, and entered and left that country without spending any money. It was still not possible for me to contemplate playing guitar for money; I was still too scared.

At last I arrived in Italy and immediately became aware of a lighter mood. I was able to order coffee in fluent Italian: *"Due cappucinni prego?"*

When two coffees arrived, I was too embarrassed to send one back. Another reminder that Gill wasn't with me, so I drank them both. The weather had turned a little sour and it was cloudy with a warm drizzle. I was close to my destination and refused to let my spirit be dampened. By the time I had rambled into Genoa I had been travelling for a week. I was in serious need of a bath, or at least a clean pair of socks.

The hostel in Genoa had been a fine old house and was now full of boring kids who seemed to me to be so young: Germans who went to bed early and got up early, and one or two squeaky-clean American hitchhikers who were out of my class as they had enough money to get across the Atlantic to start with, so as far as I was concerned they must have been rolling in wealth. That evening, tired and hungry, I swallowed down the spaghetti and asked about my old acquaintance. By now it had crossed my mind that he might well have moved on; he certainly did not know that I had left home yet. To my relief I was told I would find him in the garden and sure enough there he sat with a few people around him. He was strumming a twelve string guitar and he had the chord changes made correctly. I was impressed.

"Hello man," I said as coolly as I could, "How's it going?

He looked round and stared at me I could see he had been smoking.

"Rolf!" he burst out after a while. "You made it man, hey what's happening"?

"Nothing's happening, I just decided to come out and see you."

"Shit man I'm so stoned I have to think for a minute, you came out. Far out man, far out. Hey do you want a smoke it's good grass."

It seemed churlish to refuse and we smoked a small joint out of sight of the rest of them.

"Where's your axe man?" he suddenly panicked. "Surely you brought your guitar!"

"Yeah I got my guitar," I told him.

"Get it man, let's play some music, hey this is great, you came, you really fucking came. I can't believe you came to fucking Italy man, far fucking out!"

At this point I had started to feel pretty cool myself, after all I had done precisely that. We played and he was OK, not great but the chords were right and as always the twelve-string hides your inadequacies. My old Harmony was as loud or louder than the twelve, so I could still lead. After a while I looked up to see that we had acquired a few admirers and we basked for a while in the glow until the curfew came and we had to retire. I fell asleep quickly and the next day we hit the streets of Genova big time.

After breakfast of milky coffee and cigarette, the two of us ambled out into the sunshine. I was down to my last smokes and we stopped at a Tabaco shop and I bought a soft pack of Nazionales. I lit one up and began to take in my surroundings. Olaf knew the routes into town and he had money for the tram fare. I was rested, and felt so positive about what we were about to do that it was only when I opened my guitar bag to pull the instrument out that the full realisation hit me. I think we were back in the dock area somewhere and there were people walking about. We started playing in front of an open guitar case, and after just a few seconds people started to throw small coins into it. After a few tunes (all the tunes he knew actually) Olaf stopped playing and bent down to collect the change. I finished off and the group of people who were listening gave a little applause and dispersed. In a small café Olaf counted out the change.

"Man we are rich!" he informed me, and in fact we had earned enough

to buy our dinner already. I grinned with satisfaction. That night we went
out again and made enough to pay for our rent and we drank a little bottle
of wine and some grappa that Olaf insisted was the right thing to do. It
tasted like cleaning fluid and the next day I felt as ill as I'd ever been.

∽

disharmony

Always frugal, I soon had more money from my busking than I'd left home with—about £10. With affluence came confidence, and soon the attractions of Genoa began to pale and the desire to move on took over. We decided to visit Pisa. After an attempt to hitch together, we abandoned this method in favour of solo travel. My normal skill at the art continued and I arrived a day after Olaf. I can clearly recall, as I set out, that feeling of anticipation mixed with excitement at the prospect of playing music, because it is still with me. The petty anxieties of arriving in time for the gig and the wonder that people enjoy what you do sufficiently to pay you for the thing that gives you pleasure. It is a rare privilege.

Pisa was as magical to me as it must be to all who see it for the first time. I stood staring at the tower for a long time. It was raining, and the green of the grass around it provided a contrast to the whiteness of the building. It seemed to me that someone had noticed that the thing was leaning and had tried to correct this by altering the angle of the higher storeys, but I pushed this silly notion from my mind as Olaf and I climbed up the slippery marble steps. With all the bravado of an experienced scaffolder, I advanced perilously close to the edge of the landing and surveyed the town.

With sweaty palms I nonchalantly explained to my friend, "Heights don't trouble me. I was a scaffolder, you know."

I could see that Olaf was impressed, though he said nothing. Just as I got to the unprotected edge of the floor, my foot slipped and I made a grab for the pillar. Olaf grinned and shook his head in admonition of my bravado. I'd like to think that my grin in return was not sheepish.

We busked around the town and stayed in the youth hostel. Soon we moved on and in turn, I was moved by Florence and the beauty of Michelangelo's murals and appalled at their desecration by tourists who had stolen bits of the plaster or written their names on the bits they could reach. I returned on several occasions and considered stealing a bit of paint myself, but refrained. From my vantage point up in the gallery, I watched a congregation below take Mass. First there was a sort of procession followed by the movement of the congregation up to the altar to take the host and drink the wine, and not for the first time I felt a pang of envy at their corporate act of worship and belonging to something. I was still trying to come to terms with my growing atheism, but it was always threatened by such acts and great art. Here in this building, both were combined. It occurred then and still does that all great creativity comes either from religion or sex, and why wouldn't it, as they are the great forces of life and death?

Meanwhile I strummed on with *San Francisco Bay Blues*, and in the evenings played my fingerpicking pieces to the small groups of admirers. That stretched the evenings out till the hostel doors were closed and the German kids complained that we were making too much noise.

Florence was full of American tourists, and although I was a bit embarrassed singing only American songs to them from street corners, they tipped well and once a middle-aged guy asked me if I was from Texas, which made me feel authentic. When I asked him, however, he explained that it was my Levis that had made him wonder, as he had only seen cowboys wearing them "at home". I was happy with that explanation and even happier with the dollar bill he gave me, which I saved and took out to admire from time to time whilst I was travelling. I wondered what all the strange symbolism meant with the pyramid and the all-seeing eye suspended above it.

We found a spot on the famous bridge that crosses the river, and set up a pitch where we played for several days. Never overanxious to milk the scene, I left as soon as I thought we had enough to see us through the day. It was still raining and in the photo that survives from that episode I was damp but undaunted, and though sometimes deeply missing Gill, I was busy and had begun to consider moving further afield. Although Rome would have been the obvious place to work, I still had the memory of the last time to put me off going back, and so I suggested playing in Turin.

Once more I was lost on the road with my thoughts, daydreams and daymares. I would set myself problems and try to solve them in my head, think of friends at home, try to analyse my motives, blame myself for losing Gill, wonder if I really liked this Norwegian I was travelling with, and sometimes fleetingly consider leaving for home. In between all these ramblings I would wonder why I could not get a lift. Cars streamed by, trucks rumbled onward, motorbikes thundered and sometimes a bicycle would move silently past me.

As I stared down the road from my hitching point I saw, way off in the distance, two figures walking one behind the other. As they got closer I could see that the one at the rear was carrying a double bass, then as they got even closer that the one in the front had a huge accordion on his back. I sensed that they were gypsies, and experienced the thrill that I always get in their proximity. As the pair walked by me they took in my situation without pausing, and both spoke in greeting and one of them mentioned "guitarra" so I considered myself blessed by these two road soldier musicians. They asked me for nothing (just as well); they had sensed that I was sincere in my intent. They obviously could not seriously contemplate hitchhiking with such unwieldy instruments and so walked on. I watched them go and as they became dots on the long straight road, I realised that I still had this smile of bonded brotherhood on my face. At last I got a lift, and several hours later the grin of recognition returned as the two figures once more came into view. The pace of their walk had not diminished as they trudged purposefully onward.

I arrived a day after Olaf and found my way to the hostel, which was some distance from the main part of town. After I had checked in, I decided that I had to wash some of my clothes. This is not easy using cold water and toilet soap, but I managed to 'clean' my spare socks and pants and felt thoroughly pleased with myself. I am sure that today there are just as many travellers on the road, but I cannot imagine them to be as fired-up and evangelical as we were.

For my generation, unencumbered by the need to shower and wash our hair every day, to say nothing of a clean set of clothes each morning, the road represented a freedom that could only be imagined by today's kids. Nearly everyone has been abroad by now with the advent of package holidays, but at that time the only way to see the world was to join the navy. To leave the austerity of the fifties behind and break the future that seemed ordained for you by class or birth was totally exhilarating. Everything was different to the way it was at home. From the vehicles on the road to the taste of their coffee and cigarettes. Each corner you turned threw up new sights and sounds and you could be anyone you wanted to be. You could affect the walk that was done by that really cool kid down the road, or keep an Elvis sneer on permanently (though I'm not sure it helped with the hitchhiking). You could adopt that devil may care attitude and appear to shed the everyday anxieties that burdened you at home and be the coolest cat around, only to catch yourself in a mirror sometimes wide-eyed and gob-open at some visual feast or other.

Standing at the side of roads for hours on end was the most static I have ever been. As a kid I was always on the move, and I cannot think of any time apart from in hospitals when I would have been still. If I was on the move before my army days, I was even more so after. I ran everywhere, impatient to be with my friends to divert myself from melancholy or to share the company of my girlfriend. Perhaps I sought company precisely to avoid my own thoughts; I know I have always dreaded not being able to sleep, and as a little boy can clearly remember listening to the Croydon Town Hall clock chime away every hour from ten o'clock until it was time to get up at seven thirty.

Here on the kerbside there was no escape. I tried walking in the direction I was going with my thumb stretched out, but this method did not truly indicate the seriousness of intent that a true traveller must have. In the end there was nothing for it but to stand and try to look attractive or presentable and face the oncoming traffic with an air of studied indifference and fatalism. Unfortunately I was unable to do this, and constantly rearranged my stance, and in so doing, my body language. Thumb high, thumb low, square on or sideways, half-smile or no smile at all, big sweep of arm or just a flick of the thumb, guitar hidden in the bushes or bag at my feet. Each time I got a lift I examined my technique to see if a pattern emerged. I now know that there is none.

Trieste was full of colour and kids with carefree attitudes and loads of money. They all seemed terribly young and silly, not a bit deep and fascinating like myself. Where did all these people get their money from? Why did they all wear reds, yellows, pinks, oranges and fey pastel shades? How come they all had scooters and impossibly beautiful 'girl-child' type chicks riding side saddle on the backs? What was I doing with this Norwegian who couldn't play very well and always dragged the beat? Why did I not have a girl? What was I doing here?

It was inevitable that I would go into one of my moods sooner or later and it might as well be here. Olaf sensed it but did nothing to help; in fact he went off to town on his own, which meant I didn't even have anyone to moan at. There was this tight-assed English bloke with a very long face wearing a blue fisherman's sweater and sandals with socks. He was washing some clothes like me and I noticed he had been crying. I asked him what the matter was; he said that he was all right, but his eyes were so pink they made mine water. He looked a complete jerk, but I felt sorry for him and badgered away until we got round to the subject of his eyes. It turned out that he had contact lenses and hay fever. My interest waned when I realised he was not in trouble.

It is strange to think that in a perverse way I was a style victim. As I stood in the cool washroom pitying this bloke, he had actually got it right. The fisherman's sweater would have been very useful at night when it got cold. The shorts would have kept him cool in the hot sun and helped to give him a youthful appearance, whilst the sandals would have meant that he need not wear socks every day. Here on the other hand was I, wearing my prized brown leather jacket, Wrangler shirt (hard to wash) original Levis, hot airless leg coverings, socks hand-knitted from wool unpicked from older socks, and desert boots that had sweat marks creeping through the uppers during the day and white salt marks by the morning. My outfit was an understatement of road chic. It was based on the travel methods of a mysterious bloke called Don that my brother Bruce had met down at Brighton. His philosophy was simple and practical (but perhaps a bit too minimalist):

• All belongings should fit in a bag no bigger than one foot square by nine inches deep. A school duffel bag would make a good alternative. Rucksacks were definitely out and deeply uncool;
• One wash one wear, i.e. two T-shirts, two pairs of pants, two pairs of socks;
• One bar of soap, razor, toothbrush (no toothpaste, use soap);

• One penknife, needle and thread, aspirins and plaster;

• One baby's nappy instead of a towel. With practice you can learn to dry yourself adequately with one of these even after a bath. The secret is to push off as much surface water with your hands before you pick up the nappy and then use only a small part of it for each limb leaving the torso and hair till last.

All these items will fit into this small receptacle and you can travel that light.

My only concession to luxury was toothpaste.

When Olaf returned he was enthusiastic about the prospects of earning. By now my mood had changed, and although another attack of stage fright had hit me, I didn't let him know. That evening we did quite well playing at an outdoor terrace where several restaurants spilled out on to the square, and afterwards the two of us got pissed and wobbled back home just in time to get into the hostel—only to be loudly rebuked by some Germans. I told them to fuck off, Olaf managed a very loud fart and we both collapsed into the bunks in fits of giggles.

We were woken in the morning about seven by these same geezers loudly shaving with electric razors (uncool). I had lost some of my aggressive bravado from the night before, but I managed a few swear words. Olaf did better. Swinging his legs over the side of his bunk and landing soundlessly on the floor, he walked over to the shaver and pulled his plug out of the wall and threw the lead out of the window, then leaning very close to the geezer's half-shaved face he uttered in English, "Later."

The German was so shocked he said nothing, then as he began to complain Olaf leaned over the side of his bunk and putting his finger to his lips made the 'sh' sound. I turned over and pretended to sleep. I was proud of him. Maybe he was really that cool; perhaps we could be the all-conquering pair. I would reserve judgement till later. That evening we were thrown out of the hostel.

As we sat considering our fate on the wall outside the hostel, Olaf looked round at me and asked, "Why don't we go to India?" Before I could say anything, he quickly added, "We know we can earn enough to get by, we probably shouldn't be able to play in Yugoslavia, but Greece would be OK. Then it's just across the border into Turkey and by then we'll know how it's going and we can adjust our plans accordingly."

He seemed so assured that I hardly knew where to begin my prot-
estations. I had nothing really to go home for. I'd never been to any of
these places and I found the idea of visiting a communist country very
exciting.

"Don't we need a visa for Yugoslavia?" was all I could manage.

"We can sort it all out later, but if we're going to do it we should maybe
earn a little more money."

I clearly remember the thrill of just saying, "OK, let's do it."

As we commenced the long coastal walk into town my mind started
to think of the thwarted attempts I had made before. Gill was always
confident in me and our ability to make it, but I couldn't have done it
with her. I suppose it was the feeling or realisation that I might as well
have a go at it rather than having to look after someone I cared about. I
felt strong and I had clean socks on. My thoughts once again strayed to
the possibility of some female company, but I had sworn to stay true and
I fully intended to keep my promise.

In fairness this promise was made easier by my appearance and road
style. I was in stark contrast to the bright and gaudy Italian lads that
zoomed about the streets on fizzing scooters. I was the colour of wood-
land in November gloomed in the streets of this north Italian city; Olaf
on the other hand was the first person that I had met with that impossible combination of blond hair and beard complementing deep tanned
skin. Whilst not muscular he was athletic-looking though just a little
splay-footed.

He was also the first person I had ever met wearing the Indian sandals
that became ubiquitous during the sixties and somehow still cling to credibility today. Olaf only ever wore white, which of course enhanced his tan,
except when he wore black T-shirts which of course enhanced his tan…
He spoke English with the mid-Atlantic accent of many Scandinavians,
spoken in a deep monotone. He had travelled quite a bit, and wore the
best white canvas trousers that I had ever seen. They even had the Levis
back pocket chevron sewn into them. They were made from sail canvas
and had been put together by a tailor who kept all his broken needles to
show Olaf how hard the job had been.

By the time we had met, these trousers were as soft as corduroys but
stronger than a new pair of Yankee jeans. The only thing that blew his
cred for me was that most of the time he smoked a pipe. True, it was not
always tobacco, but the idea of a bloke not yet 22 smoking a pipe did not

sit with me. In fact I was glad that he had this road imperfection and that I could play better than him, otherwise he would have been perfect. I watched enviously as all the girls looked up when he entered a room. He affected not to notice them. They'll soon go off him when they see that pipe lit, I mistakenly thought.

That evening Trieste was busy and warm, and there was a good feeling in the air. We played for longer and made a few lire more than usual. Later in a café I took out what remained of the tatty map and we looked at Yugoslavia. It was simple: the main road stretched from Ljubljana to Belgrade and then south to the Greek border. It was pointless riding together, so we split up the next day and arranged to meet in Thessalonika. Olaf suggested about three days for this trip.

For once I picked up a lift quite quickly and spent the next several miles wondering how I had managed this. The truck was driven by an Italian, who wondered if I was going to look at the stalagmite caves. As if I was interested in things like that; I was about much more cool motivation than mere tourist visits. In fact I really did not know why I was travelling, which made it hard to explain why I was on the road. So I told him that I was going to look at them. The kindly man then drove me out of his way and dropped me at the entrance of the attraction before turning off down the road—and for all I knew heading for Greece.

Having neither money nor desire to see the bloody caves, I spent the next few hours trying to hitch back to the main road. Progress was painfully slow. There were few private cars, and the elderly trucks that thundered past belching diesel did not seem attracted to the frowning youth who stood by the road. That night was the first of many that I spent sleeping by the roadside in the open. One night I threw the bag down and climbed in only to find that I had lain it in a puddle, but as the water slowly seeped through it into my jeans I was just too exhausted to do anything about it.

Of all the places I had been this was the most different. Communist birds sang in communist trees and the sun shone. In the north, fields were green, yet there was somehow no colour. I confess to a feeling of horror when I realised that I actually missed seeing advertisements. Traffic was very slow, and apart from occasional German cars full of passengers, the lorries seemed to lumber past at a rate of about one every fifteen minutes, but perhaps I had got on to the wrong road again. More time for contemplation as I stood, trance-like with tiredness and hunger, wondering if I would ever get to Greece.

The off-white concrete sectioned roads stretching straight into the distance in both directions as far as I could see only enlarged my sense of isolation; then, shimmering like Omar Sharif in *Lawrence of Arabia*, a soundless apparition would emanate from the horizon and metamorphose into a truck that slowly became audible, and once again the heartbeat would pick up as it drew near. Each time I would try to remember the stance taken on my last success, only to have to revise my memory as the great smoking beast dopplered away from me to become another shimmering apparition on the opposite skyline.

The further south I went, the more alien I felt. As soon as you left the city, the people seemed to change. Even at the time I knew that amongst them there would be kind and gentle souls, but at the same time there was a hardness apparent in some of them, and a lack of sophistication that was present in even the lowliest working people that I had come across on my journeys so far.

My own social skills, such as they were, had no currency here and I sensed an 'every man for himself' attitude that upset and depressed me, for as a committed socialist I suppose I had hoped for more. I guessed some of my harder-left friends at home were right and that Yugoslavia was not really a communist country, but a bunch of different states held together by communism. I even contemplated taking a train for part of the journey, but after joining a rabble of people who made no attempt to form a queue for what seats remained on one of the trains, I walked the other way and took my place back on the roadside. I have always had trouble with queue jumpers, and in the terrible tragedy of modern day Yugoslavia, I recall that brief experience with horror at what things must have been like when it was truly a matter of life and death.

I have no memory of Belgrade except that of walking right through the city and out the other side. I slept on the side of the road most nights, and once a truck driver woke me where I lay, believing me to have been killed. Indeed I was lucky not to have been, as when he found me I had rolled off the kerb and into the road and could easily have been crushed by a truck as it roared by.

This driver offered me a lift and a small piece of bacon that he had in his pocket wrapped up in a grease-sodden piece of newspaper. I was warmed by the solidarity of the working class and the brotherhood that binds the poor together. I had nothing to drink for hours, days even, and this bit of salty bacon was the last thing I needed, but I had to accept only to find that it only smelt like bacon as it was actually a piece of fat with the tiniest hint of meat on it. The great globule stayed in my mouth a long time before I could muster the courage to swallow it. How I managed not to vomit I will never know.

Eventually the truck pulled into a petrol station wittily called 'Benzin', and not for the first time I missed the familiarity of brand names on fuel and longed for the presence of adverts and posters along the way to brighten the journey. I found the 'toilets' and for once there was a tap that had water running out of it. I drank as much as I could, which had the effect of having to make me stop the truck after a short distance in order to have a pee. The sun was coming up and as we rolled into Zagreb I spotted to my astonishment the two musicians plodding methodically onward, double bass and accordion slung across their backs. I wanted to greet them somehow, but we rolled past in the truck. After the driver dropped me, I too slung my bedroll across my back and walked through the town and out the other side.

Days passed and my progress had almost stopped completely. I was starving hungry and could feel spots and pimples proliferating on my forehead. Somewhere on the main road I waited for three days and on the third day, two rather large jolly Australian girls arrived at my bit of lay-by.

"G'day mate!" they chirped as they set down their two enormous uncool rucksacks. "How long have you been waiting?"

"Three days," I croaked hoarsely. I'd spoken to no-one for at least that time.

"Three days?" they chorused in disbelief. "Gee, we never wait more than a few minutes."

Very helpful, I remember thinking. Perhaps it was the pimples or maybe my near-starving, mad-eyed state that warned them away from me. Perhaps my crazed grin looked lascivious, and by now I was suffering from hay fever, which probably added to my attractiveness with red rimmed eyes and a snotty nose.

"Well as you were here first, we'll move a bit further down the road so you get the first shot," they chirruped merrily.

"Thank you," I croaked wearily, and then under my breath, "I suppose a…"

The next truck that came along drove straight past me and screeched to a halt in front of the two girls. As they clambered aboard one of them gave me a cheery wave and shouted, "Good luck!"

I grinned my acknowledgement back at her and waved stupidly. The next afternoon I too got a lift but it did not go very far. The road on which I stood was now even longer and straighter than all the others I had ever waited beside. Things really felt desperate. The trucks seemed to have dried up completely, and with no food inside me, I decided to take out the guitar and play for a bit. Perhaps this nonchalance would make me look more interesting to the drivers as they whistled past, their heavy wheels thumping rhythmically over the sectioned concrete.

I opened my case and stared in disbelief at the sight that greeted me. The body of the instrument was concertinaed into itself, the sides had split and the front had compressed into the back. The neck was intact and the strings still in place, but no way could the instrument be played. At this point I felt as low as I have ever felt. My situation now seemed utterly hopeless. Without the guitar I had lost even that precarious support. After loosening the strings, I gently laid the broken box back in the case, and a big boy's tear plopped down my cheek.

∾

crossroads

My guitar in pieces, I tried to assess the situation as my thoughts tumbled over each other. I stared at what I supposed was the direction of Greece to my right, then turning left I looked at the direction from which I'd come. Traffic moved at about the same rate in both directions, and the patch of scrub across the two-lane concrete highway looked just as appealing as the bit I was sitting on.

"I might as well cross this road and head back," was the thought that entered my head at last. Then, with a thump in my chest of real determination I thought, "What the hell, I may as well continue, things have got to get better."

I stood up, dragged a hand across my eyes, looked down the long road in front of me and took out one of my last three cigarettes. I flicked open my Zippo lighter and found that it had run out of petrol.

"Shit!" I thought, "I will not be denied!" I looked long and hard at the fuelless lighter. It still had flint in it, so how could I turn that spark into a flame? With half an idea and half in desperation, I stuck the end of the cigarette into the wind shield around the wick aiming it at the source of the spark. Furiously I spun the flint wheel whilst at the same time drawing air through the cigarette. Within a few seconds the taste of smoke reached my tongue and I removed the end of the cigarette to see that one edge had caught and by licking that edge and pulling even harder, I could get the thing to burn evenly, and soon I was puffing away merrily on one of the foul cigarettes that were all I could get in that country. They came in a blue box; inside there was not even any silver paper to glamorise them, and the brand name was something really subtle like 'Tabbac'. But that was one of the best smokes I'd ever had. My small victory in lighting it announced my new determination to overcome my difficulties.

That night I slept again by the road and woke early, shivering in the dawn. Thoughts of what had happened to my guitar kept returning. I had not played it the whole time I had been in the country, and had only spent one night under cover and that was in a student hostel that I had come across by accident. It was a crowded, hot place, and to add to my sense of loneliness, no-one spoke English. I had a reasonable night's rest but wondered if the geezer in the bunk above me had stepped on my guitar deliberately or accidentally during the night. In my mood at that time I surmised that it had been a deliberate act.

The sun rose higher in the sky. There was little shade and it was very hot. Once again I was in a dilemma whether to move to a better place or to sweat it out where I stood. In the end I was moved by thirst to find a drink of water. Everyone had advised against buying any Yugoslavian money, but I had a few notes and found somewhere to buy a coffee and a glass of water before resuming my vigil on the roadside. The day settled into an insect-buzzing, hazy, close, still afternoon. Not a soul disturbed my sojourn and the transport that passed me did so even more rarely. As my eyes sleepily stared up the road I became aware of a smaller shimmering figure that bustled along the same side of the road as me. It was a long time before I could see who it was. For a while it seemed that I would be passed by a woman in a long flowing dress before I was able to tell that it was a man in a habit.

He was in his fifties, his hair long and straggly. The sandals on his feet were almost falling apart, and the habit which at one time must have been brown was now bleached yellow on the shoulders. In his hand he carried a black tin box which he set down on the roadside.

He addressed me in a language I did not recognise and I indicated my incomprehension and uttered the single word, "English."

He nodded, his brow furrowed with compassion as he made the sign of hunger by pressing his fingers to his thumb in a cluster and pointing to his mouth. I indicated that I was OK, but he remained unconvinced. Then, leaning down he opened his metal box and pulled out half a loaf of bread wrapped in a piece of newspaper. He broke it into two approximate quarters and placed one of the pieces back into his case, handing me the other. As I took it and indicated my thanks I could feel that it was as hard as a rock. The old guy then put a hand on my shoulder and muttered something I guessed might have been a prayer of some sort. As I grinned rather inanely he turned and walked off down the road. Once more his form became androgynous before he began to shimmer. I put the bread to my lips and attempted a mouthful. It crumbled like sawdust into my dry mouth and I turned to show the monk that I was eating his gift, but by now he had disappeared into the growing shadows that indicated the beginning of evening.

I found this whole vignette incredibly moving and a very pure Christian act. I did not want to think like this; I was trying hard to be an atheist, but the old guy who obviously had nothing had shared his pittance with me. I was even more determined to carry on, and in the late evening got a lift that took me a long way in the right direction.

The road was long and straight and the surrounding countryside flat and dull. My last lift had turned off the road to some small village and I was left high and dry.

High through lack of food, and dry for lack of water. I mused on the lesson of Steve's monkey. Just when I had learned how to go without food or water I died. Way down the road was a bridge. I toyed with the idea of walking towards it, but decided as the road was so straight there was little purpose in moving from where I was. The sun was high in the sky; it must have been around two in the afternoon (you get to read shadow lengths after a while). I was gritty and sore-eyed, in need of a shower, irritable with the lack of traffic, and resigned to the unlikelihood of getting a lift.

Ever since I was a little boy I had set myself rituals that could either make things happen or stop bad things from happening, like not treading on the lines in paving stones in case the lions got me, or counting the telegraph poles that whizzed past the train carriage window to stop the train from crashing.

At first I tried not looking at an approaching vehicle until the volume of its engine had reached a certain level. Next, using the international signal of sticking out the thumb I held my Zippo in my fist. After several hours I remembered my lucky farthing (it had got me through the eleven-plus), but couldn't find it. Then I began to intone, mantra-like, the destination "Greece Greece" whilst using a rhythmic movement with my hand in synchronised movement with my lips. It must have looked to the oncoming lorry drivers as though I simply had a mad grin and St Vitus dance.

I was beginning to crack. Here I was, broke, starving, no money, a bag of grubby bits and pieces and a bundle of splintered wood and strings inside my guitar case. And my magic was not working.

I decided to move on down the road towards the bridge. As I got nearer I could see that it spanned a single track railway line which continued stretching as far as I cold see over the flat landscape. I was aware of standing in the centre of a cross, the road running north to south and the railway east to west. Leaving my small bag and my broken guitar on the other side of the road, I crossed over to lean on the railing and look out eastward. Underneath me stretched the rails, and in front of me was a largish pond, with a dead tree near the water's edge. The bark had fallen off from a large part of the trunk and my eyes slowly climbed up the tree to the skeletal bare branches at the top. There, completely at peace and a still as a statue, sat a heron.

My first sighting of this dignified bird was the day my brother Bruce stopped the train. We had been on a trip to see Grandma and Grandad in Brackley. The railway line to Brackley had recently been converted to a mere connecting service with a two-coach diesel shuttle, where previously we had been able to travel all the way there by steam train from London.

My mum and her sister had been visiting their parents, and Bruce and I had gone off to the 'echo bridge' with my pretty cousin Christine. She had been intent on picking moon daisies, and in order to impress her both Bruce and I had picked bundles. There was an abundance of flowers in the fields, but the best ones grew on the bank of the railway cutting, so we clambered down to pick them. There was never any thought of danger as we scampered about running backward and forward across the single line. Suddenly in the warm air there was a sound completely at odds with the humming of summer, as a train siren shattered the stillness. I was at the top of the embankment and Christine about halfway up. Bruce was at the bottom and the driver of the train had clearly only sought to warn us of his approach. We all looked in the direction of the train and I shouted unnecessarily at my little brother to come up away from the lines. The train looked so small and far away, but I was still concerned for Bruce; he however merely walked on to the track and assumed the position of a copper on point duty holding up his arms in the formal position of stopping traffic.

Christine and I screamed at him to move out of the way as the train grew larger and the danger more imminent. Still he stood there. The train applied its brakes and I swear it only came to a halt about six feet from where Bruce stood. Chris and I were both nearly hoarse with screaming and terror. Once the train had stopped Bruce hightailed it up the bank and the three of us scurried away over the fields.

Secretly I was impressed with his bravado, and I am sure he had hoped that Christine was as well. We soon pushed the incident to the back of our minds in the ripening fields as insects buzzed the afternoon away. After an hour or two we began our journey back to Grandma's, and after calling our names to the echo bridge and before the last stile, we saw the heron.

It was standing so still at the water's edge in the bend of the Ouse. Even though it was in its rightful place, it made me jump to see it. I thought it was beautiful and couldn't wait to tell everyone about it. As we ascended the last field before the main road a policeman apprehended us. I was terrified again, guessing correctly what he wanted.

He asked where we lived, and he escorted us home, where we were sent out in the garden whilst he warned our two mums about the seriousness of what had occurred. It finished up, so I am told, with Mum and my aunt offering to go around and scrub the police station steps so long as it was all forgotten.

In the end the railway police got involved, and I was promised a thrashing by my headmaster in front of the school, but this was finally reduced to being let off with a caution. Having experienced Mr. Wilson's savagery with a cane before, I was very relieved but still very cross with Bruce.

When I eventually told Mum about the sighting of the heron, she told me that Grandad had once found a moorhen's nest at that point and had taken some of her eggs and fried them for breakfast. It seemed wrong to steal the eggs and eat them, but somehow I was glad that Grandad, who did not seem to get much, at least had that little treat.

I stood looking at the heron on top of the tree. It was so still that I deliberately made a noise to see if it was real. A lorry thundered past, and it merely looked in the direction of the road. Eventually a train of three or four coaches passed under the bridge and into the vast middle distance and oblivion: the bird did not even acknowledge its passing. I re-crossed the road to where I could watch the bird and look towards the horizon in every direction. Then I found my lucky farthing in my Levis mini pocket.

A truck passed me and there was a shudder of brakes as he pulled up some yards away. I grabbed my bag and broken guitar and ran to the truck and surprised myself by my leap into the cab. The driver indicated that he wasn't going far, but that was OK; I was on the move again and the border was getting nearer. He let me out at a gas station and I filled my lighter with a few drops of fuel left in one of the pipes from one of the pumps. Luckily I survived the thick black smoke that came from the wick each time I lit up. The fuel soon evaporated and I rationed my cigarettes. The driver bought me a coffee before we parted and he turned off the main drag, and I trundled onward down the road and watched the shadows grow.

That evening an old Opel Rekord pulled up with four Greek guys and two English girls crammed into it. Even my broken guitar failed to put them off giving me a lift, and in great high spirits they rearranged the interior and somehow got us all back into the vehicle, its back axle periodically giving out ominous sounds as we lurched onward until, singing and shouting, they joyfully approached the border of home. The two girls and I had to get out before the border whilst our hosts did their paperwork, and we simply walked out of Yugoslavia and into Greece.

Just over the other side, the car pulled up again; we were invited back in and carried to the remains of some ancient courtyard where there was an abundance of fresh flowing water. Some of the blokes in the car stripped off and proceeded to wash themselves and so, cautiously, did I. My own skinny white body with the brown arms in contrast to their muscled olive torsos: I wondered if we were cleansing ourselves from our journey or baptising ourselves for our arrival? Suddenly the sound of jangling bells combined with ground shaking thundering made me lift up my head. Round the corner of the remains of the wall, apparently out of control, roared a horse and cart. The horse looked as shocked and surprised as we were to find anyone else there at this fine time in the morning. Soon the men were all shouting loudly and happily together, birds were singing, the sun was just clearing the horizon and there was a bright freshness at the start of this day. The contrast between the two countries was extreme. We were inside Greece and there were advertisements and posters to look at and happy people, shouting and joking together, *and* there were these two girls.

They were both from Manchester and had taken two days to hitch-hike through Yugoslavia (it had taken me a week). One, called Diane, was deeply attractive; the other one was a sweet blonde girl with larger features and her name was Margaret. Neither of them took much notice of me, but they did say they were headed for Thessalonika and maybe Athens, so I said that I would see them again. They wished me good luck and climbed back into the car with the Greek lads who had been guest Arbeiters in Germany and were returning with pockets of cash to their various villages. They told me I was welcome to join them but they were far too overcrowded; I declined and they waved me goodbye.

As the old car took off down the road with them all singing again, I took out the packet of cigarettes. There was still one left, and using my fuelless method, lit up and took a big drag. Greece looked wonderful; the early mists were clearing, and the bloke with the horse gave me a lift back to the main road with my bundle of firewood and strings rattling inside the guitar case.

From my pocket I pulled a piece of paper that had the address '*Oddos Pringiposs Nickalau*' written on it. This was the place that I was to meet Olaf and possibly these two girls. I wondered how this word was pronounced, but figured once into the town I would soon find someone who would point me in the right direction. Saloniki (as the locals call it) was a wonderful place, old and crumbling in places, with people spilling out on to the pavements and spending all day over one cup of coffee.

Outside the hostel and across the road, groups of impossibly handsome young men lounged around eyeing the girls that went in and out of the old wooden door of the student hostel. It was run by an old bloke and his wife, who were very easygoing. Olaf had been there for several days. When he saw the remains of my guitar his sympathy was great and his help practical. One evening he had been strumming along by himself and a group of young lads about fifteen years old had gathered round to watch him. Eventually one of them (Nick) had approached Olaf and struck up a conversation. Olaf had told them about this friend who could play and it seemed they were most anxious to meet me.

"They'll know someone who can help, I am sure, Ralph," he said. I was further reassured when I met these kids. They were very polite and spoke just a few words of English. Olaf got me to play his twelve-string and they told me they knew this old guitar repairer in the town who they thought could fix the wreckage of my instrument. The only problem was that I had no money now and did not feel like playing on my own with Olaf's guitar. The boys, however, had a plan. The next day when they came to take me to the luthier, they explained their scheme.

On Saturday afternoon at the local cinema there was a matinee for young people. The boys had an electric guitar that I would play, and had fixed up a microphone. They had told their friends that they had met this singing star from England and that I could play a Bob Dylan song and could play the guitar really fast and that I would perform for them all. It did not seem likely that my nerves would let me do this, but when I saw the inside of the old craftsman's shop I felt confident enough to leave the guitar with him, and now I had to have money to pay for the work, I agreed to their plan.

The weather was very hot, and as the day grew nearer, I started to wonder what a rock'n'roll singer would wear for the occasion. My wardrobe was scant, but at the bottom of my bag, and by now very crumpled, was my jean jacket and I decided that this would be the item to wow them in the aisles. A good jean jacket has been a fashion item since *The Grapes of Wrath* and I would have loved a genuine Levis one, but of course they were too expensive to take as road wear. Mine came from Millets. It was at least two sizes too big for me—and at six foot two, that made it very big indeed. But I wore it with the sleeves rolled up and was quite content.

On the morning of the show I thought very carefully about which crumpled t-shirt I should wear. In the end I opted for my denim shirt. By midday the weather was unbelievably hot, and once inside the cinema it was stifling. The noise from the audience was deafening. Finally young Nick went out and tried to calm them down before announcing me, and out I walked to an enormous noise and applause. Nick handed me the horrible guitar and plugged it in and off I went.

Immediately sweat coursed down my forehead and my hands were wringing wet within the first number. Afterwards Olaf asked me how I had managed to produce so much liquid, for after half a dozen songs I came off as if I had just swam twenty lengths. The audience went wild, and I realised at that moment what pop stars experience and knew that, although it was fun, it had nothing to do with what I hoped for from music.

On the Wednesday I went to the luthier for my guitar. He expressed doubts that it should be strung with steel strings, but I explained through Nick that it was an American guitar and he said that he thought it was a very fine instrument. I beamed with delight in the reflected glory of ownership and amazed at the price he charged me for the repair. It worked out at about three pounds, and as I had earned five for my performance, I was delighted. That night Olaf went out and played the local cafés and added to our little pile of drachmas.

There were piles of young hitchhikers and travellers passing through the town, and one day the two girls who I'd met arrived in the hostel. I introduced them to Olaf, who made his usual impression, and by the end of the evening Diane was obviously besotted. For the next few days they came out and bottled for us and we did quite well. Diane and Olaf became very intense, and I was sort of lumbered with Margaret, who wasn't romantically attracted to me but was at a bit of a loose end without her mate. We had nothing in common. Although only a working class lad from south London, I was interested in the arts and music in particular. Margaret was interested in hairdressing and in the mornings emerged from the girls' side of the hostel as if she was going to the Streatham Locarno. With coiffed hair, lipstick and makeup, she made the best of herself, but for the life of me I could not fathom what she was doing on the road (in fairness, I would have been hard pressed to explain my own motives).

Margaret was very down-to-earth, and in spite of appearances very practical, whilst Diane was not so bright and rather languid. Her skin had turned a lovely golden colour whilst Margaret was sort of pinky red and she frequently looked overheated with tiny drops of perspiration on her top lip. There is no doubt that the two girls increased our turnover, but as company I didn't really want to be around them.

Olaf was happy to be getting his oats, but slowly he realised that Diane was not the woman of his dreams. One morning I noticed bruising to her face. The sullenness from Olaf was deep and dark, and I was horrified to think that he may have beaten her. About this time I began to feel a bit of resentment towards Olaf, as I felt he contributed little to our income. He was not a natural musician but had taken up the guitar rather like growing your hair long: it was more a badge of belonging than a desire to make music. He seldom practised and had not improved at all since we started. And he hardly ever sang.

As I was doing the lion's share I felt I should be getting more out of it, yet I had to admit I was still not ready to go it alone. I never questioned Olaf about the intimacy of his relationship. He must have assumed that I knew; he did not attempt to hide his annoyance with Diane, and frequently ignored her and went out with me in the evenings. By now we knew our way around Saloniki and had found some cheap places to eat and drink. I had my first retsina there, and as all the meat seemed to be grilled and there were chips with everything I was very happy. I even began eating olives and relished the tomatoes that were served with everything.

Olaf frequently drank to excess. He could drink until he was almost incapable of speech, then go out and throw up, only to begin drinking again. He would stagger to the door and roar out into the street "I'm a focking Viking! We drink, we fall down, we throw up and then we focking drink again." With that he would poke his fingers down his throat and chuck into the gutter. Not always accurate, he would often soil his shirt and trousers, but in the morning express no remorse or contrition. I found this embarrassing. I even thought his pronunciation 'focking' sounded stupid. I was definitely getting the ache with him.

To get away from all of this I made an aborted attempt to go to Athens. My hitchhiking hit an all-time low on this trip, and I found myself stranded miles from anywhere when the heavens suddenly opened. There was no shelter anywhere, and within a few seconds I was drenched to the skin. As it was too late to do anything about my own condition, I transferred my thoughts to the guitar and to my relief spotted a bridge over a dried-up river bed. I scurried over to it with my belongings and watched in disbelief as the rain thundered down. As I gazed out from underneath the parapet, I became aware of a new sound. It was a gentle but insistent roaring, and as I looked up the river bed, I could see way off in the distance a wall of water moving down the dry bottom of the course. I reached into my bag, pulled out the little camera and jumped down into the middle of the dry stream. I looked through the viewfinder as the wall of water got ever closer. Wait—wait—nearly… right now! The water filled the frame, I pressed the shutter and let the camera drop to my chest.

When I looked up at the scene before me I nearly died of terror. The viewfinder had made the water seem small and a long way off, when in reality it was huge and only a few feet away from me. I barely made the safety of the bank before a six foot wall of water swept past which would have certainly carried me away. I sat under the bridge shaking for a long time before venturing back on to the roadside again.

Once back in Saloniki I resumed playing, and in spite of warnings by the police that it was not allowed, Olaf and I got quite blasé about the risk of arrest. A certain recklessness had begun to creep into our lifestyle and personally I felt too far away from home to think about going anywhere but onward, so I had shed what remained of my natural caution. We were enjoying a modest but reasonable lifestyle for two road rats, and for me, apart from the odd unbelievable hangover, life was fun.

I stayed most of the time in the hostel and Olaf stayed in different places with Diane, but their relationship was floundering and it was plain that they should part. It was just that to get regular sex with a pretty girl was hard for Olaf to turn down even though the result of it revealed a darker side to his nature. I was jealous but not envious of his situation; I was not tempted to pursue Margaret and was determined to keep my promise to stay true to Gill. And I was a martyr to that promise until one afternoon a beautiful sun-tanned girl called Carol arrived with two others at the hostel. Her hair was black and she wore a simple shift dress in sun-faded deep pink. She was beautifully tanned and she moved around in a totally uninhibited way with just a hint of gaucheness. I was stunned; she had a wonderful figure and my eyes followed her everywhere. She was oblivious of me, and although I was sure she must have noticed my open-mouthed staring over the next couple of days she gave no indication of having seen me. Her voice was raspy and quite deep but her accent was bloody awful. This helped me when I was all but convulsed with lust for her. Anyway, she was a party girl and had already caught the attention of some of the Greek boys who hung around the hostel. I realised I had no chance.

The next night, after repeated cautions, I was arrested and taken to the police cells. It was actually not too bad and I was not perturbed by the experience. For some reason Olaf was not banged up with me, so the following day when I was released, I seemed to have gained some cachet. As I sat outside at the café I noticed that Carol was looking at me—though she looked away as soon as I caught her eye. My heart thumped.

I could no longer play in the street without real risk, so it was definitely time to move on. That night, however, there was an outing arranged with some of the kids and a boat trip across to some beach café. This did not sound hip to me, but I was at a loose end, so I went. Carol was very close to me for part of the way, but I managed not one word. We tipped off the boat and trooped to the café, where I was surprised to find a number of Greek gentlemen, some in their forties, sitting at the tables we were to occupy. Food was ordered, and being close to Carol again I could only pick at mine. All the time I puzzled over our mixed company. I was suspicious, but I can only say that these suspicions were unfounded or plans thwarted, because at the end of our meal, with much jollity and wine, we were decanted back to the boat. Carol, who was all but falling out of her dress, was a little tipsy and was talking to me in her horrible accent, now slightly slurred.

I, too, had drunk quite a bit, and one thing led to another. By the time we were on our own we were both consumed with passion and had absolutely nowhere to go. I remembered the showers downstairs, and there in the darkness, fumbling and groping, we were about to consummate the evening. Suddenly the door swung open and a fat German kid entered wearing only a towel and proceeded to have a cold shower. His appearance had the effect of a cold shower on Carol, who hurried from the scene, and I limped off to my bunk in pain and frustration.

The next day she shipped out early, leaving me an address in Cambridge. I reasoned that it was probably for the best and my vow was still intact. I felt righteous and I really had to go. I had my reserve couple of English pounds and my dollar bill, but my drachmas were getting low. In order to soften Olaf's split with Diane, we took her and Margaret as hitchhiking companions part of the way to the border. Poor Margaret, she could not believe how long she had to wait for a lift with me. I, on the other hand, could not believe how easy it was with her.

Actually, travelling with her was good fun. We had decided to enter Turkey via Greece instead of Bulgaria, and she was happy to accompany me. She was ready to go home and our lack of emotional attachment meant that we could have a few laughs on the way—though she was worried about Olaf's temper, and thought her friend was being a silly cow. At a prearranged place the two girls met up and we said our goodbyes. We swapped addresses and I walked down the road first, leaving Olaf to sort out his departure without me looking on.

Once out of sight I felt again that delicious sense of freedom from any responsibility that I have only glimpsed since on one or two occasions. I guess you have to have a sense of responsibility in the first place in order to experience it, and there are those who need to feel it all the time. For me, though, the feeling comes so rarely that I remember each time with relish, and as I walked down the proverbial dusty road with my bedroll and guitar on my back, cigarette in my mouth and a few coins in my pocket, I was about as happy as I've ever been.

I never saw Diane again, though I did meet Carol once more one November. How strange her appearance seemed then: sallow not tanned, woollen-stockinged not brown-limbed, hair combed and parted not free and sun-bleached.

There was a detachment of the Greek army at the border, and relations between the two countries were intense. That night I slept in a noisy field where huge creatures of the night rustled and grunted, fussed and scampered all around me under a sky full of the brightest stars. I felt free and unencumbered again, and kept awake by the marvellous heart-racing Turkish coffee that the last lorry driver had bought me.

The border was a very uptight spot from the Greek side, but once across, the Turkish soldiers were just hanging about, leaning on walls and smoking, hardly taking any notice of me. True, there was not much activity at the border, and virtually no vehicles seemed to be crossing, but nevertheless they were pretty laid back. It was a very hot day and there was a lot of dust in the air; my eyes and nose were streaming as I squinted westward, searching the dry terrain for vehicles. I suppose I had been walking and thumbing for about an hour or two, when a battered saloon car screeched to a halt in a cloud of dust and a youngish bloke beckoned me in.

The inside of the car was full of dust, and my jeans resembled those of a plasterer's labourer as soon as I sat down. The road was rocky and bumpy and the driver was anxious to show me how fast he could nego-tiate the obstacles in our way. After a couple of miles, he stopped and picked up a German couple, and seemed to be more at ease with them than me. He even managed a few words of German. He then stopped for another Turkish hitchhiker, who dominated the conversation as we rattled onward.

We were a dust storm on wheels. If we closed the windows it poured through the gaps in the ancient ill-fitting doors and we nearly suffocated in the heat, so we opted for leaving the windows open and trying to breathe through the sleeves of our shirts. The good news was that he was going all the way to Istanbul. Perhaps my luck was changing.

∽

bosporus

If I had felt alien in Yugoslavia, I felt like an extraterrestrial in Istanbul. The city is awesome, not just for its magnificent appearance but because each building that glorifies God is in support of a different belief system. Here I was, trying to shake off the burden of Christianity, in the midst of a culture that I was totally unprepared for. In my boldness to reject, I had not realised the comfort still to be had from crucifixes on top of churches I had no plans to visit. Here on top of these stunning buildings rested something that to me resembled a pair of horns. Old burial grounds, their graves marked with pillars and spheres, promised a different paradise and comfort.

There was so much to feast my eyes on, and the smells of the place too, for at every street corner there was something being cooked over charcoal, and sharp smoky smells drifted in the sultriness of an overcast sky that was being jabbed by these needle-like minarets. Add to this the sounds of strange meandering music of quarter tones and cymbals, and the cantors calling the faithful to payer with the sound of sirens from ships on the magnificent Bosporus.

I was lost in a movie in which I had no useful lines to utter, and had no door by which I could leave. Of course I had no money but that was not a problem. I was approached all the time by rough looking blokes offering to change any western currency that I did have. I still had a few lire left and two English pounds that I had planned to save for an emergency and this was it. I hustled a bit and got quite a good rate of exchange, I thought, and made my way to where I was advised I could get a cheap room at the American student hostel, near the Topkapi museum.

I eventually found my way there, but it was way too expensive for me and anyway the sort of people that were staying there were on holiday! Not like me of course... Thankfully Olaf, who had arrived before me, had left me a note telling me to meet him at the Guilharne hotel which was not far away. I was unprepared for how happy I was to see him again. After a few days it was quite like old times, as there were no girls involved and we were back working the streets around the Gelata Bridge that links Europe and Asia.

The hotel was tiny with hardly any facilities apart from our tiny cell of a room in which there were three beds. We found another young English bloke there called Tim and we soon got him switched to our room and became friendly. He was younger than me and very confident in himself. I guessed correctly that he had been to boarding school. He was dressed beyond street fashion in white jeans and a checked cotton shirt and wore heavy brogues and woollen socks. He had an enormous suitcase. In spite of his confidence and our warnings, he managed to lose his passport by being bladed in the Bazaar. What happens is that the thief walks behind you and, with an incredibly sharp knife, slits your back pocket down one side from the bottom to the top. This action cannot be felt by the victim and if the thief is patient it is only a matter of time before the item slips out on to the ground.

As Tim walked into the room one night I had the satisfaction of telling him that I knew he had lost his passport because I could see the pocket flapping open. I had sewn a pocket inside my jeans where I kept my passport and pathetic valuables. Poor Tim handled his embarrassment well, and we were all supportive. After the usual bureaucratic hassle he got a new one issued in Istanbul, which was rather special.

It was noticeable how much less we were able to take from the punters on the street. At first it was such a novelty for the local population to see two western European kids busking (in reality, begging) that we did OK, but I found myself getting very uncomfortable about the numbers of dreadfully deformed beggars who were forced to make a living from our same customers, especially when I found out that they had to pay rent for their wretched pitches from street landlord gangsters.

At first, though, it was great. During the days I would wander about for hours walking in the Bazaar until the locals stopped trying to sell me things. Sometimes the merchants would invite me in to take *chai*—small glasses of tea with a sugar lump—and I would talk a little about England and tell them how wonderful it was. I bought Gill a tiny but perfectly painted segment of an ivory bracelet; I can still see the stylised face of the woman painted in miniature on its surface. The whole thing was only about three quarters of an inch square, but it was very old and I knew she would love it. I bought my mum some earrings, fashioned, I was assured, from pieces of harem jewellery (which she still has), and from my proceeds of busking I bought myself a suede jean jacket.

I am confident that this was one of the first ever suede jean jackets, and for days I worked on the tailor to get the best price from him. When we finally agreed, he asked me to let him borrow the one I was wearing for a model, and I happily left it with him. A few days later it was ready, and I can remember the excitement I felt as I went to collect it. It was made of the very softest brown suede with suede-covered buttons. The stitching was in a slightly darker brown thread and the workmanship was of the highest quality. It was a faithful copy of the original jacket that I had loaned him, and like the original it was misshapen and two full sizes too big for me! I could not believe at first that he had done this, but realised that it was all my fault because he had asked me incredulously at the time if I was sure that I really wanted it like this. I had merely been amused because I thought his implication was that I should have let him build me a beautiful coat from the high quality suede and not a lowly jean jacket. I now saw, too late, that it was the quality of the mother garment that he had alluded to. Instead of one pathetic misshapen ill-fitting coat, I now had two. Never mind, it was the price one had to pay to be a Trend Setter.

Food was cheap and mostly we ate on the street. There were street vendors all over the place, selling grilled corn on the cob to fishermen, and sardines, fresh from the Bosporus, cooked on tiny stoves in the boat and slapped between a bread roll with a sprinkle of salt. You could buy these for the equivalent of twopence in old money, and I ate one of these every day. There were kebabs, and in the evenings an occasional ice cream to complement the little hash we managed to score.

Hash was easy to find. It came wrapped in cellophane with a little crown or insignia pressed into the substance to guarantee quality. We used Olaf's pipe, and wandering around the old town in this state was a particularly pleasant experience. So was the ice cream.

One night, the most pungent smells were emanating from the next room, accompanied by the playing of the Turkish lute and flute. The smells were clearly very high grade marijuana, and the music was getting more excited and way out. Olaf insisted that we should check it out, and we knocked on their door. The occupants shouted something and we walked in. There propped up on a bed against the party wall sat three very stoned geezers, who just grinned at our look of astonishment. One of them was playing the lute, and perched on a small chair at the end of the bed sat the flute player. Without a hint of shyness, Olaf gestured rather grandly that they should continue playing, for which they needed no encouragement.

Tim, Olaf and myself crammed into this tiny room with these poor men, all of whom were manual workers and amateur musicians; they were stripped down to ragged vests and tattered work trousers whilst we were dressed in comparative finery of dirty Levis and grubby shirts. We grinned and made signs of approval at their music across a tiny overcrowded room full of smoke and sweat. It was great, and, a little bit stoned, Olaf insisted that I get my guitar and play for the men, which I did. It doesn't matter that one is no good, it is only important that music is shared.

Our mutual destination was still India, but I was beginning to be unsure. The poverty around us was impossible to ignore. I always dropped my very small change in the lap of a young lad with withered legs who sat on the pavement near the bridge where we liked to play. He certainly knew me by the end of my stay, but he never acknowledged me or thanked me for my small donation. I think I accepted this lack of appreciation as silent admonishment for doing what I was doing not out of real necessity but for adventure, whilst his very life depended on it. Certainly my life depended on this method of fund-raising, and I contented myself with the knowledge that Olaf depended on it as well.

Then there was Wendy and Tina. I cannot recall how we met, only that they appeared on our scene and, with a great deal of bravado, offered to bottle for us for the usual ten per cent. They came from Portsmouth, and were brave and fun to be around. They had great accents and seemed ready for anything, and soon they were our regular bottlers. Our income went up and we were all happy with the arrangement.

We had no particular work times, but we favoured a pitch on the Gelata Bridge where there was a slight indent, so we could stand and play while people could still pass by. Soon, with these two pretty girls bottling and the strange music emanating from our guitars, we had a huge crowd around us. I was beginning to get concerned as the crowd spilled over from the path into the road. The only thing we could have done would have been to stop playing, and we were on to too good a thing, so I just looked the other way.

Down below us in the waters of the Bosporus, boatmen ferried their craft under the floating bridge in both directions; some hauled huge numbers of barges behind them as they skilfully manoeuvred them between the stansions on the pontoons. To my horror, I looked down at an approaching boat with at least five container barges in tow, each one being about thirty feet long. He had made the mistake of slowing down slightly, the better to see what the crowd gathered on the bridge was all about. In so doing, the last barge had begun to drift round to his right and was now totally out of alignment with the arch on the bridge that he was intending to steer through.

I momentarily stopped playing to wave to him to look round at the back of his boat, but the poor man thought I was waving a greeting at him and he waved back to me. He even slowed down more and I shouted to Olaf to have a look at what was about to happen below us.

By now the last barge had pulled two more craft out of line and itself was lying at a perfect right angle to the bridge. Olaf and I stopped playing and waited for the inevitable. The boatman below us entered the arch under us at about the same time as the rear boat crashed into the upright. The whole bridge shook as the little convoy of carriers wrapped themselves round the bridge, and a great tide of swearing and shouting greeted our ears. The crowd surged forward, and we were nearly pushed over the bridge before we grabbed our instruments and threw them into their cases and made off just before the cops arrived to add to the chaos. Thereafter we selected less prone places to play.

There was a flat roof on the hotel which overlooked a small mosque, and I often sat there watching the ragged faithful going to prayers. I became fascinated, and several times visited the place with or without the congregation. It was perfectly still inside, and good to sit in contemplation from time to time. From the roof I could watch the caller psyching himself up for the job of uttering the faithful's call to prayer; he would spend several minutes walking around the platform of the minaret coughing and hawking, before a few warm-up notes emerged. Then once ready, he brought forth the most amazing noise from somewhere in his medium-sized frame. I sat partly hidden by the wall as his voice yodelled expertly between quarter tones of beauty and spirituality. Then, slowly through the door of the courtyard below, would come a trickle of men, who slipped off their shoes at the door and made their way inside for prayers.

Eventually I entered the Blue Mosque and was filled with awe at its beauty. I knew little of Islam and did not need to know much to find once again how affected I was by the corporate act of worship. Sat at the back of this magnificent building on ancient Turkish carpets, I looked towards the illuminated holy place at the front near the Imam as he took the men through their rituals. On the left stood a huge grandfather clock, to my mind oddly out of place, its slow tick there to remind us that our time is short on this Earth. I felt I had plenty of time and always felt refreshed and immortal after these short visits.

∽

spies

My daily rounds were spent in a regular fashion. For someone who had covered considerable distances overland, I moved very little from the immediate surroundings of my lodging. I would amble down to the ferry port for my bread and sardines or maybe a corn cob, and from there to the bazaar or a stroll in the Topkapi park—although I never thought of looking in the museum. I was content to soak up the atmosphere of this remarkable city and ponder not only the belief in Islam but the fact that here was the first country I had ever been in that was allied to Germany during two world wars, which felt strange. My lack of adventurous spirit provoked Olaf into suggesting a ferry trip to some places out on the Bosporus, and once convinced that I could afford it we agreed to go. The boat was reasonably modern and had a small lounge where we took chai. It was a slightly overcast day but the weather was warm. It felt odd to be travelling without the guitar, but once on our way, very pleasant.

We stopped once or twice and at the third place Olaf decided that we should have a beer. This inevitably led to another, and another, and though not drunk by any means we found ourselves relaxed enough to miss the ferry and discover that was the last one until the following day. We had nothing to get back for, and in Olaf's usual way he struck up a conversation with some local blokes who turned out to be fishermen.

As the effects of the beer wore off, the possibility of a night trip with them emerged—and as there was no way that I could get back to the city, the opportunity grew more and more attractive. Olaf had communicated that he was an ex-sailor, and they welcomed us aboard their small but efficient craft. We left the port under a beautiful sky and slid quietly over the velvety waters of the Bosporus and into the mysterious Black Sea. Slowly but certainly the night descended until the lights from shore were invisible and all we could focus on were the lights and characters on board. There were stars above us and the boat rocked gently to the hum of the diesel. It had been a long day and my eyes started to get so heavy that for once I owned up to tiredness and was shown a bunk on deck to use. In fact it was no more than a shelf that I slotted myself into. There was an incredibly smelly blanket which I gratefully wrapped around myself against the cold, and I fell into a dream-filled sleep.

I could only have been off for about an hour when my nightmares were interrupted by so much screaming and shouting that I banged my head on the low roof. I crawled out of my slot and dizzily remembered where I was. The boat was now rocking much more vigorously with the bigger swell. All around the boat, the crew of about five were screaming at each other as they pulled and hauled on nets that were bulging with an enormous catch. Olaf had his hands full and in a moment so did I. After a good fight we dragged the net over the side and a huge flipping and flopping and threshing mass of fish filled up the passageways and all around our feet, so much so that I instinctively tried to leap out of the way in case I hurt one of them. The fishermen were grinning hugely and pointing at Olaf and me as if we had been responsible for this windfall catch.

My God, I thought, how are they going to kill all these fish humanely?

My mind flashed with horror to a scene on Brighton pier during a Sunday School outing when a man, obviously in some kind of fishing competition, brought a beautiful shining mackerel from the sea and handed it to another man with some scales. My eyes wide with wonder I gazed on its shining colours as he cleverly removed the hook from its mouth and then with his index finger, he poked into the fish's gills and ripped them open. A gush of blood poured into the brass scale pan and I recoiled in horror as the creature gave a last desperate thrash and blood splattered across my arm from the twitching tail.

It soon dawned on me that this would not be the way of dispatching all of these. I remembered seeing someone once pick up a fish and beat its head on a rock to kill it and thought that this must be the way. But how long would that take? Suddenly there was a terrible scream and we all turned to face the direction of the cry. There on the other side of the boat, dramatically lit by the gas lanterns on the wheel house, was one of the fishermen, reeling and clutching his arm. All around his feet thrashed the recent catch, and lying where it had fallen from his arms was a giant ray which had bitten him.

One of the stricken man's colleagues rushed to his aid through the knee deep fish while another picked up the ray by the tail and beat it heavily against the wheel house as if to punish it for biting his friend. The ray began to die and the man it had bitten began to pass out. There was more shouting as he lost consciousness. By now another was at his side and with a knife slit open the dim mark on his arm, and like I had seen in films all my life, began to suck and spit out into the sea the poison that had paralysed his friend. The fish thrashed and the engine throbbed like some detached heartbeat.

I looked at Olaf. He looked grimly back. The injured man was now silent and I thought he had died. Blood dripped from his friend's mouth and wild eyes looked from face to face as if to see if they had missed something that might have helped the situation. Finally the man could be seen to be still breathing and was wrapped in a blanket and one of his friends sat with him as the boat turned round and headed back in the direction from which we had embarked hours before. Olaf and I had suddenly turned from good luck mascots to the bringers of misfortune; all fishermen are superstitious and we could feel their doubts. All I hoped was that we could make it back to shore before someone blamed us directly and threw us both overboard. I almost wished I was German and could remind them how we had stood together in common cause at Gallipoli. Fortunately, the man began to come round and we all gathered around him to commiserate, and as we were reassured and the atmosphere relaxed I crawled into a vacant slot and fell uneasily asleep again, to the diminishing sound of the last dying fish slapping out their long goodbyes to the evening and their unwilling participation in it.

I was awakened by a firm grip on my shoulder and being shaken by Olaf who whispered to me, "Don't say anything, just stay where you are and do not on any account move from here, I will be below you in the next bunk. An American patrol boat is pulling alongside. We've been seen trespassing in Russian waters. We must just be still or there could be a lot of trouble for all of us."

What else could go wrong? This fucking day-trip was becoming a real nightmare. I could hear the approach of the patrol boat and muffled voices speaking in English. The response in Turkish meant that there was a lot of bluff and playing dumb going on, but the clincher was the injured man who, though recovered, was putting on a good show of pain and injury. We were nearly home now and the light was coming up in stripes across the water. On inspection of the wounded man's arm, the patrol let the boat go with a stern warning. In a way our presence, which had landed them the catch and by so doing caused the injury, had paradoxically got us all out of another dangerous situation; we were once more the golden boys as we emerged from our bed-shelves blinking in the morning light.

Amongst the catch, we had brought up a beautiful orange conch shell, and as soon as he had removed the resident from its rightful place, one of the men handed it to me as a souvenir. He grinned at me, and as we said goodbye I think Olaf and I felt vindicated for all the luck we had brought them.[8]

As we stepped from the ferry that finally arrived and took us back to the city, I again experienced a lightness of step and a feeling that there was a lot of time on my side. But what I really wanted now was some sleep. Because of the size of our tiny room, I dragged my sleeping bag up to the roof of the Gulharne hotel and slept until evening when we went out to play.

I may have felt immortal, but I was not immune to the effects of an unbalanced diet and generally keeping in good health. The Turkish system of sanitation at this time was not great. True, we could flush the toilet and take cold showers, but only at certain times of the day. The reason given for this was that there was a crack in the main reservoir which supplied the city, and rather than face the cost of repair it was cheaper to turn off the water between certain hours. Of course we soon learned not to use the lavatory during this time, but some residents did. These places always stank, but during the hot weather, even after the

---

[8] I took the conch shell home for Mum, who gave it pride of place on her shelf in the living room until a horrible smell was traced to the inner ear of the shell. After a vigorous shaking some flies and maggots fell out, and we realised the fisherman had not quite removed the entire contents. We cleaned it all properly after that, and my mother has it still.

toughening-up process of life on the road, I was still nearly sick each time I had to use the place.

Hand-washing was also difficult, and washing of my nappy 'hand towel' simply never took place; it never even occurred to me to do so, and I barely had the opportunity to keep clean socks and pants together, let alone the other stuff. I did wash my jeans in the yard with a scrubbing brush, but this was more to keep them the right colour than for cleanliness.

Tim had moved on to Izmir, and Olaf and I had a Turkish bloke back in our room. I was the first one to get ill. It happened one afternoon that I began to feel hot and dizzy with stomach cramps. I barely made it back to the hotel, whereupon I threw up and had diarrhoea. I knew not to eat anything and even a drop of water went straight through me. After a day in bed in this state with just sips of water, I began to experience feelings of detachment and delirium. The bedclothes were too hot or too cold and constantly wet from sweating. I soon used up my aspirin, and knew enough to know that I must have mild dysentery. I couldn't bear staying in bed and after only a few days dragged myself up to the roof, where I rested as best I could. If you don't eat you can't throw up, so I didn't eat. After a week I was able to get about a little, and I began by eating a boiled egg, which I had to force down with a little dried bread.

Olaf had been very concerned for me, but suddenly now it was my turn. He became mega sick; his delirium was greater than mine and he was laid in a bed bath of sweat for two days. Often he was not able to hold on to the tiny amount of water that he had to drink in order not to dehydrate completely. Unfortunately this passed straight through him and soiled the already grubby bed coverings. This meant friendship above and beyond even what he had done for me, but thankfully he threw up mostly before it could arrive at the other end.

After several days in this state I eventually got him to eat an egg, and though we were both very weak we dragged ourselves out with the two girls from Portsmouth, who had begun to miss the few coins commission we had been able to provide. We must have lost about a stone between us, and we could ill afford that. Wendy and Tina were great; they both had such positive attitudes. I thought them invincible and they would have made great road companions. Wendy was the more glamorous of the pair; she wore a light denim shirt and tight blue jeans. Tina wore a dark green T-shirt and jeans, and both girls wore flip flops.

I mention this because by our standards even then, this mode of dress wouldn't have seemed provocative, but to the average Turkish male it was hard to control the passions aroused by their appearance. Olaf and I were totally unaware of any problems, then one day after a session which was cut short, Wendy suddenly burst into tears, and Tina soon joined her in floods. I was deeply shocked.

"What on earth is the matter?" I asked them.

"Oh Ralph, it's terrible out there," sobbed Wendy. "All the time they touch us and stroke us and I just can't take it any more."

I couldn't believe how naive I had been. I felt betrayed, and what compassion I may have felt for the poor repressed Turkish male vanished in a puff of righteous resentment for the way they had abused these two girls. Stupidly I had believed that the success we were enjoying was due to the strength and rightness of the music we were playing, when in reality these men (and they were all male) saw it only as an opportunity to fondle two young girls. I could only imagine the feelings of being cheap and available for these opportunistic thrill seekers. I did my best to comfort them, and indeed wished that my relationship had been a closer one to enable me to have done more, but it seemed that just being able to cry was therapy enough.

The whole Istanbul effect threw everything into a world of unreality: the minarets and wailing prayer callers, the sound of the music that wafted without beginning or end in a frenzy of what to our untutored ears sounded like acid ramblings (Turkish music is on the whole less melodic than music from further east). The strange smells and culture where ordinary men walked hand in hand down the street, the impression that dope gave that everything was vacillating between feelings of true adventure, alienation and homesickness; add to this the semi-hallucinatory and nauseous state we were in through illness, and I began to feel as if I was losing it.

Later, I realised that the reputation of English women was at an all-time low, due to various political scandals and stories of loose morals that filled the world's press. I supposed the Turkish men were rather like teenage boys who'd been told that if you blew smoke into a girl's eye without her noticing, she would not be able to resist any advance made to her, and would surrender her most intimate secrets. These ignorant boys/men must have felt Wendy and Tina were there for the taking.

Anyway true to past form, the two girls recovered themselves. Having a good cry both relieved their tension and also reassured me that they were not as tough as they would have liked us to believe (I still felt they were probably tougher than me). I determined that we would not work with them again so they should not be exposed to such treatment, and if we had to, just the pair of us would play, and so it was. I also decided that I did not want to go on any further east and I think that the girls, who had talked about accompanying us, decided that this was far enough for them too. I wanted to attack the men who had done these things, and I didn't like the way I had been made to feel. There was some satisfaction to be had when Wendy told me that she had drawn blood with the aid of my harmonica harness as she fended off a late advance from a bloke who was still trying to touch her even as we were packing up. I felt sick.

That evening I told Olaf that I'd had it and that I wanted to go back to Greece. He too had abandoned his plans to go on. There was only one problem: he felt unable to make the journey at that moment and he knew that I could not face playing on my own even though I was fed up with his contribution and felt that I did all the work.

"I've thought of that," I countered. "When I get to Saloniki I'm going to sell some blood at the hospital."

Olaf blearily looked up at me from the bed.

"You're focking mad man, you're not well enough to sell blood. You need all the focking blood you got at the moment. Stay a few days, we'll find another couple of chicks to go bottling and then we'll head back."

My mind was made up, and his inference that I was weak immediately strengthened my resolve to get back on the road to where I felt I could cope. I said goodbye to the girls, who looked a bit sad, and left for Greece the next day.

The sun beat down and I was cold and shivering one minute then sweating the next. In the cars that stopped I slept fitfully, to wake with my collar soaked. I could force no food down me, but at least I could manage to keep water inside. I arrived in Saloniki, and with almost my last money checked into the hostel and fell asleep on the bunk in the shared room. The next morning I bought a yoghurt and ate some bread. Outside, the heat was fantastic, but I felt better from my night in a real bed, even though the sounds of disjointed conversation drifted in and out of my half sleep.

With the sun blazing down on me, I wandered off to the hospital and

joined a queue of hopeful donors, all about my age, who had gathered
to sell their blood. My turn came to be assessed and the nurse strapped
on the blood pressure measure. I was turned down out of hand. I was
deeply upset and near panic; I had been relying on the thirty drachmas
that I would get for the pint and felt that this would have been enough
to get me through Yugoslavia. I staggered out into the bright sunlight
and a young American came out after me. He was looking at the tiny
plaster that covered the vein in the crook of his elbow, like a kid admires
his first tattoo. We looked at each other and he grinned.

"That wasn't too bad," he said.

"They wouldn't take mine," I told him.

"Your pressure was probably too low, try running around the block,
someone tells me that works."

I watched him move off, still looking at his plaster. It was worth a
go, I decided, and off I set around the donor clinic in the midday heat.
The queue when I returned was now much smaller, but I failed to make
the test again and wandered despondent into the waiting room to rest.
Suddenly, without explanation, I was summoned to a screen and a small
sample of blood taken for analysis. I said nothing and after a little while
a nurse came back into the room and told me they would take my pint
in a few minutes. I don't know what made them change their minds,
but I was very reassured that at least I would have enough money now
to get back to Italy.

It was very nearly my turn to go into the donor room when a young
bloke with glasses and a pretty girlfriend, who had been talking earnestly
for several minutes, stood up and made the following statement:

"Listen everybody, I think that there is something you ought to know.
The blood you are planning to sell is being paid for by gangsters. Yes, I
know that sounds hard to believe, but these unscrupulous men pay you a
pittance for your blood and then sell it to the needy patient for whatever
they can make these poor distressed people pay."

He paused to let the enormity of this fact sink in. I was appalled, but
desperate for the thirty drachmas.

Christ, I thought, I know what he's going to do, he's going to organise
a strike for more money. I'll back him up. I stood shakily to my feet.

"Hey man, we're with you, that's a terrible thing to do to someone
who needs blood, What do you want us to do?"

I had noticed this bloke around the hostel and he seemed a thoroughly decent chap, he'll see us right I thought.

"Thank you brother," he said looking straight at me.

Brother, I thought. The man's a socialist all right, he'll get us more money from these bastards.

"This shameful exploitation of the impoverished working class must stop and this is what I propose..."

Absolutely, I thought. Here we are, the working class on the roads of Europe armed only with good intent and our music, not wishing to harm anyone, and these ruthless bastards were prepared to prey on us like parasites, literally bleeding us to provide them with a living.

"Go on brother," I urged, "tell us your plan."

"Thank you for your support brother," he said again, and then turning to the other rag tag crew he continued, "This exploitation can only stop if we the suppliers get together and attempt to break their grip on the supply."

By this time one or two others were looking up and offering some solidarity, it was quite stirring actually. Our spokesman continued.

"I have been discussing it with my girlfriend and this is what I suggest we do. We give our blood..."

"Yes, yes..." I hung on to every word.

"and when they come to give us their lousy thirty drachmas..."

"Yes yes..." I was still with him.

"We tell them we don't want their lousy blood money..."

"And we demand more!" shouted an excited American across the room.

"No, no, on the contrary," continued young Lenin, "we tell them we are donating it to the hospital for free!"

At the delivery of his final comment he glanced around the room, his eyes blazing with passion, and they alighted on me. Up to this point I was sure that he was going to demand at least double for the blood, and now faced with a much more honourable choice, I was scuppered.

"What do you say brothers and sisters?" he demanded. Some of the crowd (maybe two others) agreed, and I was reluctantly about to do the same when his girlfriend chimed in, her pretty face glowing with indignation, "Well I'm selling mine! We've got no money left to speak of and he's typically trying to prick your consciences over some stupid principle that won't change anything."

Ignoring her, young Trotsky shouted once more, "All those in favour please raise your hands!" I did not raise mine and instead went out of the room for a smoke. When I got back the two young socialists were donating and I was called next and went into the bright room.

The needle was blunt when it was plunged into my arm, and the poor girl had several painful lunges before she got a satisfactory purchase. By now I was feeling sick, and they told me to pump my hand open and closed to help fill up the jar. After about five minutes and not a drop in it, they worked out that there was a blockage in the needle tube and so had to start again. Once more the bloody blunt tube was poked into another part of the vein, and this time, with the pressure I had built up, blood spurted into the jar. Of course I made the mistake of looking round at this point, and it was as if the blood in the jar was leaving my brain in equal measures. I started to pass out.

After a little while I came to, only to find that the needle tube had come loose and a rather large amount of blood had spilled on to the floor. A nurse shouted helpfully at me and lifted my now dead arm on to the bed and told me to pump my fist open and closed again. This I did until my hand was barely able to move and my whole arm was aching. Finally the same nurse came over, pulled the needle tube from my bloody lacerated arm, slipped a piece of lint over the wounds and told me to place my hand on the shoulder until the bleeding stopped. This was easier said than done, and after several checks and it was still bleeding, I tried to eat the dry biscuit they gave me but was unable. I swallowed down the tiny glass of orange juice, signed a piece of paper written in Greek and staggered out into the blinding heat of the afternoon and back to the hostel. I was nearly at my room when consciousness left me.

I came to two days later and Olaf was sitting by the bed telling me what a fool I was, as if I needed telling.

❧

tenner

Olaf, who had arrived just that morning, was perturbed by my condition and grateful for my support in Istanbul while he was ill, but as weak as I felt I just wanted to get away and get back to Italy where I felt that I could repair the damage I had done to myself and earn some money without the risk of arrest again; I had already spent one night in the cells here. I literally dragged myself out of the bed, and after sharing a coffee with Olaf I told him I was heading off to Yugoslavia. I left that afternoon.

I got one lift to somewhere near the border and then walked across the border once more. The road soon became little more than a track and I was dry, covered in dust and half delirious from lack of rest, blood and food. The sun poured down on my emaciated form and dust thickened my hair as sweat ran streaks down the side of my face, leaving small salty deposits under my chin.

Lorries passed infrequently and cars were even rarer. Not for the first time I cursed the weight of the guitar, and the weight of my bag with its few new acquisitions from the Istanbul bazaar. Each time a truck rolled by, I held my breath for two reasons: one, in case it stopped for me; and two, to avoid breathing in another lungful of the white chalky dust that blew up everywhere around me. I had decided to walk away the time because I found this made me less melancholic than standing still. I wished I was at home, I wished I was with Gill, and I decided that my attempt at dalliance in the showers that time in Istanbul did not count as a lack of faith. Then I wondered if Gill was still true to me, and the thought that she may have found someone else—or worse, made love to someone else—almost made me cry.

Self-pity turned to anger and resolve that I would see this journey through and get it over with. It was a sobering thought that I was no longer enjoying this trip, and especially dreading this crawl back through Yugoslavia, scene of the demolition of my guitar and people with haunted faces and suspicious looks at 'wealthy' strangers like me.

A truck in high revs roared along the road behind me. From around the bend all I could see was a cloud of dust then a sudden increase of noise as it hurtled into view and headed towards me. I stuck out my thumb and it thundered onward and then as if the driver had a second thought, it braked violently and shuddered to a halt. As tired and hot as I was, I managed to run to the cab and climb in, grinning at the driver. I put the guitar on the floor behind the seat under the fold out bunks and nearly knocked over a box of plums that were resting between the two seats. It was a refrigerated truck and his cargo was fruit. It was a large vehicle designed for long distance driving, noisy and high off the ground. I had to clamber into the cab by resting my foot on the wheel studs.

The driver was a thickset Greek with the traditional half tan that truck drivers wear with pride. I suppose he was about thirty seven years old. He spoke no English, but he did have a little French and some German, and with the aid of signs and looks we were soon able to communicate.

Andreas was smoking a Greek cigarette and soon he offered me one. I settled into my seat and smoked as I looked out of the window. The countryside was yellow and dry, but I was all right. He offered me some of the fruit which I had knocked over as I clambered into the cab, and I accepted a couple of apricots. I was touched by the look of concern in his eyes, and as I reached over to take the fruit, he noticed the plaster over the bruised area in the crook of my arm and asked me what had happened. I managed to explain that I was short of money and that I had sold blood in Thessalonika to try to make it back to Italy. He nodded his understanding but clicked his tongue to indicate that I was perhaps foolish to have done this as I looked weak and in need of sustenance.

As the hot day progressed, the thump of the diesel and the bumpy road rocked me into the best sleep I'd had for several days (I still sleep great in cars). I woke as the first shadows of evening were lengthening, and we took a left hand turn into a sort of road café area. Andreas directed me to a water tap in the yard, where he stripped down to his trousers and gave himself a refreshing sloosh. I did the same and with hair dripping and still a little damp we entered the café, where he ordered some food for both of us. It was my first hot meal for days and it tasted great. It was only a thin steak with chips with some tomato ketchup, but I can taste it still. Afterwards I offered my pathetic leftover dinars from my trip through the country, but magnanimously he refused, waving the few coins away with theatrical emphasis. I mused on the solidarity of the working class and the fact that we were all brothers and should help each other in our times of need; my faith in human nature was restored.

I felt terrific, restored even, and we were on our way all the way to Belgrade as well. I had no idea how far we had already come, but the light was fading fast and I noticed that with each passing hour the yawning from my driver was getting louder and more frequent. I judged the time to be well past midnight when I noticed his eyes begin to close whilst still driving, so I loudly cleared my throat. Fortunately this woke him immediately, and for the next hour or so I kept him awake in this fashion as we steadily lumbered into the mountains. Virtually no cars or trucks were coming the other way and no lights shone in the distance over a welcoming town. It became obvious that we would have to rest up for some time, and with a grin Andreas noticed my anxiety and pulled the lorry over in a sort of lay-by above a ravine and, heaving on the handbrake, brought the hissing truck to rest.

He got out and took a piss and as he got back in I thought I should do the same. As I clambered back inside the truck I could see that he had lowered the bunk and had climbed in having moved my guitar and bag and placed them on the engine housing inside the cab. Outside the sky was overcast because in spite of the altitude there were no stars visible. With the engine off it soon became chilly even inside the cab. I shuffled down on my seat and tried to make myself comfortable as my friend snuffled and snorted until his breathing became quite steady as he began to fall asleep. I decided to have a last cigarette and opened the window just a little to let out the smoke. As I finished and threw out the dog-end,

Andreas grunted that there was room for me to lie down on the bunk where I would be more comfortable. For a second I wondered if I would be safe, and then realising how ridiculous any doubt would have been, I crawled over the seat and lay down.

I pondered the day and all the days and thought of Gill and where we might be at this moment. I thought how good it would be to be back in Italy, where I was sure I would be able to go out busking. I tried not to move too much in case I disturbed my host, and I was very nearly asleep when I felt a bristly chin on the back of my neck. At first I thought that I must have moved into his space and moved my head forward, but within a second or two the regular breathing had been replaced by silence as this huge macho lorry driver started placing tiny kisses on the back of my neck. I froze in terror, then I cracked and my sense of betrayal turned to unbelievable rage.

I leaped up from the bunk and started shouting at him in English, "You fucking bastard what the fuck do you think you're doing? What gave you the fucking idea that you could try this on with me? You fucking bastard what am I supposed to do where the fuck can I go? If you try to touch me again I'll fucking kill you, you fucking horrible piece of shit you stinking queer how dare you lay your fucking hands on me you fucking piece of shit."

I was frantically trying to pull my bag and guitar over towards me in order that I should get out of the truck and then I realised that there was no shelter for me and if this bastard had wanted to, he could have probably overpowered me—or worse, clubbed my head in with a rock and tipped me over the ravine. I stopped my hysterical ranting, noting that my outrage had no effect on him. After a while his breathing returned to the steady snore and whistle, and I slept holding my bag on my lap with my head lain on the door window dozing on and off awake all night until the threads of the dawn slowly crept over the hills and a different reality came to rest on my jangling red-eyed consciousness. Slowly the form of my driver stirred and in one movement, swung his legs over the bunk and into his work trousers. I noted with horror that he was down to his underpants in readiness. I was still fully clothed, and with trepidation wondered what he would say now with me still sat there like an idiot.

He said nothing, but opened the door on his side got out and took a piss, I did the same on my side and got back in. It was actually cold outside and without a word he started the engine and we pulled out and on to the highway again. After only half an hour he pulled into another café area and insisted that I had a coffee and some bread with him. It was then that he apologised for his advances the night before, explaining it away by stating that he had not had a woman for over a week. I was nonplussed by his excuse, and although grateful for the food and appreciative of the fact that he had sort of said sorry, I could not comprehend that he did not understand my feelings of outrage. I was totally shaken. All my judgements about people were under threat: my fellow feeling for the working class; doubts about myself; what of self-control? Had I somehow given him a signal that I might be open to this type of advance? I felt as if all my values were under threat and this bastard had managed it all with just one misjudged move. I did not say anything to him about his excuse and when he turned me out before he turned off the main road, he pointed out the way I should go. He waved me off, and it was as much as I could do to wave back. It was with a heavy step that I wandered into the centre of Belgrade. I don't recall how I made it to the border with Italy, but somehow I did.

I met Olaf in Trieste as we'd arranged—again he had beaten me to it. He looked even thinner and a little road-weary, but he still looked better than I felt. How come he always got there first? I even started to wonder if he took the train. Did he cheat? Cheat at what? Was this a game with rules? No, of course not. The rules of the road are get there any way you can. If you have the money, take the train; if you have the money, eat steak. I still couldn't get out of the habit of saving just a little bit, so consequently I was always poor or felt poor. In spite of these doubts it was good to see him, and it sure was good to be back in Italy ordering *due cappuccini* and smoking the old Nazionale again. We got some accommodation for a night, earned some money playing and then sat up for a long time telling each other about how we got back to where we had just met. Olaf listened patiently to my tale of near rape at the hands of the lorry driver and helpfully opined that if it had happened to him, he would have waited till the man was asleep and then stoved his head in with a rock.

"Oh yeah," I countered, "and just how far do you think you would have got on a mountain road covered with blood in the middle of fucking Yugoslavia?" He said nothing, and I added, "I wouldn't have minded but he never even blew smoke in my eyes."

It was good to have company again. We drank more wine and smoked more cigarettes (by now I had a spectacular hacking cough), finally turning in after discussing where we might go next. Olaf wanted to go to Venice where he was sure we could really earn a fortune, but I was tired. I had not embarked on it to see things and tick them off like a tourist; Venice held no more attraction to me than Frankfurt. I had begun to travel to be in it, to be part of the scenario, playing my small part in the events mundane or special, like a time traveller who momentarily interrupts the ordained course of events—and I could do that anywhere, I didn't need Venice. Then suddenly I decided to give it another go, although my resentment at Olaf's lack of musical progress was getting me down.

It's only now that I see my attitude may have been that way because I was still not ready to go it alone, and somehow I blamed him for it. I also failed to see that my slightly better musical skills were what provided equality in our relationship; if he had not been an admirer of what I could do, our relationship would have been impossible, as he was superior to me in many ways and much tougher and more confident.

Olaf had taken to wearing shorts, and was constantly going on about his elegant legs, which were if anything on the skinny side. He was luxuriating on his new meerschaum pipe, and kept on repeating how you should only smoke it wearing white gloves, so that your fingers didn't mark the bowl and make it colour unevenly. I was really starting to get irritated, but our combination still worked well, and after a brief rest I wearily plodded my way to Venice.

The place we stayed was somewhere around a heavy industrial complex—I recall power stations or electricity substations—but the hostel was old and adequate, and I met a French bloke who wanted to swap me his rather smart Fred Perry shirt for a set of guitar strings. I had brought a few spares and had been very fortunate in breaking hardly any on the trip, so I was able to cobble together a set. And I loved that red shirt. It was my lucky shirt, and I still had it in 1970 at the Isle of Wight festival.

We had to take a ferry across to Venice itself. Sadly its crumbling grandeur was lost on me. Busking was a bit difficult, but we did OK in a very short space of time as the tourists were as plentiful as the pigeons in St Mark's Square. I added the tower to my collection of tall buildings when I climbed it one day. The truth is that my abiding memories are: a comparison of the way the tourists looked and my by now tramp-like appearance; meeting a young harmonica player from Norfolk who could play Sonny Terry style; and a photograph on a café wall somewhere of the pigeons that had been persuaded to feed on carefully laid out letters of the Coca-Cola label.

The weather was warm but overcast and I was incredibly tired, the canal stank and I wanted to move on. Milan sounded promising, and Olaf, the harmonica player and I made plans. A photo of Olaf and I exists showing us outside the hostel and we both look surprisingly fit. I am proudly wearing the red shirt and leather flip flops, looking more like starting out than ending a trip.

I headed off for Milan on my own as usual, but once there met up with the other two who—surprise—were there before me. We must have sounded quite good, as the harp player was always asking when we were next going out to make some money. It amazed me to see that he actually saw this as an earner, when all I was worried about was just making enough to get by on, and once that had been achieved I wanted to have the day off. I guess I'm still the same. It was all right for these two, as neither felt competent to go it alone and I was resenting taking a third share when I felt I was holding it together. I had conveniently forgotten that I was still too scared to go it alone, and needed them just as much as they needed me.

I had found a room which I shared with Olaf, the harp player and another bloke called Nick. This guy was about three or four years older than me and very cool. He wore glasses and had his hair cropped unfashionably short. He stayed silent while he listened to our various tales, but when he did talk I found myself quite mesmerised by his understanding. This still happens occasionally. Generally speaking, experience is available to all, though we learn at different rates. My favourite comparison is that of someone who drives around a big city for years and then makes a 'wrong' turning that leads to a street he already knows. The relief at the discovery of familiarity is the same as when someone is able to link the things that you already know so that you don't feel stupid; on the contrary, you have been guided to a conclusion that you would probably have come to after a 'wrong turning' just a little quicker. So it was with Nick; over many long night chats and discussions, he shepherded my rambling thoughts and steered them safely into pens where I could call on them as proper themes rather than rambles. Such are the building blocks of reason.

I remember nothing specific of our conversations, except that he was incredibly knowledgeable about the coded messages wrapped up in the radio series *Beyond Our Ken*, which he revealed was a show written for the enjoyment of camp and gay audiences. My recent close encounter had not exactly endeared this minority to me, but as he explained the strange jokes and mummers lingo, I was entertained and couldn't wait to tell Les (who thought this was the greatest show on the air) what it all meant when I got back.

Nick had worked for the BBC and had been in the theatre, and although I was not sure at the time, I am now positive that he was gay in a very non-camp way. One by one as I delivered my prejudices and fears about 'queers', he demolished them with reason and humanity that made me a little ashamed.

When I protested at my recent experience he told me, "The ultimate fantasy for a gay man is to be loved by a straight one; this is not possible, and therefore a gay man's ultimate fantasy is never possible."

Even after my outraged feelings, I could see the poignancy and sadness in that situation.

Olaf moved to other accommodation nearby, and an American named Gerald Bergstrom moved in. He was a friendly geezer, and knew something about the music I loved. He offered to collect for us, and for a little while things slid along in an easy manner. A couple of times Olaf cried off from busking; he was getting stoned a lot and I went out with the harp player, until one afternoon he left my bag of harmonicas at the railway station where we'd been working. I'd had enough by now, and with Olaf throwing more moodies, I decided I was strong enough to head home.

It was Nick who casually said one evening, "Why don't you take the train, it's only ten pounds to Victoria."

It sounds little enough now, but it was a fortune to me and I said so. Nick immediately offered to lend me the money as he could tell that I would post it back to him. I gratefully accepted, and within a day I had said my goodbye to Olaf and the lads and was on my way. So exhausted was I that I slept nearly all the way. In any case I had no money for food and this is a good way of suppressing appetite. I had my cigarettes, a couple of snide lighters, a conch shell, the remains of some socks and underwear, my mended guitar, a glass animal from Venice and some jewellery from the bazaar. I also had two ill-fitting jean jackets, one in flimsy denim and the other in top quality suede. My passport was full of stamps, and I had what I feared at the time might be terminal athlete's foot.

A few days after I got home, my small gifts shared and my suede jean jacket sort of admired (it was strange explaining that the man who had made it was a master craftsman as it looked like it was tailor made for Quasimodo, but all admired the quality of the material), I was frantically trying to sort out the ten quid that I had borrowed to pay back Nick in Milan when a note arrived from Olaf from an address in Milan:

> Dear Ralph,
> I am sorry to have to ask you but I know that things are not good between us. I hate to ask you for money but I cannot turn to anyone else. Please send me some dollars to the address on this letter.
> > Olaf

I was overwhelmed with compassion and guilt, for without me Olaf was unable to support himself. By the end of the week I had raised the dough. I changed it into dollars (ten pounds worth) and sent it off.

Six months later the letter was returned to me with the money still inside, with a message that simply informed me that my letter had remained uncollected. I was completely puzzled and finally found Olaf's original letter and checked the return address. To my horror I saw that I had sent it to American Express (which for some reason was where all travellers normally got money sent to) when Olaf had asked for it to be sent to Thomas Cook's.

I wrote several times to his address in Norway to apologise and explain what had happened, but my letters were never acknowledged and I never heard from him again. He talked of going to work in the city of Brasilia—I hope he made it.

As for the ten pounds, Nick knew I would return it to him. I regret to say that I still owe him it!

∾

And once I walked a million miles
All of the way to Yugoslavia
And I carried you all of the way
For where I was, then there you are

Now I cannot speak for everyone
For they got their reasons
All on this road
But heron, would that I had your wings
For then I'd know where I would go

PART FIVE

PARIS

tubs

Almost certainly I first met Tubs at the Olive Tree coffee bar in Croydon. The Olive Tree was just a little converted shop, so above the ground floor were a few tiny rooms that were occupied by a vague assortment of beatniks or apprentice beatniks, and in one of these dingy little rooms lurked Tubs.

The first thing to say about Tubs was that he was not fat. He had a shock of blond hair that was so thick and curly that the only thing he could think to do was to part it down one side and try to make it lie down. He showed a great deal more imagination about every other aspect of his life, however. He'd lost a couple of teeth along the line, though you would never know unless he deliberately showed you. He had a penchant for white jeans and leather shoes that clicked as he walked. His eyes were small and never stopped moving about. He had less of a Croydon accent than me in; in fact at first I thought he might be posh. He'd attended secondary modern school when he'd felt like it, and though he was capable of better things, he just wasn't interested.

Tubs's family were what I would describe as upper working or lower middle class; he once told me that his father worked at the Savoy—'bowing and scraping' Tubs called it—then imitating the characters in the

Styx cartoons he would flex his fingers as if tapping in exasperation and say "Scra-a-a-a-pe". This was one of his trademarks that we were all to copy. To me he had a strange sense of humour, in as much as he admired comedians like Jack Benny and Bob Hope alongside such British stalwarts as Peter Sellers (my all time comic hero) and Frankie Howerd. Tubs's speaking voice was sort of smoky and cracked in tone, and was a fairly unreliable accompaniment to his playing; his laughter was a wheezy, almost silent chuckle that frequently brought tears to his tiny mischievous eyes. He was one of the few people I've met that laugh out loud at cartoons or jokes in newspapers. One such joke from a Playboy magazine (no-one else I knew would even admit to reading such an item, but Tubs had no problem with this) showed two city gent type characters walking down a street passing a skeleton with a begging cup in front of him, with a card reading 'thank you' around his neck; one gent turns to the other and observes, "Some people can't make a go of anything!"

Tubs thought this was so funny, I must have heard him repeat that punchline dozens of times. He was also a master of the double take, reacting to movements that in no way threatened him as if he was about to be slapped.

Tubs was ideally suited to the apprentice beatnik lifestyle, but had adapted it so as to dispense with the search for enlightenment through poetry and jazz, preferring to reach the answer by sleeping, shagging and getting pissed as often and as cheaply as possible. He did however have a flirtatious interest in acoustic blues guitar, especially a number by Big Bill Broonzy called *Hey Hey* which he played all the time. Tubs seldom arose before mid-afternoon and had somehow convinced the owner of the coffee bar to employ him behind the jump on a 'live-in' basis.

Val Liloff lived downstairs below Tubs's room. Val was of Polish origin and was full of all the angst and passion of the true beatnik. His bible was the Alexandria Quartet and he was engaged in an impossible affair with a middle-class girl from the suburb of Shirley, who was probably a lot brighter than he was, but who seemed to enjoy the intensity of the relationship as much as Val loved the constant arguing and passionate raging this love provoked. He was never more fulfilled than when he carried the weight of yet another breakdown in their on/off affair. Val knew that the best way to understand the meaning of life was through art, literature and music, though frequently he would resort to the *Sporting Life* for relief from his pain. Sometimes he would drag me with him to the betting shop, and we would sit next door in the little Greek café whilst he daydreamed over the heavily pregnant wife of the owner.

"Isn't she beautiful?" he would ask me, and eventually I began to see why he found her so sexy. I ventured that most men have a mild attraction to waitresses and a pregnant one is even more dominated by man, as she wears the proof of carrying his child as evidence of her willingness to serve his every wish blah blah blah, but Val said it was just the way she moved and the tiredness in her languid movements and he'd just seen *The Fugitive Kind* and was in love (sort of) with Anna Magnani. We both wanted Marlon's snakeskin jacket, but it was Val who had noticed Leadbelly's signature on the guitar Brando carried.

One night Val introduced me to Tubs as "the noisy bastard who's got a thing for Ma Parker". It transpired that Tubs knew I played and liked what I did, and thus was born our musical friendship, which spilled over to the Whitgift Arms. Maurice and Rene were happy to tolerate this younger breed of drinkers to enliven the place from the usual type of cider head with their twitching hands, stammering and eye tics. We strummed guitars, got drunk, groped girls, swore undying friendships, fought and fell in love just like any normal post-war broken-homed teenage kids.

There was always a bit of grass about, and also some purple hearts which we could get hold of. But I was already going off that and I'd never been into speed really, so I suppose you could say that I was fairly relaxed on the subject of dope. Tubs, however, was fascinated and would constantly ask me about it—what was it like, what did it do? No-one openly sold any gear down at the Whitgift, so Tubs, like the rest of us, had to be content with the stuff you could get across the pub counter. I enjoyed the feeling of being more experienced than him, at the same time knowing or sensing that Tubs had an almost dangerous obsession with finding out as soon as possible what it would be like to turn on.

Henry had started to get heavily into the Cyril Davies Band that used to play at Eel Pie Island on the Thames at Twickenham. He still loved his jazz, but for sheer excitement and what we took for pure authentic-ity, Cyril's band was hard to beat. The journey to the island was part of the adventure; a platform ticket from East Croydon station, change at Clapham Junction for the Twickenham train and either get off at St. Margaret's and walk, or pay from St. Margaret's at Twickenham the 6d fare. However once at the island it cost 2d to go over the bridge, where two little old ladies used to stand in all weathers to take our tolls as they huddled round a paraffin stove. Wearing plastic raincoats in a little sentry box, they addressed everyone as 'dear'. They never looked up as they took the money, so I couldn't say what they looked like.

The venue itself was a great big abandoned hotel with a sprung dance floor and a stage at one end. It was between two and three shillings to get in most Saturday nights. Once when one of our friends complained about paying half a crown and asked who it was that should command such a high price he was told, "The Paul Butterworth *(sic)* Blues Band."

There was a huge long bar in another room which also sold strong cider and I remember a handwritten note on the wall high above the bar under the outline of two footprints with the legend 'Mr. Bunce jumped 10 feet'.

The plot was to freight up with a few pints and then bop and dance away to the great sounds of Cyril Davies and later Long John Baldry. During the break we would repair outside for some air or occasionally a draw and a few pulls on a joint. Weed had not taken any real hold on me. My preference was for rough cider, cheap, and in the quantities that I drank it, cheerful. I seldom bought dope as I could never achieve the precise balance to gain the desired effect. You knew where you were with cider, and you also knew where that extra pint would take you. Also I seldom if ever had a drag on any dope without having had some drink first. This is a dangerous way to handle things. A couple of hits was all I usually wanted anyway, and only then where music was involved. Up until this time all smoking materials had been marijuana or Golden Virginia and odd 'tailor mades'.

Stan had just returned from India after more than a year on the road. His hair was an admirable below-shoulder length and he was a rich golden brown colour. His Levis were the colour we all wanted ours to be, and above all he looked the real thing; a gentleman of the road, a beatnik. But although he had managed to smuggle a couple of pounds of hash across a dozen borders and convince the Egyptian authorities that he was probably a holy man and should not have his hair cut when he was arrested for begging, he was still Stan Tether from Mitcham who couldn't wait to get back on his 350 Velocette and go ripping round the lanes and roads of south London again. I was totally impressed by Stan, who had achieved what I had always hoped to have done, but I had been beaten back by hunger, insecurity and cowardice, and had on one of my early trips suffered the indignity of repatriation from the British consul in Lyon. Perhaps it was the fact that Stan was not really arty, although he loved music like the rest of us.

In the end it was music that was the glue that held us all together, but it was not his driving force. Stan was practical, good with his hands, that sort of thing. I questioned him constantly as to how he made out, and to this day I wonder if his travels changed him in any major way. In the end it didn't matter. We had returned home after brief adventures whilst Stan trekked onward through to India with not a penny to his name and did not return until the call of the Velo was louder than the pull of the road.

When I asked him how he'd managed to keep the dope hidden across all those borders, he just said that no-one seemed very keen to question him and that he only carried the most distressed of his few undergarments on the top of his travel bag, so that whenever it was opened no-one delved very deep. Stan sold his stash slowly in small amounts for about ten shillings a deal, which was a cube of hash about the size of a dice for a game of snakes and ladders. Hash was fairly new to us at this time; we soon learned to love the ritual that went with the preparation of the joints, but Stan simply broke a bit off with his thumbnail and smoked it in a conventional briar pipe with a bit of Old Holborn.

One Saturday in September I went to Eel Pie Island with Tubs and a bunch of friends. Having recently returned from the Istanbul adventure, there were still some physical effects, and as usual there was the anticlimax of home, where you find little has changed and people don't seem to be impressed with your exploits, especially post-Stan. And there was of course Gill's continued absence. Whatever the reasons, I was desperately unhappy and went for the drink even harder than usual.

I lost Tubs somewhere during the evening, and staggered outside during the break to where I knew someone would be smoking a bit of stuff. I found Stan with a couple of other mates and Stan's pipe, and their joints were soon being passed round and I greedily had my share. On my return to the dancefloor I surpassed myself with my technique until the pillars were moving with the walls and ceiling. Soon I entered the swirling pit and threw up all over myself before collapsing on the sympathetically heaving sprung floor. My friends realised I was in some trouble and dragged me outside and were persuaded by me to leave me on the steps where I promptly vomited again. People were now giving me a pretty wide berth and although I can remember events clearly, I was in no state to do anything about it.

It was here that Tubs found me, and in all honesty would probably have left me if I hadn't mentioned the word dope to explain my predicament. His first question was as to whether or not I had still got any on me. I think he'd had a few on board anyway and without much resistance from me decided to help me across the bridge and take me home.

"Good night dears," cooed the paraffin stove ladies as Tubs manfully hauled me over the bridge where I threw up again—this time partly over him. "Ne-e-e-e-xt," said Tubs (his favourite catchphrase). He dumped me on a bench and disappeared from my blurred double vision.

I began to enter the swirling pit again when I became aware of a scuffle. It seems my friend, in a misguided attempt to help me, had decided to steal a motorbike and had been observed by three off-duty policemen trying to kick over at least five different bikes. His excuse that he was drunk and couldn't remember what his machine looked like had not impressed them, and they were about to cart him off to the nick when he kindly remembered me. When the cops realised that I was unable to walk unaided, they deduced that I was intoxicated and arrested me for being drunk in a public place. We were both taken to the Twickenham nick and banged up for the night in different cells, as even my friend could not stand the smell of my regurgitated cider and was given his own room. I doubt they would show the same consideration to an offender today.

In the small hours of the morning, some other mates turned up and bailed us out, took us home and returned us to court the following day where I was fined £5 and Tubs £15. Rumours started that we were both under the influence of drugs and it now became a matter of urgency that Tubs get hold of the real thing. Up until this point I had attempted to keep him away from the gear because I knew there would be no half measures with Tubs. Now having disgraced myself in a marvellous exhibition of not being able to handle it, I could no longer ignore his incessant nagging to score a deal for him. In the end Stan relented and sold Tubs his first ten bob deal. He soon became an expert in rolling and scoring, quickly building up his own network of contacts for his needs.

Before long he was travelling up to the Front Line in Brixton and talking in West Indian patois, until one day when slightly high he got one of their swear words confused with a term of endearment: he greeted a black guy in a doorway with the salutation, "To Ras clart mon," and was immediately nutted, knocked to the ground and given a kicking. Although bewildered by the experience, he continued to make regular journeys up there. Soon Larry, a small time dealer, was part of our group, and Larry explained to me why it was OK to smoke hash.

"You see man, when they go into the tomb of Christ an' found him gone, they look around and them find only traces of his dried blood from his wounds. Them take it a sign and the roll up the dried blood of Jesus man an' them smoke it ya hear sah. Then they have visions and all things are clear to them man. Thas why it OK to smoke the blood of Christ!"

What could anyone say against that? Larry had almost turned it into communion. The religious significance was of no matter to Tubs, and I am absolutely sure that, although up until the island escapade he had not partaken of anything stronger than his mum's slimming pills, he was determined to make up for lost time.

waterloo

When I had asked Gill to marry me, I had actually asked that question. Some people asked to get engaged, which is different, like asking for a trial period. We had been through that. However marriage was never on my mind, although I supposed one day we would get married. I just wanted her to know that I only wanted her and, equally if not more importantly, that I wanted to be assured she would not look elsewhere. Engagement was really a way of making a claim on someone. I offered her nothing except my company and some slightly rudimentary guitar playing. She did however say yes. We never lived together, although we did once go and look at a flat. It was dismal and my wages would have confined us to the two rooms. I never wanted to get a career job, and I could stay at home until the summer came and we could be off again.

Gill never pressured me. I know it was not just my apparent lack of commitment that may have helped her make up her mind to go to the States. We had been through a great deal together. Some price had to be paid for the reckoning of the equation of reckless love over fun, divided by responsibility for each other and our actions, multiplied by intensity of needing to possess without proper sharing.

Gill's American employers thought I might be able to get a job playing out there, but I was still too worried about my ability to consider working as an illegal alien. Besides, I had no money to buy a ticket and so continued to beg her to return.

Her social circle widened a little more, and of course it was not long before her beauty effected introductions to more people. At one time she was an escort to a gay Hollywood minor celebrity who needed to have a pretty girl to be seen with. She found him amusing and I was mad with jealousy.

In the summer of 1965, rioting broke out in downtown LA, in the black area called Watts, and Gill tried to interpret for me the causes of the unrest. My politics were naive, and her views and interpretations were perceptive and more mature than my vague grasp. The civil rights campaign held no real resonance with me as there was no really disenfranchised minority I was aware of, at least until six years later in Northern Ireland. Of course I supported the aims of the movement, and as a very left-wing young man deeply suspected the true motives of some of the shirt-tail grabbers attached to the protest movement.

All the time I was aware of Gill's growing maturity and broadening horizons. My only concern was when I would see her again. It's not that I didn't want Gill to be happy; I just did not want to be unhappy. Her absence seemed to be the cause of my unhappiness and therefore if she returned I would be happy. And she...?

Finally my begging and pleading worked. Perhaps she was tired of it all out there (who was I kidding? I mean what could sunny California and open-topped cars possibly have to offer compared to Croydon in October?). Gill talked to her employer, and the understanding couple released her from her contract and wished us both well hoping that we would be happy.

I had no plans in place as to how we were to carry on, but once she got back something would work out. I had kept my promise to stay faithful almost to the end. I had been faithful to her in my mind. I would deal with this lapse eventually, I promised myself. But what if Gill had slipped? The realisation that she might have was almost too hard to bear. In the end the thought of seeing her again vastly outweighed that doubt. Her ticket home was booked and I did my best to prepare myself.

On the day of her return I found myself at Heathrow Airport in a state of inner turmoil. Most of my feelings began with "what if...?"

I stood at the arrivals gate of Terminal 2 awaiting her appearance with my heart pounding as the minutes ticked by. I knew she had landed because it said so on the board. Might she have changed her mind at the last minute? I watched other passengers coming through the terminal gate. I paced up and down and moved further away from the exit and then after a short gap in the passengers coming through, there she was.

Grinning and waving, she came hurrying over to me. I was over-whelmed and tongue tied. She was brimming with affection and confidence and I was the same way I was when we first met, stumbling, mumbling and feeling slightly weak and wobbly-lipped.

Taking her back to the dismal flat in Miller Road was in such sharp contrast to California, it is hard to imagine how she felt. Mum made up a bed in our tiny front room and Gill was soon asleep. I lay in the room I used to share with Bruce wondering if all was as it should be. Some-thing was different; I was scared. Naturally I wanted to consummate our relationship as soon as possible and to start where things had ended. We had a little time together the following morning, but things were not right; conversation was stilted and I had so little to tell her except to confess my one slip-up, and this was not the right time.

Gill had so much to tell, but I could not differentiate her enthusiasm from the thought that she might have met someone else, and I didn't want to hear about all I had not been able to participate in.

She had to pay a visit to her parents' home. I decided to go with her, frightened to let her out of my sight. We left the next day for Bourne-mouth.

Waterloo.
Within a day of her being back, Gill and I were on the train to the south coast. Her parents were anxious to see her and I could not provide anywhere for her to make her stay longer in Croydon.

We had been alone together but there was an uncertainty and a coolness that had settled on Gill and I did not know how to deal with it. The feeling was like having a hunger that no food could satisfy and experiencing the same weakness resulting from lack of sustenance. Your arms and legs sort of lose their strength and all attempts at light con-versation sound mundane and ordinary. The little jokes and asides that lubricate conversation dry up and you sound like a stumbling fool. I could only evince one or two words from Gill, despite my best efforts. Most of the journey was spent with me trying to make conversation and Gill seemingly wishing that I would stop talking. Finally I could stand it no longer. My voice was faltering and I was trembling slightly. I asked her to step into the corridor of the train so that we could talk without being overheard by the other passengers.

"You're just not sure are you, Gill?" I said.

The empty pit of my stomach seemed to appear as a hole in the floor of the train, and as she answered quietly "No," I began to slide into it.

Through the blackness of the outside a few lights were appearing as we neared our destination. Rain distorted the view and I was aware of the train slowing down as my heartbeats increased. The train stopped. My heart pounded and I felt myself moving along the corridor. The door had become so heavy I had to push hard to open it on to a small platform. I half stepped and half fell out and without a backward look slammed the train door behind me. I walked steadily to the ticket barrier, there was no-one to take my ticket. I had no idea where I was except that it was near Bournemouth. I felt faint and the rain fell on me.

I was in a film. I could not stop the camera; the train was pulling away. I had no money as usual. Out on the street the cars went by, people scurried to wherever they were going. No-one knew me or what had just happened. No-one knew what I had just done. To these strangers it was just a rainy night and they were going home. To me it was like the world was ending. Nothing eased my feelings of desperation and numbed senses. I did not write songs then but if I did this would be my first one.

My girl left me—no that wasn't right.

I left my girl at the station—where was I? I looked around and saw that I had alighted at somewhere called Pokesdown.

Fucking Pokesdown for Christ's sake! There was a name that was never going into a romantic song of love and loss.

What could I do? Should I try to get to Bournemouth and see if her family would put me up? I thought if Gill tells them it's over they would already have the bunting hanging out by the time I got there. The evening drizzle had soaked through my coat shoulders and I was crying but no-one would have noticed. I would have to hitch home. Where was the London road? Shop signs and traffic lights reflecting on the otherwise unyielding pavement. My desert boots are sodden, I can feel the water inside my socks. I am drowning from the feet up. My balance is affected,

I am disorientated by the immediate and waterlogged confusion spreads like ink on blotting paper in my head.

"...the road is so hard..."

That time I took the bend on the motorbike
and Gill sensed I wouldn't make it;
she jumped off and came to no harm,
I landed on the road and my jaw hit the gravel
which also scraped the skin off my knee down to the bone.
My leg was so shocked that it forgot to bleed for a while
and then it poured.
My chin swelled up on one side
and I couldn't shave for days until the cut had healed.
My eyebrow was torn like a boxer's.
I did not mind the torn eyebrow.
I left the racing green Francis Barnett in New Addington
and sold it a few days later.
My motorbike time was at an end.

Gill had got off the bike, now I had got off the train.
"Do you know where the London road is?" I asked someone.
"No mate."
Where the fuck is the London road?
Curtains are being drawn in houses along the way. Slowly I am being shut out. There are fewer and fewer people on the street as I wander working my way out towards the road to London via the urban road signs. Now and then I make huge shuddering sighs. Past more shops closing and shutters going down.

"The riots are all about prices in the Watts district being too high for the poor black people who live there. All the shops are owned by white people. From where we are we can see the smoke and everyone is worried," wrote Gill.

Civil rights and the back of the bus. I have no money for any part of the bus. I just keep on walking.

"...I'm going where the weather suits my clothes," sings Woody.

Dear Woody,
I am writing to you to tell you that I have sung your songs in Franco's Spain.
I have your picture inside my guitar case.
Yours sincerely with huge admiration, Ralph May.

Dear Ralph,
Thank you for writing. Keep singing, signed Marjorie Guthrie.

My first lift is taking me the wrong way towards Bournemouth. I ask to stop, at least I am on the right road, should I continue or cross the road—how different will my life be? My next lift takes me near the New Forest.

Hide and seek
the smell of summer
insects buzzing
soft bracken
two days to go before she flies.

"…baby please don't go…"

"…I love my baby
and she's bound to love me some.
she used to throw her arms around me
like a circle round the sun…"

My head is bouncing gently off the window of the car Gill is nudging me.
I am on the wrong side of the vehicle. Where are we? Italy.
"He keeps touching me."
"I'll kill him," I murmur.
"Don't hit him, he'll crash the car. Let's get further down the road," whispers Gill.
"I won't fall asleep," I say, but I do.

I am woken by my head banging against the window. I am on the left side. My clothes are warm but damp.
"Are you all right mate?"
"Yeah."

"You had a bad dream?"
"Yeah."
"How long you been waiting?"
"What time is it?"

"Does anybody know what time it is?"
Brighton beach. March.
Christ it's cold
lying on the pebbles
with Judy in the bag.

"About two hours I suppose."
"You look like a drowned rat!"

Rats swimming around in drains
dragging the debris pulling it under.
In the red sea an arm waves.
It's OK it's already dead.
They go for the throat.

I sit up.
"Do you mind if I smoke?" My eyes are so sore.

"…I love my baby
and she's bound to love me some…"

"Here have one of these."
"No, I roll my own." My hands are shaking still the tobacco falls on my lap. I make the smoke; it is badly rolled; I inhale deeply.

The windscreen is misty and everywhere is black except the dashboard and my red glow from the roll up reflection. I drift into a red miasma… rat's teeth nip at my skin jerking me back to startled wakefulness. I am shivering in short rhythmic bursts just like Teddy Wolf.

My donkey jacket smells like a blanket. The car steams like a wintry stable.

She is riding over the hills and New Forest,
her hair blowing in the wind.

Her hair flicks at my face
as we drive the coast road on the scooter.

"…she used to throw her arms around me
Like a circle round the sun…"

I doze; the car is heading for a wall, I instinctively lean away; my head hits the driver's shoulder as we drive straight on. "Sorry," I say.

"You OK mate?" he asks again.

"Yeah." I roll another fag. It stops raining and he drops me outside of Epsom. I walk and walk, eke out my tobacco. My Zippo held tight in my fist. Maybe she will write in a few days.

I knew she wouldn't.
She needed more time.
She was jet-lagged, except the term had not been invented
and it would have meant nothing to me.
This is not a nursery game, ending prematurely.
I am not a baby, I am a man.
This is not some lovesick teenage boy here.
These are a man's feelings—does she not know?

"…you should have gone to the States man…" chorus the nipping, squeak-
ing, red-eyed rats.
She cannot know.

"…baby please don't go…" sings Big Joe.

I am sinking like a stone,
I am drowning,
I am being pulled under a red river.
The headlights are rats' eyes in the dark.
I am not waving.

I never wavered, except once or twice.

I am back on the train.
Some soldiers share some cake with me
and my mum says it's OK to eat it.

The men laugh a lot and offer her a cigarette.
She politely refuses. I think they like her.
The cake is nice. It came out of a mess tin.
I am on the train; her eyes have a deeper knowledge than me.
They look at me but I am barred from access to move her heart.
Shutters have been pulled down.
The victim cannot forgive.
The judgement extenuated.
The jury is excused.
We will never forget.

"Now you understand.
This is not to hurt you,
the teeth marks will fade.
You will swim away one day," sings the wind through the pylons on Factory Lane.

I am under the shadow of the gasholder and it has been raining for the last hour. I tap the letterbox. Eventually my mother answers the door.

"What on earth is the matter?" she asks with a worried look.

"It's over," I say, and the tears fall again.

"...the sun gonna shine on my back door some day
And the wind's gonna get up and blow my blues away..."

❧

timber

Once again the cast of thousands that populated these years came to my rescue. I spent my 21st birthday alone and drunk, but friends were supportive and in their pre-hippy way tried to offer advice and comfort. Between bouts of severe melancholy I did begin to eat again, although I lost an awful lot of weight in a few weeks.

Jobs were quite plentiful and I found work in a timber kiln drying unit in Beddington Lane, Mitcham, where I worked with Tubs' bosom pal Bunny Doyle. The job was actually quite a gas, and soon we had Tubs working with us as well. We had a great little cockney foreman called Fred, from Rotherhithe. He looked at us with a mixture of pity and curiosity. We had decided to eat in the modest staff canteen, and the normal boys' talk was interspersed with political chat and conversations about obscure jazz musicians. We discussed news items and general issues whilst wading through the typical English stodge that passed for food for the working man. Our little foreman listened to us and threw in the odd comment now and again. Once when Tubs was recounting a time when he managed it four times with a very pretty girl called 'dirty Di', Fred stood up, shaking his head in disbelief.

"Four times in one night?" he said. "You must be like bleedin' bunny rabbits, that's all I can say. When me and my missus is finished we're both completely knackered and sweating hot." It was not a pretty thought but a good point.

Once when we were talking about child psychology, little Fred told us, "During the war my old man bred rabbits. We was all allowed to call one of them our own but we didn't realise he was breeding them to eat did we? So one day my little sister is watching out the window when she sees my old man going to her hutch. He takes out her rabbit, Snowy was his name as he was nearly all white. And the next thing, bosh! he kills it ready for the table. Well you know my sister went really peculiar after that and got St Vitus' Dance and had fits. Funny that..."

Fred had been listening to a conversation about capital punishment. We were all fervently against it and were deeply engrossed in argument with one of our number. He was a real racist called John. Lunch break was nearly over and none of us had made any advance on John's view.

The bell sounded to resume work, and as we stood up from the table Fred solemnly announced his philosophy thus: "If you debolish the hangin' you ain't got no detergent!"

Tubs' last mouthful of mashed potato hit the wall opposite, and this phrase entered our vernacular for years.

Jacqui McShee and I were friends from the Olive Tree, and our common love of music was one of the bonds that saw us on a weekend away with Henry, who had newly passed his test. Henry had acquired an elderly hand-painted Bedford Dormobile with a sliding side door that was very good at sliding open, especially on bends.

Somehow we made the long and pleasant journey back to Poole for old times' sake and spent the day ambling about the old place washed in nostalgia for events that had only occurred a couple of years before. I had my Harmony Sovereign and soon we were sitting outside the Angel pub; I was playing songs and Jacqui was singing along, with a small group of admirers watching us.

I guess we must have impressed, as after a short while a tall young fair-haired fellow came up to us and engaged us in conversation, saying that he had really enjoyed our playing. Henry acted as intermediary as we discussed music in general and guitars in particular.

"Actually I have a guitar I want to sell," said the young fellow.

"Oh, I'm suited," I said. "I love this guitar, I've taken it all over Europe and I hope to get a Gibson."

"I think you'd like this guitar I've got," interrupted the young bloke. "It's called a Martin."

"A Martin—" blurted Henry as I kicked out at him and hit him smartly on the shin.

All of this was duly noted by the young bloke who said, "I know what a Martin is. I know they are valuable but all I do is keep it under my bed and polish it. I can't play it like you would, so I'd like you to have it."

Henry and I looked suitably chastened. Henry asked, "How much do you want for it?"

"Well it's very old, it's a 1936 00028. It's smaller than your guitar but it sounds great and I think you ought to have it."

Martin is the acknowledged Rolls Royce of acoustic instruments, and as such was completely out of my class. The only people I knew who played them were pro musicians who needed them for their work or their ego. In the days before PA systems in folk clubs the Martin reigned supreme as it was both beautiful in tone and huge in volume. The guitars also started off at about £200. My Harmony had cost me £29 and that had taken me a year to save for.

I repeated Henry's question: "How much do you want for it?"

The young man seemed to think for a moment as if trying to access what we could reasonably pay and then he said, "I must get £25 for it."

He might as well have said two hundred. As usual I had a few coins and my emergency ten bob note folded into my Levis 'pick pocket'. Jacqui had a couple of quid, and Henry said, "Twenty five quid? I've got some money but not that much."

"Well why don't you come and look at it?" offered the bloke.

We agreed and drove him to his address where, as he told us, the instrument was stored under the bed. He pulled out the old shaped case and opened the lid and there, nestling in its faded blue lining, was a near-perfect vintage 00028 Martin guitar. I carefully took out the instrument and smelled the strong aroma of lavender polish and must that accompanies old instruments kept in cases.

The strings looked like they had never been changed, but the sound! The sound was of bell-like clarity and I gawped in wonder at its simple beauty. The back and sides were of rosewood and the top a splendid piece of pine; the bridge and finger board were of ebony and the body was bound in herring bone purfling. It had a slotted head and the Grover machines were adequate, if not perfect. There was a small mark on the front and the usual little scratches earned through proper playing and ownership.

"It used to belong to the guitar player in the Billy Cotton band," the bloke informed us. I looked at Henry and Henry looked at me. Jacqui looked at both of us and we all looked back at the bloke. We simply did not have £25 between us.

"It is beautiful," I said, "but it's not really my guitar." In truth the action had risen over the years and I could not easily get the response from it that the instrument merited but it was almost a religious experience to hold the thing.

"Look," said the bloke, "I know it's worth about £250 but I really would love you to have it." Henry told me he had his holiday money on him and that if we pooled all our dough we would have sixteen pounds ten shillings. We told the bloke more to provide him with the information than in hope that he would be interested.

"Are you going back to London today?" he asked. We nodded that we were. "Can I get a lift with you then?" he said.

"Yeah," said Henry, "I suppose so."

"Well maybe I'm mad, but you can have the guitar for that money and a lift to town," he said, so we shook hands all round and gave him literally all our money and the guitar was mine.

It was a Sunday evening and Henry wanted to get back to the Red Lion in Sutton, where we met some old friends. I shared the news with them and Cliff Aungier who was the guest that night at the folk club there.

"You jammy sod!" he laughed. Everyone was slightly incredulous at my good fortune. We had dropped off the bloke somewhere along the line and all the time I was wondering if the guitar could have been stolen. The bloke had got the guitar from an old Irishman he had met in a pub. It all seemed a bit shady.

As soon as I could, I wrote to Martin Guitars with the serial number; they wrote back to confirm that it was shipped to England in 1934 and that it had never been reported as stolen, and I sighed a huge sigh of relief. It was a long time before I tried to get it worked on and made easier to play.

Over the years, I have used it on record and Bert Jansch once borrowed it for a recording. It is a real treasure of a guitar and it is still in great condition. I have never played it on stage, but I once used it in public a few years ago when I performed with John Williams on a Melvyn Bragg programme to publicise a concert we gave for Chile.

I do hope the bloke who sold it to me happened to be watching, because the last words my generous guitar donor uttered to me before leaving Henry's old Bedford were, "You never know, one day I might see you on the telly playing my guitar and that will be great."

A week or so later, Henry, Jacqui, a girl called Alison and I went for a mooch about in Cornwall. I was never one for camping, but during our short stay in the West Country that was what I was forced to do. My clearest memory, sharpened by some photos, is staying in a caravan near Penzance and playing and singing together. We heard about a folk club down at Bottalack, near Land's End, called 'The Counthouse'. We managed to play two or three numbers there. We were received well, and who could fail to be impressed by Jacqui's marvellous voice and Henry's jug blowing?

I am pretty sure that I wrote *Sleepy Time Blues* in the rainswept caravan park just behind the heliport in Penzance. It was somewhere in St Ives that Henry bought his first fisherman's smock and I remember his dad asking me what I thought he looked like. I responded that he looked all right, I supposed.

"All right?" he queried, "I think he looks like a bleedin' terrapin."

Back at the timber yard, Bunny managed to keep me from the deep darks by his enthusiasm and ever-optimistic plans. Bunny's dad was Irish, and for some reason had settled in Alderney. From his accounts it was a very quiet place, which was amazing because Bunny had a sense of survival and an eye for a situation that was so far in front of us town boys; he shamed us all and he would have a go at anything. He was the sort of bloke who wouldn't impress Mums but, providing he was not trying to get off with your sister, might impress your Dad.

I think it was Bunny who first realised that one of the black guys used to come back from lunch with a big grin on his face, and it wasn't long before we were all sitting in his old Jag having a draw after the canteen. It was as a result of this partnership that the three of us started harmonising whilst we were loading the timber on to pallets on rails for the kilns. We used to get off on it and no-one ever took the piss so I guess we sounded all right. I remember one time as we stood in the machine shop on wet time, we even started harmonising with the lathes, creating dissonances and eastern tones as well. Most of the other workers were sure we were quite mad, except the black guys who just shook their heads and smiled.

One day in late November or early December, we were loading stacks of timber in the pouring rain when Bunny suddenly said, "Sod this, why don't we fuck off to Paris?"

I knew that Gill would not call me again, so after thinking about the proposition deeply for about ten seconds I said, "I haven't got any money."

Bunny said, "Where would you rather be broke?" We both climbed off the stack and turned the job in. Within two days Bunny and I were in Paris.

∾

matuzzi

The Hotel du Commerce was already a well-known cheap lodging on the Rue de la Montagne Ste Geneviève. To say it was run-down implies that at one time it must have been fairly decent. Its present state belied that it was ever anything other than dark, dingy and smelly, with minute rooms barely big enough to take the bed, a cupboard and an evil smelling hand basin, set off with oddments of lino and rough painted walls. My army days were only five years behind me, and to give myself some sense of order I tried to make my bed most days—or at least to straighten it out. Once I even stripped the sheet away from the mattress, but the sight of what lay underneath lives with me still. The mattress looked as if it had been used as a dissecting table for about thirty years, which was probably half its real age. To this day I try never to read other people's love letters written on mattresses.

The whole place was presided over by Madame Matuzzi *"et mon fils, Jean."*

She was five foot two with eyes of blue and about the same size waist measurement, grizzled grey hair, rolled down stockings which revealed varicose veins and a jovial face with a ready smile. I can't recall her smoking but she sounded as if she did. After living there about a month I was awoken one morning by a lot of activity outside; Madame et Jean were hanging out bed sheets, and that night when Bunny and I got back to our room we had different linen—I can't bring myself to say clean, but it was not the same as we'd had up to that point. It cost eleven francs per night and we paid every night after working the cinema queues.

Madame appreciated our promptness, and not only got us a room on the ground floor out the back in the courtyard near a WC (there was another one on the first floor landing) but one night she insisted that we had a little drink from a bottle that she kept hidden.

"Attention flics!" she used to say, rubbing the side of her nose with a grubby finger. She dropped a sugar cube into each tiny glass and bade us throw it down. It was so strong that after two glasses we had to go and lie down. I seem to remember saying something about alcohol made from wood, but anyway we didn't notice the dampness of the beds that night.

Another little act of kindness towards us was the provision of a small paraffin stove which she put in the room one freezing cold night in January. The problem was that all the wallpaper left its moorings as the heat pulled moisture from the walls and steamed it off on to our beds. The next day the stove was gone and dry wallpaper had been pinned up on the crumbling plaster with drawing pins.

There was no doubt that Madame quite liked us, mainly I suppose because we paid nightly for our accommodation. But rough as we were, we were positively upmarket compared to the usual clientele. Across the courtyard from us lived two ladies of the evening who entertained their noisy punters through the small hours, but in the end we took hardly any notice of the crashes and bangings, and I never even saw them in daylight—though Bunny did, and commented that you could understand why they only went out after dark.

The two WCs that served all the patrons were of the 'bomb aimer' type and were really awful even by Paris standards. The one on the first landing had a wooden shed-type door and the walls were covered in graffiti in most European languages (plus Arabic). One notice in French had been translated into English as 'Please do not flush the dismembered bodies of your unborn children down the toilet as it blocks the drains.'

Because of the late hours many of the guests kept, and the occupations of some of the others, the front door was always open, enabling anyone to get in. There was little reason to lock the door as no-one living in this place would have anything worth stealing. There was the little window in the hall behind which Madame used to sit, fat knees apart, scratching her veins which ought to have been a deterrent to anyone planning on gaining entry for any criminal intent, and in front of her window were the stairs to the first floor.

One morning as we were leaving the hotel, I happened to notice that someone had taken a shit on the uncarpeted third stair, just out of sight of Madame's window. It remained there for several days. Neither Bunny nor I liked to say anything about it in case it was construed as a complaint. I don't think Madame Matuzzi knew anything about what went on upstairs, as she found moving about a bit of a nuisance as well as tiring. Although she would probably not have approved of the wording of the notice, she would have gone along with its practicality. I doubt if Jean could read, and if he could have, would have cared. As for the turd, no-one would have noticed the smell.

Madame Matuzzi favoured the toilet on the courtyard level as it was near her lair. Unfortunately it was also adjacent to our room. The smell from it was unbelievable, so the door was always left open to help disperse the build-up of dangerous gases. If you required privacy when forced by nature to enter this foul cabinet, it was necessary to turn the little lock on the door which was cleverly arranged so that a light went on at the same time. Unfortunately, once the electrical circuit was complete, you also received a rather nasty shock. I personally could not bear to go inside unless I had first thrown in a lighted newspaper in order to obliterate some of the excess smell (it brings a whole new meaning to taking a newspaper to the loo). Then by skilfully adapting a rubber band and hooking it over the lock, privacy and light could sometimes be obtained.

Usually though, by the time you had got properly into position with any degree of confidence that you might be on target, you began to get overcome by the fumes once more, and were forced into running the gauntlet of a short sharp shock and bursting into the morning air of the courtyard having aborted your mission. Besides, the local café was just around the corner and marginally less pungent.

Madame Matuzzi however was made of stronger stuff and was far more practical; she simply didn't bother closing the door.

"Bonjour mes enfants!" she would shout as we attempted the near impossible task of walking past her without looking directly at her,

responding only with as nonchalant a *"Bonjour madame!"* as we could manage whilst she grunted and puffed, poised in a most precarious position that was not quite squatting and not quite standing. As far as anyone could tell though her aim was perfect and she never missed the hole.

"For fuck's sake don't start her talking mate, we'll never get away," Bunny would warn me. I would find something deeply fascinating to study on my left sleeve as we scurried by.

"Il fait beau ce matin eh?" she would offer. *"Attention flics mes enfants eh!"*

"Oui Madame, a toute a l'heure," we limply chorused down the hall past the turd on the third step.

There was a bar on the corner of our street and the Rue des Ecoles, and we would start the day with a cup of coffee and, in my case, a hard boiled egg and a piece of baguette and butter. Then I would either go back to the hotel and play guitar for a while or mooch about the area of St Michel. My only source of income at this time was busking, which I dreaded.

The day we arrived in Paris I had just five pounds in my pocket. It must have been Bunny's idea to go to this particular area, as it was all new to me.

We stood on the Rue des Ecoles—bag in one hand, guitar in the other—and Bunny said, "Well how about it then, are you hungry?"

"Yes," I replied.

"Well let's go to work then."

"What right here, now?" I enquired, the nervousness creeping up on me.

"No mate," said Bunny, "there's these two cinemas down the road. We'll play there." So we made our way along the road to where two small cinemas were situated, one on the corner and the other just inside a tiny turning. To my relief there was no-one there, so I reasoned with my mate that there was no point in playing. So he explained to me the way Paris cinemas work: people do not enter the picture house once the film has begun, preferring to form a line outside where of course they are a captive audience. My heart was now beating as fast as it does before going on stage, and as we sipped a coffee across the road and watched, a queue began slowly to form at first one and then the other movie house.

Bunny and I had played together before on many occasions, and he was a very competent strummer with a slightly nasal voice with a good bit more penetration than me, but our repertoire was very esoteric, made up of 1950s blues, bluegrass and folk songs.

I wondered if we perhaps should have had something better known, but it was far too late to worry about things like that now. Both queues were now considerable and I knew it was time to move. My hands were trembling and I needed to go to the lavatory. The awful thing was, every one of my friends knew that I had carried myself around Europe playing guitar for a couple of years already, but due to my shy personality I had always played where the people had an option to avoid paying me anything, i.e. street corners. Here we were on a street where the audience had only the option of refusing the hat when proffered.

"I need to tune up," I announced as I returned from the loo. We managed a rudimentary A-string agreement and in a rare act of French café proprietor kindness, he allowed us to leave the guitar cases in the café and we crossed the road ready to take up position to play. As we drew near I excused myself again and went for a little stroll around the block to try and calm my almost uncontrollable shaking.

By the time I had regained my composure enough to play, Bunny was really agitated. "Come on mate for fuck's sake, they're about to let them in."

There was nothing left but to go for it, and as soon as the sound from my old Harmony Sovereign boomed out I was OK. Halfway through the second number the queue started to move. Suddenly Bunny stopped playing, put his guitar down and ran to the front of the queue. He pulled his cap out of his pocket and started bottling the line. I manfully continued on my own until the last of them had gone in. There was no time to count the money as the second queue had started to move.

"Oh shit man," said Bunny, "we'd better hop it, lively, lively."

With pockets jingling we ran across the road and over St Michel to the Rue Racine where there was another small picture house. Here we did our first proper busking, playing four numbers which became our staple show over the next few weeks.

We began with *San Francisco Bay Blues*, then *Hard Travelling*, followed by *Roll in My Sweet Baby's Arms* and finishing with *The Saints*. The first number was played halfway down the line; the next was played on the hoof as we slowly moved up towards the front. For the third we moved back down the line, bottling as we went; and the fourth we played as an unrequested encore. This generous performance was soon cut to three numbers, with the bottling being done by a third party for 10% of the take.

After our little show we returned to where we had left our cases and excitedly counted our small change. I don't remember how much we got, but it was more than we expected and we were able to pay for our drinks, a snack, and most importantly a room for the night.

Some people would have gone on to do much more playing, as there was certainly a good living to be made on the street if you were bold enough. I was content just to get by; in those early Paris days we got merry and occasionally pissed but we didn't drink a lot.

∽

musketeers

All northern European cities are cold in winter, but Paris, so far inland, was bitter. Part of the reason we played such a short set on the street was that we could not feel our fingers after the first number, and whilst sensitivity is not normally a quality that is in high demand as a busker, it does help to know what string you are pressing down. String breakages were common, but because there were always two of us we could cover for each other and we'd get away with it. I remember one freezing night I broke a B string and carried on playing, and at the end of the number I noticed that it had entered the back of my hand. To my amazement as I pulled it out I realised that it must have penetrated nearly half an inch and I hadn't felt a thing. Luckily it did not become infected—I don't suppose any germs could survive in that temperature.

I have always been a creature of habit, and I never ventured very far out of this small group of streets around St Michel. I hardly remember eating anything hot but occasionally one of those thin steaks and chips that you can get in nearly all French cafés. I drank coffee, developing a strong taste for espresso, and smoked Gauloises *sans filtre*, hardly slept, played guitar, laughed a lot, talked about what it would be like when Tubs came over, and in the main loved this existence.

I still experienced this terrible void whenever I thought about Gill, but in my heart I knew it was all over. I knew that somewhere she was living, working, maybe even loving someone else. When these thoughts of her came to me, the emptiness I felt almost made me sick. Since we were seventeen we had done everything together and now she was gone. I had tried to be faithful to her while she was in the States, but had slipped a couple of times, only to be consumed with guilt afterwards.

I knew in my heart that she would have erred as well, because no girl as beautiful as her would have been able to avoid the attention of men for very long. I knew that some of the time she had been the escort of some gay bloke who worked out of Hollywood but needed not to be perceived as homosexual. I also knew that there was a guy that she occasionally mentioned in letters, and if the thought that she may have loved him hurt me then, the pain I now felt was hardly bearable. I constantly went over our last few days together, wondering if it had all been my fault or was it just the payoff line for all my immaturity and insecurity. I constantly asked how she was feeling and constantly told her how I felt. Most of the time when I looked at her I could not believe she was mine, and the fact that she was so completely mine and had gone through so much with me made the pain of her going even harder. Sometimes I just felt like crying out like a wounded animal, such was my desolation.

My companions knew of as much of my hurt as I chose to tell them, and as the pain produced by the awful realisation that our affair was over began to subside, I found as any young man does that pretty girls still affected the vital parts, if only the heart would mend.

In truth the city provided so many distractions, and instead of a constant ache, the pain used to suddenly flood over me like a wave that hits you when your back is to the sea. Gradually the gaps between the waves grew further and further apart until, like giving up smoking, a whole day might pass without thinking of her at all. I had to wait a very long time for that to happen.

I also knew I had to do something about the female situation. I would have loved to have met a French girl, but it was as if they were on another planet as far as we were concerned. Also you have to put out the signs that you are interested in becoming involved with someone new. I guess I was still walking around wearing my mourning in a very visible way. Of course there were girls all around us from all over the world and even at street level there was a foreign community of sorts that we were becoming aware of. This area centred round the Boulevard St Germain and Odéon but I guess through shyness or British reserve we made very slow progress. Except for Tubs, who was convinced that everywhere we went girls were undressing him with their eyes.

Just before I left England I'd had a brief encounter with a girl called Anita. She was really beautiful, tall and slim with a lovely complexion, blue eyes and a pretty mouth and a cascade of blonde hair which she pulled up at the sides in a ponytail and left some to fall over her shoulders. She had a lovely south London accent, but after the admiration of her beauty there was not much to be said to each other really, and after a couple of dates I went cool. I was so lonely in Paris for girl company that somehow I prevailed on her to pay a short visit to Paris.

It was not a great success, and after the brief joy of a companion in my room/bed I lost interest and was unable to disguise my lack of depth of feeling for her. I'm sure her feelings were hurt; I just felt like a heel. I needed some sexual satisfaction and I really convinced myself that we could make it. Maybe that is the difference between my generation and the one my children have grown up in. It's funny how my generation never seemed to have friends of both sexes. We were all ensconced or involved sexually; working class kids got engaged then, and I had been engaged to Gill for about two years on and off by this time. Now it was most definitely off.[9]

At some point I decided I had to go home at Christmas. This again was probably an obligation that I felt towards my mum, and anyway I

---

[9] Years later I chanced to meet 'Slim Tony' and MB (two old mates from the sixties) in a pub in west London. It was one of those chance things when someone you haven't seen for years turns up out of the blue and you stand reminiscing over a few pints. Both blokes had been part of our late adolescent scene and we had lots to reminisce about.

At one point MB went to the gents toilet and Slim Tony said to me, "You nicked the best looking bird I ever had."

I was stunned and certainly couldn't remember at that point who he could mean.

"Her name was Anita and you pulled her off me at a Bonzo Dog Doo Dah Band gig at the Old Tiger's Head in Lee Green."

"Did I?"

I could not deny knowing Anita but I had no recollection of pulling her from anyone. I certainly went to plenty of Bonzo gigs with Henry, and Anita came from somewhere. Actually I had only to look at him as he spoke these words. The look in his eyes clearly showed pain even after all the intervening years. I felt terrible and thirty years later found myself apologising for something I did not remember doing. He laughed and said it didn't matter now but for a moment there in his eyes I saw all the pain of remembrance and knew that he had experienced that aching void that I had gone through with Gill.

Summer Lightning

have never spent a Christmas away from home to this day. I was back in Paris before New Year. If anything it was colder, but we still had our cinema queues and Bunny had met some more people. Tubs had arrived and we all shared the fortunes of the streets.

Tubs had brought a friend from Croydon who couldn't play guitar but who wanted to earn his living with us. His name was Robin Best and he had earned something of a reputation back home for being somewhat difficult and dangerous.

Robin was older by a few years than all of us and walked in subtly different worlds to our little trio. It was years later that I found out that he had been rejected by his mother and raised by his grandmother, which gave him a very strange attitude to all his women. Nevertheless he was from the now almost obligatory broken home, and was attracted like all of us to the music that gave us commonality. I had to believe it was the music because he was so successful at all other aspects of his social life. If it had not been the music I doubt very much if our paths would have crossed at all. Robin was a real predator and enormously experienced as far as girls were concerned. He was possessed of very good looks and more front than Blackpool. Even if a girl showed immediate distaste for him it would seldom put him off and whatever his formula was he never had any trouble pulling a new 'chick'. I had not taken to him and I was prepared for the worst.

Although the Olive Tree was the place where most of us met in Croydon, there was another coffee bar called 'The Chalet Suisse' which was frequented by a different class of kid altogether. Most of them had cars or access to them, and all of them had money that they did not earn. I suppose they were all middle class young people from the more prosperous parts of South Croydon and the suburbs of Selsdon and beyond. I only ever went in the place once, but Robin, who spoke with a posh accent (to my ears) used it on a regular basis, only latterly becoming a visitor to the Olive. Tubs was a sometime visitor to the Chalet Suisse and I suppose that's how their friendship developed. Robin had a reputation as a good man in a fight; the only trouble was that it was often he who started them.

I remember one night on the door of the Olive there was a little fracas and Robin who was smoking a small cigar stepped in to help out. Quickly weighing up the situation and realising that actions would be more effective than words, he moved into the group and hit the first one with a straight right hand which caused the chap's nose to sort of explode. The blow sent the chap reeling back down the narrow passage of the club entrance taking his three mates with him. There was no room for a full scale bundle and they were soon thrown out the door humiliated and damaged, with the promise they'd be back. They never did.

Robin sauntered back up the passage and leant forward to the girl taking the money and jutting out his chin wordlessly bade her take the cigar from his mouth, he then stepped into the gents to wash his hands (of blood) returning a few seconds later to jut out his chin to receive his cigar back from the girl. This all happened so quickly hardly a word was said. I thought it was pretty cool.

Some time later I learned that for a very brief period Robin had been an apprentice policeman but had decided to hold up a petrol station for some cash and had been nabbed as he drove off straight into the path of some of his colleagues. He had spent his twenty first birthday in the nick. Robin was very volatile and had little tolerance of gentler souls except for women. Up until this point I'd hardly ever been in a fight, and hearing of Robin's impending arrival I feared the worst. I needn't have worried however, as the bloke who arrived in Paris was very different to the one we knew in Croydon, both in looks and personality.

Bunny and I were out on the street as Tubs and Robin arrived, we were coming back from Place Contrescarpe where we occasionally went for an evening beer and had just arrived at Rue des Ecoles as they walked up Rue de la Montagne.

"Jesus, look at Bestie," sniggered Bunny. "What does he fucking look like?" Then after a moment, "Fuck me, he looks like Barnacle Bill the Sailor!"

We both burst out laughing. I have to admit it was embarrassing. There was Tubs in a white polo neck sweater matching jeans and jean jacket, leather Chelsea boots with guitar slung over his shoulder and a carrier bag holding his worldly goods.

'Bestie', on the other hand, looked like he'd done a smash and grab raid on Millets and a fancy dress shop. He was wearing flared sailor's trousers, a reefer jacket and white leather boots, and to top it all off he had a peaked naval cap on his head. His bag of belongings was vast by our frugal standards, and over his shoulder sticking out of a military duffel bag was what looked suspiciously like a guitar. Definitely uncool, I thought!

Gone was the over-confident swaggering self-assured bloke from the smart set of Croydon and in his place stood this risible caricature of what he thought a busker should look like—and he couldn't even play an instrument. Bunny was unable to hide his amusement but I started to feel sorry for the poor sod. Robin was plainly excited by the prospect of Paris street life and it showed in his eyes that were taking in everything we said. I remember thinking that we'd better enjoy his brief moment of insecurity because it wouldn't be long before he had it sussed.

The implement he carried in the duffel bag turned out to be a collapsible bass guitar which he intended to learn to play so that he could earn his share of the take. This was all very well, but no-one knew how to play one and no-one even cared about Robin's position—after all he'd let others suffer plenty of indignities in the past. I realised this wouldn't do however, and later spent some time showing him what not to hit if he could help it. After a week the bass was abandoned and Robin took up the job of bottling, at which he was superb. Though some of his methods for extracting money may have been illegal; I think particularly of the very firm thrust of the hat under the rib cage if someone refused to donate, and the long cold stare that implied he might be waiting for them after they came out of the cinema. For whatever reason, our take went up when Bestie bottled the queue.

Until this time we'd had a girl called Marie, who appeared from somewhere and offered to do the job, which she did very thoroughly and for 10% of the take. She was an Irish girl who had spent a bit of time in London and was here in Paris for reasons she never explained. Bunny was sure she was a 'brass' and Tubs hoped she was and certainly tried it on, but she wasn't having any from us boys.

It was extremely hard to determine her age because she wore so much make-up and was from a very different world to us, but I liked her. She had lovely unusually deep brown eyes and she always turned herself out well for us when she worked the queues. The boys were sure she was dipping us, but I think that would have been beneath her dignity. When Robin took over she accepted it without complaint. Once to see who was the best we let them both do the queue and though we let her go first, Robin still managed to get nearly as much again.

It soon became obvious that Robin's pride would not allow this situation to last, and one afternoon after he had got rid of the offending bass implement and acquired a Spanish guitar, I gave him a start with a few rudimentary chords. By the time I returned to Paris after Christmas, Robin was just about holding his own with the others and well on the trail of female company.

One Saturday morning just after New Year I met Marie with four of the roughest looking blokes I'd seen in a while. It was not yet midday but they were drinking champagne and were on the way to getting pissed. They could not have been more conspicuous as they had arrived in Paris in an old London taxi cab. Marie introduced me to them, herself a little squiffy, and they all offered me drink. I definitely didn't fancy getting to know them better and after about two weeks they all mysteriously disappeared.

Marie later confided what we already sussed—that they had done a bank job somewhere around London and were having a bit of fun in Gay Paree. I deliberately did not get close to them but it was a matter of some pride to me that Marie chose to confide in me, and I was proud that I managed to keep her confidences. I found it amusing watching the villains getting slowly more bored with their high life; the cultural differences began to wear them down and their frustration with the language and inability to communicate with anyone but themselves started to lead to tensions.

One of them in particular, called Pete, was a nasty paranoid piece of work, who thought everyone was taking the piss out of him. His hair was very dark and he had a pointed undamaged nose. One of the things that was pointed out to me early on in my travels is that it is sensible to respect a man who has a broken nose because he probably sustained it in a fight. The fact that he wears it like a badge warns other men that he might be dangerous (what it also signifies is that he has been hit and if he's been hit once he can be hit again). Anyway Pete, after flaunting his new money and getting pissed, his chat-ups misconstrued and misunderstood, just got angry.

"Who's he fuckin' lookin' at?" was his most commonly spoken or shouted remark, and several times before they all got bored and went back to England, the others had to hold him back from dangerous close calls with the locals. In a way I felt sorry for Pete as he would probably have enjoyed his trip to Paris if the others had let him have a punchup.

I am convinced that robbers don't steal just for the money, because when they have had a result they usually can't wait to get rid of it and usually in the most ostentatious manner. This unloading of spoils seems to give them a little satisfaction but cannot be the reason for robbing in the first place. Over the intervening years I have met a few villains including 'Jacka' Goody, the Great Train Robber, along with several other lesser ones, and most of them say they do it for the rush.[10]

1966 had come in on Boulevard St Michel with a chorus of car horns and a slight uneasiness that the general movement against America's involvement in Vietnam and the call to rational debate about politics, drugs, the meaning of life and the awareness fostered by the music of Bob Dylan had permeated the consciousness of French student life. The city was buzzing and we three musketeers had learned a Donovan song!

As someone who had written to Woody Guthrie, sung his songs all over Europe, defended Dylan's actions and songs from the outrage of some of my contemporaries (one of whom had accused Bob of 'crawling over the dying body of Woody Guthrie to success'), and as someone who loved the work of Bert Jansch, I was deeply resentful of Don. He has since become a good friend, but at the time I perceived him to be an exploiter of the vacant position of British Bob Dylan, and to my mind he did not deserve it. But then some have greatness thrust upon them, and Don handled it as well or better than most would have done. He's given the world a bunch of memorable tunes, loads of hits and has always been generous with his patience and time with others. Of course at the time I didn't know any of this, and having taken the piss out of his song about contagious flatulence, I ended up singing it on the Paris streets in fairly close Everly Brothers harmony with Tubs and Bunny. The French cinemagoers loved it. Thanks, Don.

∿

---

[10] One long-time friend of ours and almost reformed minor villain used to say when describing armed robbery, "Ralph, it's better than a bunkup."

joints

Snow had fallen some time in early January and settled around our neighbourhood. Christ, it was cold. As the boys and I wandered home to the Commerce at night we frequently saw 'clochards' sleeping over the hot air gratings above the metro, often with their boots under their heads to prevent them being stolen. Occasionally we would leave the smallest of our change in a shoe if it was visible, and we became on friendly terms with one or two old winos up at the Place Contrescarpe.

We were stunned to learn after a few nights elsewhere that one of them had frozen to death on the street the previous night. It was perhaps a couple of days later, turning left out of the hotel, that I noticed a pile of snow about a metre high begin to move. A couple of people shook the blanket that had covered them free of snow and brushed themselves down. I began to form the idea of a song about the poor people of Paris, but that had been done before. Maybe Paris boulevards or Paris streets? Streets of Paris even? I put the idea on hold for a while but it never left me.

Thinking only of ourselves and being away from English media, I was largely unaware of the things that were going on at home. Sometimes we glimpsed a copy of the Herald Tribune which was sold each evening by a very self-contained Finnish girl who was very fanciable in her blue jeans and jacket and fair hair. The odd perusal of tabloid French papers indicated that there was growing unrest with the influx of foreign flotsam that was finding its way to Paris. As spring approached, more and more penniless kids arrived: Americans, Dutch, some Germans, more English and soon every busking site was a jealously guarded property. On more than one occasion encroachers had to be reminded that these were our pitches, sometimes with threats levelled at their instruments and more rarely at their person. Pitches you could protect, but street corners were up for grabs and on every street corner there was someone doing something: conjurers, fire eaters, sword swallowers and strummers of every type of ability and nationality.

One street entertainer caught my imagination, and some years later I wrote a short instrumental and named it after him (*The Wino and The Mouse*). This little old man used to sit outside the self-service restaurant on St Germain des Prés on a piece of cardboard. He played little meandering notes on a penny whistle whilst a little mouse ran up and down the length of the instrument in an appearance of dancing. It was not a great show and not much else happened, but it was enough to catch the eye and earn the old boy a little change.

One day I observed his preparations for the performance which entailed dipping the tiny creature into a glass of water which along with the mouse's showbiz nerves and the extreme weather conditions made the poor thing shiver which added to the dancing effect. I liked to think that he was able to warm his little mouse hands over the warm air coming out of the finger holes on the instrument. Usually though the corner musicians would be strummers, and Bunny's most often repeated judgement was "crap" as he walked past, usually loud enough to be heard.

Nat Schaeffer was a piano accordion player from London who every year came over to Paris to play for the tourists.

"What do people come to Paris for?" Nat would ask rhetorically. "I'll tell you, they want to see the Eiffel Tower, the Mona Lisa, the Seine. They want a bit of romance and they want piano accordions. And if the French don't want to dress like Frenchmen and play their accordions, I will."

Nat was about forty five years old, of medium height and slim with a small French-style moustache. For professional purposes he wore a beret, striped matelot tee-shirt and black trousers. Although some of the buskers were really getting on our nerves, for Nat the situation was almost intolerable. One night Tubs was sitting in a café in the Rue Seine when he overheard Nat talking soothingly to some young girl at a table just behind where he was sitting. By his tone of voice he was obviously trying to pull her and as it became more and more obvious that he wasn't going to succeed, his tactics turned from trying to impress her to sympathy for his situation. His pleas grew more plaintive and desperate as he realised the situation was moving further away from his grasp, whilst nearby Tubs (who had probably had a joint) was finding the situation more and more hysterical. Tubs reported it this way.

"I know what it is, you think I'm too old for you don't you, you want another drink, I suppose you think I'm trying to get you drunk, listen babe I could have any woman I want in this town, you think you're special, you're not so special, is it because I'm old, listen there's many a good tune in an old fiddle, it's because I play accordion isn't it? I suppose you like them bleedin' guitar players don't you? why? they can't play, do you know most of them learn to play on the boat coming over here..."

At this point Tubs could hold his laughter in no longer and sprayed whoever he was with with beer, and having made such an outburst attracted Nat's attention, which alerted him to the fact that he may have been overheard, so Tubs had to pretend to have been hit by a really good punchline to some joke to divert Nat's attention. When the situation was back under control Tubs swore he heard Nat lean over to the girl and ask in a softer even more hurt tone, "Is it because I'm Jewish?" After spraying everyone for the second time Tubs was forced to make his excuses and leave.

One night on the Rue de Medicis we were playing the queues as usual when a young American made himself known to us. He had been standing in line for the movie, but decided that we looked more fun. He was with his wife Melinda, and after our performance they joined us for a coffee across the road in the bar, then invited us back to their hotel, the Juliana.

Gary Petersen had recently turned twenty one and had inherited a trust fund from his dad. Mr. Petersen Sr. was a very wealthy man who had many wives and offspring. To satisfy his obligations to his children he had created these funds that became available on maturity. Gary had managed to convince the draft board of his unsuitability for service by affecting to be homosexual and then mentally unstable. He was frighteningly thin, with barely enough on his hips to hold up a pair of Levis.

He made a passable lisping gay boy, although he was totally straight. However I'm sure he got out of service on the grounds of being mentally unstable.

He was a very strange but enormously talented young man. He ran from California for New York where, while studying guitar with the legendary Rev. Gary Davis and jazz with Les Span, he met, fell in love with, and married Melinda Patton. Gary was kind and generous and Melinda was warm and eccentric. They were a wonderful crazy irresponsible couple who slept a lot and smoked an enormous amount of dope in a little pipe with no tobacco. With his trust money Gary had purchased a Gibson Les Paul, a 1941 vintage Martin D-28 and two one-way tickets to Paris with his new bride. What I was to hear later that night would change my life again.

The two of them were so nice that we could not resist the invitation to visit. After offering us a smoke, which we accepted to be sociable, Gary took out his beloved Martin and played for us. That night in their hotel room I heard the best live guitar playing I'd ever heard in my life. The moments flew past as if he was a weaver of magic. Notes of unheard syncopation floated around their tiny room as Bunny and I sat totally entranced whilst Melinda shyly relished our enjoyment of her young husband's ability.

Amongst my friends I was regarded as a pretty good guitarist, but in Gary's company I was a rank beginner. His classical ragtime playing was sensational; my jaw literally dropped at the things he could do and it stayed dropped. The boys got me to play my bits of Blind Boy Fuller, Anji and so on, and although Gary was complimentary I knew he was out of my class. When I got back to my place I tried to emulate what he had done. I managed to get some way with his version of *Buddy Bolden* which I subsequently recorded on my first album under the wrong name of *Blind Blake's Rag*.

When I had learned to play the guitar there were no songbooks to teach you, like there are now. My method comprised lifting the needle on and off a record, listening carefully to try and work out what was going on. Even with the best ears in the world this was a highly unreliable plan, and I often convinced myself that something was correct only to go back to a piece years later to find I was miles off.

Gary not only had a remarkable set of ears, he also understood music in an intellectual way, he could actually tell you what chord something was just by listening to it, e.g. E minor 6th flattened 13th sus 4th. What to me was even more amazing was his deep affection for country blues, never 'correcting' musical naivety with what would be the correct musical thing; if someone played a twelve-and-a-half bar blues, then that's how Gary played it. Obviously if you can sit at the feet of someone like the Rev. Davis you are in touch with a living thread with the past, and you learn an even deeper respect for these masters of their instrument. Gary also composed tunes of wonderful melody coupled with beautiful bass harmonies as he employed his almost double-jointed finger style to tremendous effect.

For example, Gary often played the A chord in the first position with the first joint of his second finger only! It was awesome for us skifflers and because I'd grown up playing with guys who jealously guarded all their knowledge to the point of turning away when they were about to play a particular part they knew you wanted to know, I could never look directly at Gary's fingers for fear he would hide his skill from me. On the contrary, he was generous to a fault and I was mesmerised by his ability and so grateful for his willingness to share his talent.

I think if you truly love music there are few things in the world that compare to making it: the first time you can cleanly play the (aptly named) F chord, the first time you play a tune you have composed all the way through, the time you share a newly completed song with a trusted friend, the thrill of anticipation you get when you open your guitar case to take out your instrument to play. That's how I felt again with Gary; each day I was learning something new. I was discovering new harmonies and my right hand was beginning to master the mind-over-matter techniques required to play ragtime properly. On top of this, Gary and I were beginning to play together, though he never contemplated busking with me; his playing was too subtle for the street.

Gary and Melinda had a friend called Isobel from New York; she was very interested in pornography and delighted in telling us all about her goofy cousin who could only achieve a climax if a woman abused him by calling him names and making him lie on the floor. It was all a bit strong for me, especially as I felt sorry for the poor bastard, but she said I shouldn't be, because he was very happy with this arrangement. Through Isobel we met some other Americans; I particularly remember George who was a genuine draft dodger. George had a slight lisp and was nearly broke, but he always produced some candy after everyone had been smoking for what he called the 'munchies'. We would meet up at Gary's room and play guitars, smoke dope and wander round the streets of the quarter.

These sessions were never enough for Tubs, who always wanted to get that bit further out than everyone else. The joints he rolled were twice the size of anyone else's, and he developed a technique of using loads of 'skins' when manufacturing. His preparations for take-off became more and more elaborate and pedantic. Soon he realised that the paper that tampons were wrapped in was as thin as the cigarette papers he used. He started to collect them, and to ask girls of our acquaintance if they were having a period. If they replied in the affirmative he would ask them for their wrappers and ask them to open them as near to the end as they could manage. After mixing the tobacco and other materials together, he would painstakingly stuff the empty wrapper, making the roach out of cardboard and putting this in the open end resulting in him having what resembled a white cigar. He would then smoke until he could hardly move.

I was becoming concerned for him. All he seemed to want to do was get wasted. The strange thing was that he was not unhappy, but he was increasingly drawn to the low life and the junkies that you can find any-where if you try. He became fascinated with an American banjo player called Curran, and whilst I was away in England began to call round to see him, allegedly to play music together. Curran was a junkie and Tubs was fascinated by the ritual of preparing his fix.

Tubs wasn't using at this time, but under supervision he helped Curran with his strap and spoon and learned how to load the syringe. It was, from what Tubs told me, an almost doctor/patient relationship. Tubs watched enthralled as Curran became stoned and spoke softly to his new friend. Their bonding was confirmed when one day Tubs called round unexpect-edly to find his friend collapsed across the sink in his tiny room, blood all up the wall from a fix that had gone wrong. Tubs relished his role as saviour and was very soon using the needle himself. It was classic, him trying to convince us that he had it all under control and that he was cool, and to be fair he was still smoking and drinking.

We all gave him our fears and advice but he ignored all of us and did his own thing. He was always looking for quick money and hatching crazy schemes. Sometimes he would seem mildly deluded, saying things like "that girl over there keeps on undressing me with her eyes," or "she fancies me gutless."

We found this way of talking quite amusing, but sometimes I wondered what was going on in his brain. Our morning rituals gradually began to change, and more and more we found ourselves across St Germain where we might eat a croque monsieur or spin a coffee out for an hour or two. Around Rue de Seine there were a lot of small bars and all sorts of fascinating characters. Most of them had money of some kind and I think we had a little kudos by virtue of the fact that we took care of ourselves via the streets.

One little group caught my eye who always sat at the next bar to us but in the way that bars touch each other on the crowded streets we could all hear each other's conversation and anyway these three guys were American, and Americans always seemed to talk to each other in public as if they were deaf. These blokes couldn't care less who heard them. They always seemed to be having a good time, and it slowly dawned on me that they were always stoned.

Tubs was fascinated by them, especially when it became common knowledge that they could get LSD. It also became clear that they were gay. I was intrigued by their behaviour and astonished to hear that they spoke to each other just like the gays back home, only with American accents. The ringleader was the most outrageous in his mannerisms and I doubt he would have been able to flaunt his sexuality with as much abandon back in the USA. He was going for it, and we all found it quite amusing and just another rich seam of the eccentricity that so enhanced our Left Bank days. Soon rumours started to go around as to how they used some of these new drugs to seduce young boys, and we all watched in helpless fascination as one young fellow was gradually absorbed into their clique. He seemed happy enough, so then there were four of them.

Tubs had made friends with another strange bloke, a South African called Dennis. He was a classics scholar and a very intelligent and funny guy. He was both fascinated and appalled by Tubs. Dennis seemed so straight, with his spotless shirts and immaculate pressed trousers, and always clean-shaven. Tubs kept up appearances in the main, but he was starting to let go a little. It appeared that Dennis liked to let Tubs draw him into these scrapes he would not ever allow himself to have entered on his own. I particularly remember his shame when I enquired what was in the bottle he was carrying wrapped up in a paper bag. He leant towards me to confide that it was a lotion for the treatment of 'crabs' (crab lice).

He blamed Tubs for this problem because he got them from some chick that he and Tubs pulled somewhere. But if he hadn't been somewhat proud of this street-cred affliction, why hadn't he lied about it? None of us would have ever known. We later heard that he'd had a terrible bad trip on some acid in the States and never came back from it.

One day I bumped into Tubs by the Café Seine and he was quite animated.

"I've got a great ruse afoot," he said, "a ru-u-u-u-se." He stretched the word to enjoy it the more. "I've got wind through one of the blokes in the Café Bussey that there's this African diplomat that's coming through and he wants a white girl for the night and he'll pay 10,000 new francs for the privilege."

"Tubs," I said, "that would make you a pimp or a ponce. You're not going to be able to get any girl to do it."

"We'll see about that. I've already got someone in mind," he replied mysteriously.

Nothing more was said, but a flurry of excitement went round our small community as speculation began as to whom the girl might be. Tubs enjoyed the task immensely; chatting up girls was always something he enjoyed, but this quest added a whole new piquancy to the challenge. As the day grew closer and no candidate had emerged it began to seem more unlikely that the arrangement would take place, but Tubs had not given up and with about one day left to find a girl he was successful. Far from being a brassy type, she was a slightly round mousy little thing, American and broke. She was trepidacious but had no problem with the morality of the thing. Talking to her before the event, I was amazed at her matter-of-fact attitude. Croydon seemed very far away.

The assignation duly took place in some small hotel nearby on the appointed day. Tubs confirmed that it had taken place, but we didn't see the girl for some days and when we did I was shocked. She was wearing shades but she was still bruised under the glasses. She was shaking a little, wearing no make-up or stockings, smoking heavily and not saying much. I felt a mixture of compassion and curiosity. I never heard the details, but it was clear she had been very badly abused, and to make matters worse she was never paid. Tubs was vaguely sympathetic but uncontrite. We began to drift apart, and anyway I had met Nanna.

nanna

I first saw Nanna standing outside the big bar at the end of Rue des Ecoles: a very pretty girl wearing a very green coat and black suede boots that were too wide for her slim legs. Her haircut reminded me of Leslie Caron. Her friend Karen was American; she had long dark hair and huge brown eyes. She too was pretty but not as slim as Nanna (the suede boots belonged to her). The two girls shared a room in the Hotel Welcome in Rue de Seine with a Swiss girl called Eve that Tubs fancied.

Eve had a job but the other two girls were broke and found it quite a gas to work with us. Nanna was Norwegian and engaged to an American army guy; they had been together some time and Bill had visited Nanna's folks back home. Karen was unattached. Tubs introduced us all and as far as I could tell I made very little impression on either girl, but it was so nice to have female company again. I found that I was prepared to shave in the freezing cold water that came out of the smelly sink in my room before going out and meeting the girls. Some nights after playing we would meet some of their acquaintances and everyone would sit and talk quite frankly about their lives and morality. My recent past was still too painful to discuss so I told them of my days as a boy soldier. They seemed to be impressed.

As far as getting money from the cinema queues went, neither of them was very good. Nanna was far too gentle to bully the small change out of the reluctant Parisians and we were all beginning to feel the growing unrest amongst the locals about the foreigners who found their way to Paris expecting to find a living there. Stories had started to reach us about arrests and even instrument confiscation, as well as the proceeds from buskers who were nabbed by *les flics* (the police) whilst bottling the crowd. We were all a little wary and tense with the situation. Once or twice we ventured out of our quarter as far as the Champs Elysées, where the money was very good but the chances of getting nicked were even higher. Sometimes we played sidewalk cafés and this too could be good. But, creature of habit that I was, I still preferred my own patch that we'd managed to cling on to. Our circle of friends was changing too, and my friendship with Nanna was changing at the same time. She still saw Bill, but we two were keeping company even when we weren't working the cinemas.

Somewhere around this time I'd met a German called Bernard Grey. He was a lot older than me and as Tubs was more and more working his own scene and still being a very nervy street performer I threw my lot in with him and we started to play together. Bernard found it necessary to call himself Grey after his 'Scottish' grandmother. I never believed his granny was Scottish, but it clearly suited him not to have a German name.[11]

We all got along together, but I think Bill was beginning to get the ache with me. Although Nanna and I were still just friends, I was certainly harbouring stronger feelings for her and I hoped she felt the same. Nanna spoke very good English with a charming Norwegian uplift at the end of sentences. In spite of her knowledge she still made small mistakes with her vocabulary. One evening we were playing some sidewalk cafés near Pigalle and it was pouring with rain. I thought I might get a few more sympathetic francs from the punters by continuing to ply my trade as the rain came down. I sort of stood outside the awnings over the cafés with the guitar just under the protection of the material. The effect was that I became quickly drenched and my old Harmony guitar stayed dry. Unfortunately the audience found more humour than sympathy in my

---

[11] A couple of years ago I was looking through some snapshots in Pete and Gill Brown's collection from their days in Paris and among the names like Alex Campbell and the Thompson Brothers from Croydon and an earlier time, I spotted a snap of this Bernard who was working the streets or just hanging out at least three or four years before I arrived.

plight. I seemed to be making out all right, though, and I suppose I was trying to impress Nanna with my boyish, devil-may-care bravado.

We finished playing one café, and as we hurried across the boulevard she looked at me and said with real concern, "Oh Ralph, you must get your wet clothes off or you might catch nymphomania!"

I hoped that it might have been a Freudian slip. It gave everybody a few laughs in repetition. Nanna had by now met Gary and Melinda and we increasingly went around together. One day they took us to see a concert by an experimental group who were playing instruments of extraordinary construction. Mainly glass rods of various lengths and thickness, some had long wires attached to them and reflectors for the sound; they were variously tapped or struck but mostly caressed with fingers or gloves to give an ethereal sound of immensely soothing effect. The piece was continuous and apparently improvised, occasionally dissonant but never discordant and harsh. We were transported and delighted, perhaps enhanced by a little dope beforehand but certainly abetted by our now mutually growing feelings for each other. The effect was both intoxicating and erotic, and later that afternoon in my grotty little room Nanna and I became lovers. From that moment everything changed.

Paris, they say is made for lovers. I don't know if this is any more true of the Latin Quarter than, say, Sutton Coldfield—lovers are probably so self-centred that they just think the world smiles on them wherever they are.[12]

The thing was, we were in Paris, spring was on its way, we had somewhere to stay together, our lives revolved around music, and we had mad and eccentric friends. So all things considered, we were in with a chance. We also had Bill.

To say that Bill was not best pleased with the situation was an understatement. News filtered back to us that he was determined to seek revenge. I was very uneasy and wished that Robin was still around, instead of having departed with his three chords to Geneva in an MG. I saw Bill everywhere and once even thought he was skulking around the inside of the hotel. The locks on the doors were not strong enough to repel a cat so we slept with a large piece of wood under the pillow. It was an uneasy time.

On Rue Xavier Privas there was a little bar called the 'Bombarde', and this became a hangout for us as we could sit for hours with a beer and

---

[12] As my old manager Joe Lustig used to say, "When you're in love the whole world is Jewish!"

play guitars quietly—which made a big change from having to thrash it out on the streets every night. We actually became friendly with some French people, in particular a youngish guitar player who thought I was the bee's knees because I could play finger-style.

It's hard now to realise the effect guitarists who played with their fingers had on other musicians, because nowadays so many use this method, from Mark Knopfler in the world of rock, to Jerry Donahue in country rock, and all the folkies from Bert Jansch on down, but at that time it was almost the exclusive preserve of British and American players who had acquired the techniques from their black American cousins. I am sure that most guitarists will admit that the first time you hear some picker playing Scott Joplin's *Maple Leaf Rag* is a moment you never forget, that an instrument with just six strings and with only one hand to be able to project the melody, rhythm and bass all at the same time is really awesome (the other hand meanwhile is as it were manufacturing the notes on the fretboard).

I really enjoyed my moments of fame at the Bombarde, and when I got to persuade Gary to come and play there too our reputation was secured. Gary would seldom sing and when he did it was a strange sound, somewhere between the voice of an old lady and a guy that had had a couple to get him going. He sang *Diving Duck* and *Buddy Bolden* and would patiently accompany most of my repertoire. He loved some of the Beatles tunes and did a stunning version of *My Babe*. I did not however share his passion for endless and repetitive twelve bars, which seemed pointless to me. Tubs would get loaded and quite cheerfully spend a half hour vamping away on his three chords. This part of the session usually had the effect of me leaving the smoky room and going for a wander outside.

One day Melinda noticed an advert in the paper saying that Memphis Slim was playing in a bar called 'Le Chat Qui Peche'.

"Why don't we go and play there?" asked Gary with a huge stoned grin.

"You must be joking!" I said. "Because we're not good enough."

"Oh yes we are," said Gary, and try as I might I could not get him to relinquish the idea. We began to practise more earnestly together, but when we heard how much it was going to cost to get in I felt relieved because now I certainly would not be going. Then Melinda bought the tickets for the four of us and I reluctantly dragged my guitar with me to the club where Gary and Melinda were already seated.

Gary had been smoking extensively for the whole day and was fairly relaxed by the time I arrived. Memphis Slim was genial and clearly enjoying being in Paris. His style is not my favourite but if I hadn't been so nervous at the prospect of our impending debut I would have enjoyed him. When the great man took a break Gary went up with me and asked him if we could play.

"Oh you can play the blues can you?" said Memphis Slim.

"Yes sir," answered Gary politely and smiled his stoned friendly grin.

"Sure!" said the great man. "Let's hear what you can do."

Perhaps I was wrong, but I thought I detected a patronising note in his response, and that was enough to undermine me completely. I told Gary I couldn't join him, but Gary didn't seem to mind. He went up on stage and played his old Gibson L5 and sang in his creaky stoned nasally voice. He should have played the old Martin, because there was poor amplification on stage and even a great guitar like an L5 can sound tinny. The public largely ignored Gary's efforts and Melinda sat breaking the contents of an entire box of matches into tiny fragments before her new husband left the stage to indifferent applause. I certainly respected Gary for his courage and could never have done what he did myself. I felt I had let him down, but Gary was pretty pleased with himself. I am afraid that I was embarrassed and after a discreet interval we left, went back to their hotel, smoked a little dope and played guitars together.

Around this time we met Cindy, an American girl who was striking without being pretty. She was several years older than us and had money. She lived in a nice hotel near the island in the Seine. She had captured a huge young, shy, probably virgin male football college student who was attending the University of Hawaii, and they were hugely happy.

One day Cindy announced that a hamburger bar had opened on the Champs Elysées and it was her intention to introduce all of us lowlifes to the culture of the good ol' US of A by treating us all to a burger. For a lad who had only had the Croydon Wimpy Bar experience to go on (where the likes of Kercher, Liloff and Atkinson discussed Ginsberg, Corso and Ferlinghetti whilst being waited on by Shirl the fat waitress), a real hamburger was quite a treat—if a little decadent and frivolous. Our days were like that, often punctured by spontaneous indulgences. Nanna liked ice cream and sweets which I thought immature and unhip, but I found myself joining in with these moments. Maybe I'd been old too long. Gary and Melinda were much the same and after my initial reluctance to let go, I joined in with them too.

Rumours greeted my return that an even more disgruntled Bill was on the prowl again. In spite of Nanna's assertion that their relationship was already over because of his assumption that it was OK to pick up other girls, Bill was not able to come to terms with this fact. One night I had arranged to meet Nanna at the Bombarde, and when I arrived there was quite a crowd of us. As I sat down I was immediately approached by Cindy telling me that Bill was in the place up at the bar and was seriously pissed off. I decided that I'd had enough of all this cloak and dagger stuff and I went over to talk with him in a reasonable way.

"Look Bill," I said, "it's crazy going on like this. Nanna wants this to be over between you and her, and she's going out with me now so can't we just try to get on together?"

"I'm not talking to you, you fucking bastard," he hinted. "I want to talk with Nanna."

I went back to Nanna and explained the situation. "Why don't you see him just for a minute," I asked, having not read the madness in his eyes to be anything other than hurt pride.

Against her better judgement, Nanna went outside to talk with him on the street and the heavy wooden door of the club swung shut. For some reason we sensed that all was not well and Cindy opened the door to look outside. Bill in his rage had knocked Nanna to the ground and started kicking her. Cindy screamed, at which point I jumped up from the table and raced round to the door, but Cindy's cry of shock had alerted Bill who pulled a huge Bowie knife from his boot. The next few seconds flew past.

"Christ he's got a knife!" yelled Cindy, as everyone rushed for the door. I could see what was happening, but as I struggled to get out of the door it was pushed wide open as the huge bulk of Cindy's boyfriend from Hawaii hurtled past. In the time-honoured manner of all heroes I was still trapped behind the door as Bill took off down the tiny street. Everyone was running and girls were screaming when Cindy's boyfriend produced what can only be described as a near perfect American football tackle, the kind you dream of making. He dived full-length with no thought of his own safety or the solid nature of the road and grabbed Nanna's assailant around the knees at the same time that his shoulder crashed into Bill's waist.

The effect was spectacular as both of them careered through a restaurant plate glass window and landed on a table where a couple were dining, showering glass and food everywhere. Nanna was on her feet being comforted by Cindy, so I ran past her into the restaurant and hauled Bill to his feet, pulling one of his arms behind him and forcing it up his back. I was shaking with anger and fear and so was he. I wanted to kill him for what he had done and I wanted to die for what I'd been unable to do.

I had to be content to hold the creep until the police and ambulance arrived. All hell was going on around us with people screaming and men shouting. Bill said nothing and waited without resistance until the authorities arrived. I felt so frustrated just holding him there. I really wanted to hurt him, trapped as he was and unable to escape, but apart from giving his arm the odd tweak to let him know I was still there I took my lead from the quiet American from Hawaii who calmed the proceedings down with his height and unassuming authority.

Later Nanna told me that Bill had watched his mother kill his father with a shotgun.

Nanna was allowed out of hospital later that night with severe bruising, but sadly the woman diner on whose table the two Americans landed had her leg broken, something we all deeply regretted. The hardest thing to come to terms with was that, as Bill was an American GI, he was back out on the street within hours of his arrest. I had a few sleepless nights thinking I could still hear him creeping about the Paris streets, but he never troubled us again. For as long as I live I will wish it was me who had rugby-tackled the rat.

fin

Life on the street was improving as the weather got warmer, and consequently playing got easier, though my rituals before performance remained fairly elaborate, just as now, nearly thirty years on—just one more cigarette, one more tune up, mislaid the pick etc. etc.

In early spring, Bernard told me he was going to Brussels to visit his girlfriend and did I fancy a change of scene? I told him I did. On arrival Bernard got me a room and deposited me in the Café Welkom—and that was the last I saw of him for two days while he made up for lost time. I only have so much time for 'café society'—the endless hanging about doesn't sit easily with me and I usually find that I get impatient with circular discussions about art and the meaning of life.

The same goes for sitting around someone's pad smoking joints and giggling or hammering out endless twelve bars, or worse, tuning guitars. It was interesting to be somewhere else but I wondered how long I would be able to stand not doing anything. I was sitting halfway down the bar when a group of young people about my age came in, and after lighting up and ordering coffee they began to talk in very loud voices, arguing and bantering like students everywhere. I had decided that they were very un-hip but I had nowhere else to go so I stayed put and tried to understand a little of their conversation. It appeared that they were mostly talking about the night before when a generally good time seemed to have been had by all. Then suddenly in the chatter I heard the name Derroll Adams, and shortly the name came up again.

There could only be one Derroll Adams, surely; my heart picked up a bit and I concentrated even harder to understand what they were saying.

Derroll Adams, in partnership with the wonderful Jack Elliott, had made one of the most influential albums of the sixties as far as those of us who wished to follow in the footsteps of the great Woody Guthrie were concerned. The album was called 'The Ramblin' Boys' and had changed the lives of several people that I knew who had willingly bought into the lifestyle and philosophy contained in the grooves of this record. Could Derroll be in Brussels? Did he live near here? Finally I plucked up courage to ask in French, *"Excusez moi, mais je pense que j'ai entendu le nom Derroll Adams, est-ce qu'il habite ici?"*

"Yes, he lives here," said a tall young man in English. "You can meet him if you like." Some of the other kids tittered in the background, and I was embarrassed. I asked if this was the same Derroll Adams who played the banjo and was assured that it was. The tall young man explained that usually by prior arrangement somebody accompanied Derroll to the bar as he was often unsteady in the mornings due to drink. I felt I understood and asked if I could bring him to the bar the next day. Would he mind being met by a stranger? The young man assured me that it would be OK and I felt quite excited by the prospect. The young man turned out to be more simpatico than he first appeared as we chatted—then he revealed that he was the grandson of the artist Marc Chagall. My trip to Belgium was really becoming an adventure.

I woke early the next day and followed the directions to where Derroll was living, located the number of the apartment and nervously knocked at the door. After a few seconds the door half opened and a harassed looking youngish woman looked out,

"Je m'excuse, je viens à accompanier Derroll au bar," I offered.

"Oui, je le sais," she replied in a heavy resigned tone and pushing the door to a quarter closed, called in a soft voice to Derroll to come to meet the stranger out on the street.

I wasn't prepared for the sight of the man who arrived on the doorstep and carefully stepped down to the pavement. He looked like a real old man. He was taller than I'd imagined he would be and very pale. He was unable or unwilling to speak, and his walk was unsteady. Supporting him slightly on my arm I began a non-stop babble of how pleased I was to meet him and what his music had meant to me and how Max Faulkner and I had hoped to emulate him and Jack by hitching across Europe playing guitars and trying to become the Ramblin' Boys of Croydon...

Derroll's response to this was zero and we shuffled along to the bar where some of yesterday's crowd were already sitting. Most of them acknowledged him in some way, but none of them afforded him the respect I felt he deserved. I asked him what I could get him; he motioned towards the bar with a wave of his hand and one of the students whispered that Derroll would like a whisky and coke. I happily ordered Derroll's usual and was only slightly shocked when I was given a quarter bottle of the stuff and a single small bottle of coke. I had to help Derroll get the top off the whisky as the poor man had little strength in his hands. He took a moderate swig and then topped up the amount he had swallowed with a little dribble of coke. By the time he was halfway down the bottle he had begun to talk. At three quarters down the bottle he began to take an interest in me, though clearly he didn't remember my meeting him at his home. I told him of my desire to sort of follow in his footsteps, quickly adding "not all of them" and I asked him if he had any plans to play.

"I don't play much any more. It's the drink," he explained in his gentle bass baritone voice, but for once I wasn't going to stand for 'no'. I worked on him for a long time and eventually he agreed to get his banjo. It duly arrived from somewhere, and after more drink and tuning the thing to his satisfaction, he began to finger the instrument. For me it was a moment of pure joy and as I just happened to have my guitar with me I asked if I might pick along. He played so softly that my guitar kept drowning him out and he kept telling me to play quieter. I found this so hard to do because of my excitement and pleasure but I had several flat picks and eventually found the softest one so that he didn't object to my duetting.

I was so happy and was able to offer accompaniment to most of what he could play—which wasn't much because drink had made him forget lyrics and a lot of tunes—but his demeanour improved so much so that I managed to get him to agree to do a little busking with me in one or two places nearby. Reluctantly he agreed, and I am proud to say that I worked a couple of bars with the great man. He kept telling me to play softer and I ended up using a shirt collar stiffener to strum lightly behind him. The only words he could remember went with a song called *Little Birdie*, and of those the only ones which came to him were "little birdie little birdie." It was not a session of great variety but I shall never forget it. Derroll cannot recall any of it!

We have become good friends and still meet occasionally, most recently at a concert that Billy Connolly gave in Glasgow when he invited me and Derroll to be his special guests.

As my memorable night with Derroll came to a close and he became more and more lucid, he confided in me, "You know Ralph, the thing with an alcoholic is that when most people say, 'Boy did I get drunk yesterday,' I say, 'Boy did I get sober!'"

I left Bernard in Brussels and returned to Paris; I was missing Nanna and wanted to tell someone about my adventure. It was good to be back even after such a short time away. We got to know different people and our circle of acquaintances continued to grow. After getting the minimum from the street to sustain me and pay my rent, Nanna and I would wander slowly through our patch and make our way to Rue Xavier Privas and into the dark womb-like safety of the Bombarde, where we were regarded almost as regulars.

Gradually over the evenings spent there we became aware of a quiet and intense young guy who always wore black gloves. He was an American and gradually he was pulled into our company. Our conversations were rambling, funny and disjointed and I suppose we all assumed that because we were in Paris, we were bound together by some obvious arty interest. At best our politics would have been described as vaguely left wing. Sexual matters were discussed with more candour than I was used to especially in mixed company. I know now that it is one of the most commonly used tricks to show how liberated one is. Those of us with girls were usually the first to leave the company, but Nanna and I often stayed up until the very early hours. I always preferred the softening to the conversation that female company brings. The young American was called Steve, and apart from the eccentricity of his refusal to ever take off his gloves he was a funny, average sort of bloke.

Late one night he told us that he had seen active service in Vietnam. This was a war that had hardly registered with most of the people we were with. We listened eagerly to his stories. All I knew at this time was that it had been Kennedy who had sent the US soldiers into southeast Asia,

SUMMER LIGHTNING

but we were all largely ignorant of the horrors of that conflict.

The stories and coverage that we knew about were somehow related in my mind to the riots in Watts in Los Angeles that Gill had brought to life in her eagerly awaited letters to me whilst she worked there. My knowledge of the civil rights movement was still concerned with the very basic and sentimental views that were all mixed up with the songs of Bob Dylan and my early attempts at songwriting.

It took a little time before Steve really trusted us enough to stop trying to be funny all the time. He definitely wanted to unload on us, but just as he seemed to be nearly ready he would change tack and make a silly joke. Slowly as his confidence grew his stories gained a greater intensity and it began to emerge how deeply affected by his war he had been. At one point, when our naive understanding of the rights of the people of North Vietnam to self-determination was being aired, and by implication our support for the Viet Cong, he leaned forward, his eyes blazing and said in an eerily calm voice, "They use little kids you know."

My politics at this time were pretty far left, so obviously I sided with the people of Vietnam to decide their own destiny; this was all right so long as I was in England and perceived the US army as a bunch of John Wayne types slaughtering poor peasants in a land far away. Here in Paris, though, these soldiers were as young or younger than me, often confused by their role and needing to unwind. These were young men made old by their experiences and wanting to be young again. To find people that were my age and who looked like me, yet had quite different views, was a shock.

"I went into this village one time," he continued, "and we were just mopping up. We'd practically wiped the place out, when suddenly out of a doorway steps this young girl about nine years old with a grenade in her hand."

At this point he paused while we confronted the scene in our imaginations.

"So what did you do?" I asked.

"Do?" he responded, "I blew her fucking head off!"

I can't possibly describe the effect of these words on those of us listening to him, and seeing them written down doesn't convey it either.

"It was her or me," he explained.

I understood, and in that one short sentence the real horror of that terrible time came home to me. There was simply nothing more to be said.

We were looking at a man who had knowingly responded to his training and shot dead a nine year old girl in the name of what, I wondered? Unlike Pilate he could never wash off that stain; gloves would have to do.

My main busking associate now was Tubs, though I felt his performances lacked conviction. He often arrived late and would never rehearse new numbers, and yet we made a living. The tightening up on the street people was making me very nervous, as police were regularly to be found in cinema lines. If they got you, you would be cautioned and your money confiscated. Adding to this was Tubs' cavalier attitude, my run-in with Bill and the growing intensity of my relationship with Nanna.

The lines outside the cinemas contained the money that only needed to be extracted from the punters. They had also contained the police that had on one occasion stepped from the queue and arrested me, only to release us after confiscating our takings. It was from one of these lines that Gary and Melinda had emerged and become good friends. I had begun to come up with little riffs and finger style driven melodies; I think it was Melinda who first suggested I write some words to one of these songs, and that's how *Nanna's Song* was born. Now the queue on Rue de Medicis was about to throw up another adventure.

One evening Bernard and I were working, and a small Frenchman in a red shirt and glasses stepped out and asked me in an excited voice if I could play the guitar finger style. I could not quite make out what he was driving at, so Bernard translated for me and answered that I could. The Frenchman asked us if I would like a job off the streets, and when I said that I would, gave me a card with his name on and asked me to report to the address on the back the following morning. I said that I might, and we finished our show and crossed the road to the bar to divide our tips. Bernard was staring at this card and finally he said, "You know, I think this could be very important. I think I'll come with you."

I must have looked up with an 'oh yeah?' look, because the next thing he said was, "They want you to play an audition at l'Olympia, my friend!"

L'Olympia is one of Paris's most famous music theatres; Piaf played there and countless others. It was like being summoned to the London Palladium. The next day the three of us duly arrived, to scenes of utter chaos. I was soon glad that Bernard was there because at least he could speak French well enough to find out what was going on and to make sure we were in the right place when the time came. Backstage musicians were riffing and tuning up, scene shifters were shifting scenes, people were shouting, a bearded giant of a man was mooching about and the little Frenchman with the red shirt and glasses was conducting it all with much gesticulation and screaming. A beautiful Swedish girl kept walking on stage and I became aware of a very gangly French lad about my age who was keeping a nervous eye on everything.

At last in the chaos I was summoned to the centre stage. Bernard came with me and translated. The little Frenchman said something like *"Commencez s'il vous plait,"* and Bernard said, "Play something really fast like *Freight Train* or *Railroad Bill*."

At the end they all clapped and said *"Formidable!"* and Bernard announced that we'd got the job. What job, I wondered?

The music of Bob Dylan had finally reached France, and just as France had its own Elvis in Johnny Halliday, they now needed their own Bob Dylan. His name was Antoine, the skinny lad I had seen earlier at the auditions. His backing group were called 'Les Problemes' and the bill also comprised a skiffle group from Belgium featuring the bearded giant I had seen earlier and the pretty Swedish girl with her backing.

I was employed to play the accompaniment to two quiet songs in the middle of the show called *Pourquoi les Cannons* and *Je Vie Comme Je Veux* (which couldn't have been further from the truth). This was the moment of the show when he was supposed to truly communicate with his audience in a very intimate manner. He had to sit on the edge of the stage languidly picking his guitar but not actually touching the strings whilst the music was provided by me. There was even a subterfuge here as well, in case the audience might have been too impressed with one guitarist making all the music, they made three of us stand on stage (that's where Bernard came in, and another slightly plump French guy who lived at Robinet) and in case any of the audience might find any of us attractive we all had to wear 'le Smoking' (tuxedos) to add to our anonymity.

When asked what they should play, the other two were told, *"Faire un blanc."* In other words, pretend.

I was horrified by the level of deceit and showbiz; surely this was not what the new music was about! I had severe problems with all of it, but because the whole thing seldom rose above the level of farce I managed to see the funny side.

The contrasts between the acts was quite extreme to begin with. The

Belgian skiffle group had a singer with a voice that could stop a train, which was in direct contrast to Antoine, whose voice would have had trouble stopping a bicycle. The Swedish girl was mostly decorative and everyone wanted to screw her; stories were fed to the press which upset her because they were all lies. The promoters needn't have worried, as the shows were all sold out, even the matinees.

The papers were also full of stories about the clean-up of foreign bums from the streets of Paris. It seemed our timing was good for once and we were in the warm with guaranteed money. Les Problemes had an excellent lead singer and though I can't say much about the content of their songs, they were professional and competent. As they only had a couple of songs on their own they gave them their best shot. When they came on with Antoine it was a different story. The stage director had decided that the band should be arranged on a system of ladders and planks, but had not allowed for the bass player's vertigo. I will forever remember his expression of total fear as he perched in the middle of a plank between two trestle ladders moving involuntarily with his own slight weight. Every time there was a sudden movement by one of the band he took his hand off the bass to steady himself, which didn't do a lot for his rhythm.

Les Problemes also had another problem: the keyboard player. He was a perfectly ordinary chap and one of the better musicians, but he was a little overweight, and they made him stand behind a curtain so that he wasn't seen. I found this both unnecessary and cruel. I still see the hurt in his eyes, and as far as I remember none of his so-called friends in the band protested on his behalf. Whatever I could have said would have been ignored, as we were so low down the pecking order we didn't even have a dressing room.

Bernard always wore his sunglasses on stage, which I thought a bit over the top, but I soon realised that it was so that he might be remembered—or at least noticed—as we walked out the stage door and pushed our way past the adoring fans that nightly clogged the passage up the side of the theatre.

Antoine had long hair, and although certainly this had been the fashion for some years at home, most of us hip chaps had rejected that style. Indeed, Tubs and I were both totally through that phase, and Croydon chic dictated we cut our own hair and slightly back-combed the crown for effect. In Paris, though, there was no time for all that old moody so we just kept it fairly short but always looking grown out.

France it seemed took no notice of long-haired foreigners any more, but Antoine was French and his hair was a sensation. Suddenly, French kids were all turning up with shoulder length hair. This fashion spilled over to the student population and consequently they got lumped together with the rest of the street bums. I've often pondered whether the crackdown on the streets was observed by French youth and in some way contributed to the student unrest that finally degenerated into the violence known as the Paris riots. It's odd to think that a hairstyle might have had something to do with it.

The Antoine shows were a huge success and sold out for every single concert. I must say I enjoyed my fifteen minutes of fame as his backing guitarist, although any kudos I might have gained was diluted by the presence of the other two guys who had to pretend we were all making the music. Each night we would change in the wings and step out into the rainy early spring streets. Bernard usually hesitated for a moment and looking around through his sunglasses in the darkness flared his nostrils in a thespian way. Actually his nostrils were already flared now I think about it.

One afternoon after the matinee performance I became very disorientated. I found my way to an empty room near the side of the stage and passed out on the floor. I was still in my tuxedo when they found me. A sort of paralysis had kept me locked on the floor. I was pretty scared and totally aware of not being able to move or get up by myself. A doctor was summoned and he gave me a shot of something, which enabled me to get up and eventually be able to perform in the evening show.

It was a very frightening experience, and from what I gathered later had been brought on by exhaustion and lack of proper food. This situation improved slightly for soon Nanna found a friendly restaurant back in our area of the Quartier Latin. We were looked after by a youngish waiter who had an incredibly deep voice. We always ordered the same meal of spaghetti and we always got huge portions. Paris did seem to have a special understanding and regard for lovers, and people smiled at us and were sympatique and gentil. Our waiter was working like a slave and probably raising a couple of kids on his meagre salary and tips, yet he was kind to us and we appreciated it.

The last Saturday's performance had a special appearance from Dave Dee, Dozy, Beaky, Mick and Titch. They looked like creatures from another planet, which I suppose was their intention. These events only served to point up more emphatically that the music I wanted to play, learn and eventually write would have nothing to do with show biz if I could help it.

At the end of the run, the musical director who had found me in the cinema queue came and asked me to go on tour with the company. The show's phenomenal success meant that the provincial theatres were crying out for the production and I was offered good money by busking standards. I was flattered, but to be truthful I'd had enough of *Pourquoi* and *Je Vie*.

I also suspect that young Antoine was a bit disillusioned with the 'biz'. We spoke only a few times, but to me he seemed sincere and had had the mantle of 'the French Bob Dylan', or perhaps more accurately that of Donovan, thrust upon him. The culture of France at that time could not have coped with his gentle rebel image, and without the media, who had a field day inventing stories about the artists, especially the pretty Swedish girl, he could not have enjoyed such success. I declined the invitation to join the tour and wondered what to do next. The comparative security of the Olympia had softened me a little and the prospect of running the gauntlet of le flic busting the busking fraternity helped me to make up my mind. There is no doubt a lot of confidence had returned to me; my guitar playing was rated enough to be taken on tour with a top act.

I was in love with a beautiful girl who also loved me. There was so much I wanted to do but I did not know what it was. There were still places I wanted to see but I did not know where they were. My original street friends were otherwise disposed. Tubs was by now addicted to heroin although he maintained that he was 'cool'. I was hurt that I had absolutely no influence on the guy when once I seemed to have so much. I soon learned that you can't argue with a junkie. Tubs was resolute and had formed a business plan. He would return to England where he would become a registered addict and then sell his surplus prescription to produce income. I could not persuade him against his logic but having observed his intake going up all the time I feared the worst. Bunny, arguably Tubs' best pal, had all but given up on him too and had plans to quit the 'overplayed' streets of Paris for Geneva. He wanted me to go with him, but I was drained by recent events and missed my friends in England, like Henry, who were perhaps less radical than my Paris mates.

Robin was about his business and progressing well on his quest to be self-sufficient with his guitar playing. I did not see him again for eight years as he set off around Europe on his own adventure. Gary and Melinda were talking about coming to England. My excitement for the guitar that was glowing pleasantly was now blazing merrily with the new breath of life breathed into it by the insights revealed by Gary's wonderful playing techniques. I had begun to write songs. The depth of feelings I had for Nanna worried me too. We were in love and never out of each other's company, but I was not ready for any new real commitment. It was 1966 and the last year had been a roller coaster of a ride. Nanna, who had also been through a difficult time, understood that it was probably best to put some space between us and we agreed to part for a while.

It was April when we said goodbye. She on the train to Oslo and I on the boat to England. Spring was occasionally promising Summer, lightening my footstep and expectations. In a lower key, the turn of the ship's screw hummed the deep rumbling song of freedom again. I stood on deck and watched the white cliffs come into view. As the ship rhythmically dipped and rose through the water, it seemed to harmonise with my mood. Down with one wave, and up with the next. A sad developing acceptance for things past, only to have the sickly comfort of melancholy lifted by the next. A glow from knowing that although we were apart, I was a mere stretch away to things not entirely out of reach.

I was once more back on the lorry that took me away from Parkhall Camp and my brief military service. The wind and spray on my face was exhilarating. The offshore breeze sent a shiver through my two-shilling jacket and thin clothes, but part of the shiver was anticipation.

Something else was in the air.

∾

In my dreams you're dancing
In the embers of an evening
And I'll hold your hand a little tight
As if by this I'd stop the night
From running into morning light too soon

Acclaim for the first volume of Ralph McTell's autobiography

ANGEL LAUGHTER

"What we have here is a beautiful social history of life in post-war south London, with the young Ralph May acting as the still centre of the narrative… his take on growing up in Croydon is never judgmental and always full of acute insight and gentle humour."

– Bill Bellamy, *Taplas* magazine

"Given Ralph's already celebrated qualities as a storyteller, it is the dreamlike objectivity—almost as if writing about someone else—that most surprises and impresses. This poignant, compelling tale of post-war poverty through adolescence… should be regarded alongside the social history of *Angela's Ashes* as much as the cultural history of British music."

– Colin Harper, *Mojo* magazine

"McTell is a natural raconteur and the book is unashamedly anecdotal, recounting the author's childhood and adolescence in postwar Britain in a readable and whimsical style."

– Andy Farquharson, *Birmingham Post*

"Ralph writes well about childhood, particularly on the way that a child perceives the adult world… a moving, often very funny account which will throw light on the lyrics of some of Ralph's songs, though it is an enjoyable read simply as an autobiography of a young man growing up in the post-war period."

– Grahame Hood, *Traditional Music Maker*

"A vivid and touching evocation of [postwar south London] as viewed by an anxious, insecure little boy… it's a real child's eye view, delivered warts and all in an uncomplicated conversational style. McTell's prose is not as eloquent as Flora Thompson's, but there's something in the vivid, powerful evocation of another time and place of the sort that I get from reading *Lark Rise*. I found it an extremely enjoyable read."

– Maggie Holland, *Folk Roots*

"Ralph's wit and determination shine through the grime and hardship of post-war south London. While it will appeal to the over-40 age group, nobody can fail to be moved by the love and devotion of his mother in raising two young boys… of all the many books I've read in the past year, this is the one I remember with most affection."

Brian Tansley, *BBC Radio Nottingham*

"Evocative of Laurie Lee, it's an affectionate childhood memoir, from toddler to the bitter experiences of being a bullied army cadet. Full of pain, love and laughter, it recalls such familiar experiences as school bullying, puberty, being caught swearing and (very funny) that first fumbling date in the cinema."

– Mike Davies, *Birmingham What's On*

"*Angel Laughter* will swell waves of nostalgia in any reader of 40 and over, and curiosity in younger readers. His honesty is impressive and he skilfully captures the angst of young adolescence."

– Roger Bing, *Croydon Advertiser*

ANOTHER amber waves BOOK FROM HEARTLAND PUBLISHING: ISBN 1-902684-02-8